Faith Working through Love

Faith Working through Love
The Theology of William Perkins

Edited by

Joel R. Beeke
Matthew N. Payne
J. Stephen Yuille

Reformation Heritage Books
Grand Rapids, Michigan

Faith Working through Love
© 2022 by Joel R. Beeke, Matthew N. Payne, and J. Stephen Yuille

Reformation Heritage Books
3070 29th St. SE
Grand Rapids, MI 49512
616-977-0889
orders@heritagebooks.org
www.heritagebooks.org

Printed in the United States of America
22 23 24 25 26 27/10 9 8 7 6 5 4 3 2 1

Library of Congress Cataloging-in-Publication Data

Names: Beeke, Joel R., 1952- editor. | Payne, Matthew N., editor. | Yuille, J. Stephen, 1968- editor.
Title: Faith working through love : the theology of William Perkins / edited by Joel R. Beeke, Matthew N. Payne, J. Stephen Yuille.
Description: Grand Rapids, Michigan : Reformation Heritage Books, [2022] | Includes bibliographical references and index.
Identifiers: LCCN 2022009132 (print) | LCCN 2022009133 (ebook) | ISBN 9781601789761 (hardcover) | ISBN 9781601789778 (epub)
Subjects: LCSH: Perkins, William, 1558-1602. | Puritans--Doctrines. | Reformed Church—Doctrines.
Classification: LCC BX9339.P43 F35 2022 (print) | LCC BX9339.P43 (ebook) | DDC 230/.59—dc23/eng/20220321
LC record available at https://lccn.loc.gov/2022009132
LC ebook record available at https://lccn.loc.gov/2022009133

For additional Reformed literature, request a free book list from Reformation Heritage Books at the above regular or email address.

Table of Contents

Preface

William Perkins (1558–1602), often called "the father of Puritanism," was a master preacher and teacher of Reformed, experiential theology. He left an indelible mark upon the English Puritan movement, and his writings were translated into Dutch, German, French, Hungarian, and other European languages. The 1631 edition of his English *Works* filled over two thousand large pages of small print in three folio volumes. These *Works* were recently published in a newly formatted ten volume set, thereby making this towering theologian accessible to a new generation of readers.[1] It is hoped that this accessibility will translate into a renewed interest in Perkins studies. To that end, Reformation Heritage Books is pleased to publish this companion volume, *Faith Working through Love*—a compilation of the research of twelve "Perkins" scholars.

---

1. *The Works of William Perkins,* 10 vols., gen. ed. Joel R. Beeke and Derek W. H. Thomas (Grand Rapids: Reformation Heritage Books, 2014–2020)—hereafter *Works*. Unless otherwise stated, references to Perkins's writings throughout this book relate to this set and typically give a short title of the book along with volume and page numbers (e.g. *Reformed Catholic,* 7:5).

Introduction

William Perkins's legacy is multifaceted. He was instrumental in securing the Reformation in England, and his works became the standard polemic against Rome. He made an incalculable contribution to the advancement of Reformed theology, leaving a discernible imprint upon the development of the five points of Calvinism. His role as a physician of the soul became paradigmatic for succeeding generations of ministers. His method of preaching shaped the English pulpit well into the eighteenth century and is still felt in some quarters of the church today. While all this is true, behind the industrious scholar, combative polemicist, exhaustive expositor, and prolific author stood a pastor deeply concerned about the spiritual condition of the individual in the pew.

Perkins was troubled by the prevalence of what he called "false" faith. In his estimation, too many people made an outward profession of faith in Christ yet demonstrated little vitality.[1] While this concern was shared in the late sixteenth century by Protestants and Catholics alike, their proposed remedies were markedly different. Perkins acknowledges this in his sermons on Galatians 5:6, "For in Jesus Christ neither circumcision availeth any thing, nor uncircumcision; but faith which worketh by love."

According to Perkins, the "papists" interpret this verse to mean "that love is the form and life of faith, not because it makes faith to be faith, but because it makes it to be a true faith, a good faith, a lively faith." He labels their doctrine "false and erroneous" because it implies that faith is "acted and moved by love," meaning it receives its "efficacy" from love.[2] For Perkins, the Roman church has fallen into this error because of its failure to recognize that "true faith is lively and effectual in itself and has a peculiar form of its own, and that is a certain power to apprehend Christ in the promise." This is the case because faith consists of "knowledge" and "apprehension" (also called "application" or "special

---

1. *Exposition of Jude*, 4:49, 73–77.
2. *Commentary on Galatians*, 2:332–34.

affiance"). Because it rejects this definition of faith, the Roman church is "constrained" to insert love into faith, to distinguish between "true" and "false" faith.

In marked contrast, Perkins does not attempt to remedy the problem of "false" faith by making love "the form and life of faith." Rather, as per Galatians 5:6, he insists that love is the "operation" of faith, writing, "Faith and love are two hands of our soul. Faith is a hand that lays hold of Christ, and it does (as it were) pull Him and His benefits into our souls. But love is a hand of another kind, for it serves not to receive in, but to give out the good it has and to communicate itself unto others." Faith, therefore, is the "cause" of love while love is the "fruit" of faith. As the apostle Paul writes, "Now the end of the commandment is charity out of a pure heart, and of a good conscience, and of faith unfeigned" (1 Tim. 1:5). Logically, a cause (i.e., faith) does not receive any "force or efficacy" from its effect (i.e., love).

Perkins's position regarding love as the "operation" of faith is informed by his understanding of (1) the nature of saving faith, (2) the relationship between the mind and the will, and (3) the difference between the instrument of salvation and the way of salvation.

The Nature of Saving Faith

Perkins insists that faith is a supernatural gift of God, "not only because it is above the corrupt nature in which we are born, but also because it is above that pure nature in which our first parents were created."[3] In the state of innocence, Adam and Eve had no need for faith in Christ. Saving faith, therefore, "is a new grace of God added to regeneration after the fall and first prescribed and taught in the covenant of grace." In this way it differs from "the rest of the gifts of God" (e.g., fear of God, love of God, love of others, etc.), which were in man's nature before the fall. Whereas these gifts are renewed at conversion, faith is not; rather, "the first engrafting of it into the heart is in the conversion of a sinner."[4]

It is by means of this supernatural gift (faith) that we are "approved of God."[5] This is the case, not because it is "an action of a sanctified mind and a good grace of God, for so are humility, love, fear of God (all which are graces of the sanctifying Spirit, as faith is)," but because "it is a worthy instrument in the heart of the believer, which apprehends and applies to the soul that righteousness of Christ by which he is justified."

---

3. *Exposition of the Creed*, 5:11–18.
4. *Exposition of the Creed*, 5:11–18.
5. *Commentary on Hebrews 11*, 3:13–15.

Perkins affirms that "Christ, as he is set forth unto us in the Word and sacraments, is the object of faith."[6] This faith consists of two essential components.[7] The first is knowing Christ and His benefits: "And this is life eternal, that they might know thee the only true God, and Jesus Christ, whom thou hast sent" (John 17:3). The second is applying what we know (namely, Christ and His benefits) to ourselves "in particular." According to Perkins, application is "the very substance of true faith, which is not caused by any natural affection of heart or action of will but by the supernatural action of the mind enlightened by the Spirit of God, resolving us that Christ and His merits belong unto us in particular."[8]

In sum, we must receive "in particular" that which God offers us (John 1:12; 6:35). He offers Christ and all His benefits to us in the Word and sacraments. And, therefore, we must believe it (that is, apply it to ourselves). This is the "principal" thing in saving faith.

The Relationship between the Mind and the Will

From the above discussion it is evident that Perkins places faith in the mind. However, this point is less than straightforward than initially appears, and has caused significant challenges for interpreters.[9] Perkins states that,

> The place and seat of faith (as I think) is the mind of man, not the will; for it stands in a kind of particular knowledge or persuasion, and there is no persuasion but in the mind. Paul says indeed that we believe with the heart (Rom. 10:9). But by the heart he understands the soul, without

---

6. *Exposition of the Creed*, 5:11–18. Elsewhere, Perkins describes faith as "a special gift of God whereby we believe Christ and his benefits to be ours.... Now God gives Christ in the Word and sacraments. And in them He does (as it were) open His hand and reach forth all the blessings of Christ unto us. We must not, therefore, imagine to find Christ where and how we list, but we must seek Him in the Word and sacraments, and there we must receive Him if we desire to receive Him aright." *True Gain*, 9:64.

7. *Exposition of Jude*, 4:58–64. Elsewhere, Perkins employs the traditional tripartite division of faith—namely, knowledge, assent, and persuasion. *Exposition of the Creed*, 5:11–18. At other times (as in the present discussion), assent is included under knowledge. He is convinced that knowledge (with assent) alone is not true faith. There must be "a certain and particular persuasion, whereby a man is resolved that the promise of salvation belongs to him." *Exposition of the Creed*, 5:12. Perkins follows Ursinus in this. See *Summe of Christian Religion*, 257–69.

8. *Exposition of Jude*, 4:58–64.

9. The most prominent example is R. T. Kendall's claim that, based on Perkins's thought as a whole, he "should" have said that faith is located in the will. R. T. Kendall, *Calvin and English Calvinism to 1649* (Oxford: Oxford University Press, 1979), 62. See discussion in Matthew N. Payne, "William Perkins's Doctrines of Faith and Assurance through the Lens of Early-Modern Faculty Psychology," *Westminster Theological Journal* 83, no. 2 (2021): 319–23; and Richard A. Muller, *Grace and Freedom: William Perkins and the Early Modern Reformed Understanding of Free Choice and Divine Grace* (Oxford: Oxford University Press, 2020), 136–43.

limitation to any part. Some do place faith partly in the mind and partly in the will because it has two parts: knowledge and affiance. But it seems not greatly to stand with reason that one particular and single grace should be seated in divers parts or faculties of the soul.[10]

This appears straightforward, yet Perkins goes on to claim that the formation of faith by the Holy Spirit "stands in two principal actions: first, the enlightening of the mind; the second, the moving of the will."[11] Further, while insisting that the mind is the exclusive seat of faith (that is, of knowledge, apprehension, and persuasion), Perkins's repeated use of the voluntaristic language of "applying" Christ indicates that the will performs a central and active role in his account of faith. Just as the acts of apprehension and persuasion are functions of the mind, the act of application is a function of the will. The will is a "blind" faculty, incapable of knowing anything in itself, and so its applicatory role must be entirely guided by the knowledge provided to it by the mind. Thus, for Perkins, the mind "apprehends" Christ, which leads to the will "applying" Christ and His benefits to the individual. Faith, as it were, flows downstream from the mind to the will as the Holy Spirit's regenerative work gradually takes more pervasive effect through the faculties of the soul.

Therefore, Perkins can summarily describe faith as involving both apprehension and application: "to apprehend properly is an action of the hand of man, which lays hold of a thing and pulls [it] to himself; and by resemblance it agrees to faith, which is the hand of the soul, receiving and applying the saving promise." He also insists that this "apprehension of faith is not performed by any affection of the will, but by a certain and particular persuasion whereby a man is resolved that the promise of salvation belongs unto him, which persuasion is wrought in the mind by the Holy Spirit (1 Cor. 2:12)." However, this persuasion then flows on to the will: "And by this, the promise, which is general, is applied particularly to one subject."[12]

This formulation is also central to Perkins's understanding of the relationship between faith and assurance. Along with many later-sixteenth century thinkers, Perkins distinguished faith and assurance without separating them, arguing that they are to be understood as organically related stages of spiritual growth. Indeed, an organic metaphor drives one of Perkins's most important works on assurance, *A Grain of Mustard Seed*,[13] which describes how the "seed"

---

10. *Exposition of the Creed*, 5:11. For a full discussion of this theme, see Payne, "Faith and Assurance."

11. *Exposition of the Creed*, 5:13.

12. *Exposition of the Creed*, 5:12.

13. *Grain of Mustard Seed*, 8:639–58.

of regenerate spiritual desire grows into the "tree" of faith and full assurance.[14] Regenerate spiritual desire produces faith in the mind, which ultimately develops to become full assurance. As Perkins states, "No Christian attains to this full assurance at the first, but in some continuance of time, after he has for a long space kept a good conscience before God and before men, and has had divers experiences of God's love and favor towards him in Christ."[15]

Thus, for Perkins, assurance is of the essence of faith, even when it merely lays seminally dormant in the heart.[16] In contrast, Perkins treats love as an action which is not of the essence of faith, though it does inescapably flow from it. Indeed, love is the principal operation of faith. For Perkins, love is not "the very nature and form of faith," but "an effect which proceeds from faith."[17] He maintains that faith and love differ greatly in "nature." Christ is the fountain of the water of life. Faith is "the pipes and leads that receive in and hold the water," whereas "love in some part is as the cock of the conduit, that lets out the water to every corner." He adds, "The property of the hand is to hold, and of itself it cannot cut. Yet by a knife or other instrument put into the hand it cuts. The hand of the soul is faith, and its property is to apprehend Christ with all His benefits and by itself can do nothing else. Yet join love unto it, and by love it will be effectual in all good duties [Gal. 5:6]."[18]

The Difference between the Instrument of Salvation and the Way of Salvation

As noted above, by regeneration the mind knows and applies Christ and His benefits. The will then freely accepts this knowledge and application of Christ, and thereby puts faith in operation. In this way, faith becomes operative in the way of salvation—namely, good works (e.g., love for God, fear of God, obedience, etc.).

For Perkins, this way of salvation is summed up in repentance.[19] He is adamant that repentance "is not a *cause* of salvation but only a *way* wherein men

---

14. Similarly, Perkins describes the formation of faith in the soul as occurring "not suddenly but by certain steps and degrees—as nature frames the body of the infant in the mother's womb." *Exposition of the Creed*, 5:13.

15. *Treatise Tending unto a Declaration*, 8:477.

16. "A little faith then is in the heart of man, as in the spring time the fruit is in the bud, which yet appears not, but only has its nature and substance in the bud." *Treatise Tending unto a Declaration*, 8:475.

17. *Exposition of the Creed*, 5:13.

18. *Exposition of the Creed*, 5:13.

19. Perkins acknowledges that "divines" understand repentance differently. "Some make it a fruit of faith containing two parts (mortification and vivification); some make faith a part of it by dividing it into contrition, faith, [and] new obedience; [and] some make it all one with

must walk to life everlasting." He adds, "We are slandered by the popish church, while they exclaim that our doctrine requires nothing but faith to be saved by, and so we become enemies to all good works. But this is not our doctrine, for we hold the works of repentance to be the *way* of salvation. Indeed, when we speak of the *instrument* whereby we lay hold upon Christ, that we say is faith only, not hope, love, or any works. But when we speak of a *way* to life, then faith is not alone, but repentance is required, hope, the fear of God, and every good work."[20]

According to Perkins, we become members of Christ's "mystical body" (thereby gaining Him and His benefits) through faith. It is the only "instrument" by which we receive what is "given by the Father, procured by the Son, [and] applied by the Holy Spirit." However, when it comes to the "way" to eternal life, faith is not alone, but is accompanied by good works (which arise from the operation of faith). "If we speak of the *way* to life," says Perkins, "then we are not saved only by faith. For though faith is the only *instrument* to apprehend Christ, yet it is not the only *way* to life. Repentance also is the *way*, yea all virtues and all works are the *way*."[21]

We are justified by faith without the works of the law (Rom. 3:28). For Perkins, this includes "the works of moral and ceremonial law, works of nature and grace." He elaborates on why "works of grace" are excluded from justification.

---

regeneration. The difference is not in the substance of doctrine, but in the logical manner of handling it. And the difference of handling arises from the divers acceptation of repentance. It is taken [in] two ways: generally and particularly. [It is taken] generally for the whole conversion of a sinner, and so it may contain contrition, faith, [and] new obedience under it, and be confounded with regeneration. It is taken particularly for the renovation of the life and behavior, and so it is a fruit of faith. And I only follow this sense in this treatise." "To the Reader," in *Nature and Practice of Repentance*, 9:125–26. Perkins acknowledges that Calvin speaks of repentance in the "general" sense—that is, of the whole conversion of a sinner. He provides the following marginal note: Calvin Inst. l. 3. c. 3. par. 9.

20. *Exposition of Jude*, 4:72–74 (my italics). Perkins's emphasis on repentance raises the issue of how he understood it in relation to faith. He clarifies, "Some may object that repentance goes before all grace because it is preached first.... The answer hereto may be this: If we respect the order of nature, there are other graces of God which go before repentance, because a man's conscience must in some sort be settled touching his reconciliation with God in Christ before he can begin to repent. Wherefore, justification and sanctification in order of nature go before repentance. But if we respect time, grace and repentance are both together. As soon as there is fire, it is hot. And as soon as a man is regenerate, he repents. If we respect the outward manifestation of these two, repentance goes before all other graces because it first of all appears outwardly. Regeneration is like the sap of the tree that lies hid within the bark. Repentance is like the bud that speedily shows itself before either blossom, leaf, or fruit appear. Yea, all other graces of the heart, which are needful to salvation, are made manifest by repentance. And for this cause repentance (as I take it) is preached first." *Nature and Practice of Repentance*, 9:130.

21. *True Gain*, 9:37 (my italics).

First, "works of grace" would give us a reason to boast (Rom. 3:27). Second, "works of grace" would mean that our justification would stand by the law. Third, "works of grace" are those which God has prepared for us to walk in (Eph. 2:8, 10). Fourth, "works of grace" follow justification.

> Yea, and as all works are excluded, so all virtues also (excepting faith) are here rejected. For as in a man that stands to receive a gift no part does anything to receive it but the hand, yet, having received it, all other parts testify thankfulness—the tongue, the feet, and all the body. Even so, we receive the matter of our justification by faith alone, not by hope or love, but after the receiving of Christ these with the other graces work and show themselves.[22]

Summary
From this discussion, it is evident that Perkins has no place for a truncated gospel—a Christ who fails to transform. While excluding good works (including love—the fulfillment of the law) from justification, he most certainly does not exclude them from the Christian's life. The *instrument* by which we lay hold of Christ is faith alone—the knowledge and application of Him and His benefits. However, when we speak of the *way* of salvation, good works (including love) are essential because they are the necessary operation of faith.

Troubled by the prevalence of false faith in his day, Perkins made it his apologetic aim to demonstrate that true faith never remains indifferent to eternal realities. In short, to know God is to be changed by God because there is an inseparable relationship between faith and its operation (namely, love). Perkins insisted that we are saved by virtue of union with Christ through faith (the knowledge and application of Christ and His benefits); however, he was equally adamant that such faith is always operative. "Knowledge in the brain will not save the soul; saving knowledge in religion is experimental; and he that is truly founded upon Christ, feels the power and efficacy of his death and resurrection, effectually causing the death of sin and the life of grace which both appear by new obedience."[23]

For Perkins, the gospel (union with Christ through faith) is always transformative because faith is always operative as it works through love. It is this conviction that is on full display in the present volume.

---

22. *Exposition of Jude*, 4:58–64.
23. *Sermon on the Mount*, 1:725.

1

The Triune God

Wyatt Graham

William Perkins did not write a treatise on the doctrine of the Trinity. When he does speak on the doctrine, he says almost nothing surprising or novel. The most unique contribution he might have within the history of dogma is simply his agreement with a common Reformed notion of the Son as *autotheos* (God Himself). Even here, Perkins rather faithfully preserves Reformed and Catholic Trinitarian thought. This is because he affirms the truth of creedal statements on the doctrine of Trinity. He describes the Apostles' Creed as "the very pith and substance of Christian religion."[1] As part of the Church of England, Perkins likewise maintained that the Thirty-Nine Articles had "set down the foundations of Christian religion, allowed and held by all evangelical churches."[2] Article 1 preserves a creedal and scriptural understanding of the Trinity when it affirms: "There is but one living and true God, everlasting, without body, parts or passions, of infinite power, wisdom and goodness, the maker and preserver of all things both visible and invisible. And in unity of this Godhead there be three persons of one substance, power and eternity, the Father, the Son and the Holy Ghost."[3]

Perkins affirms such creedal and ecclesial documents because they accord with Scripture. They have authority then only insofar as they represent the teaching of Holy Scripture. When they do, Perkins will go so far as to say that creedal and ecclesial writings can even be called the Word of God. He explains, "Now both these kinds of books may be called *God's Word*, so far forth as they agree with Scripture."[4] They also are "the word of men, because they were penned by men, and have both order and style from men; and in this regard, that they

---

1. *Exposition of the Creed*, 5:4.
2. *Sermon on the Mount*, 1:310.
3. See Gerald Bray, *Documents of the English Reformation* (Minneapolis: Fortress Press, 1994), 285.
4. *Sermon on the Mount*, 1:651–52.

were partly men's works, they are not authentic of themselves, but depend upon the authority of Scripture."[5] Thus, Perkins maintains a creedal understanding of God not because of the authority of the creed itself but because the creed finds its authority in Scripture. His scriptural focus means that his dogmatic theology often ties itself directly to the text through his commentaries. Even in his explanation of the Apostles' Creed, Perkins starts with Scripture.[6]

It is this union of Scripture and creed that illustrates the ongoing importance of Perkins for Trinitarian theology today. He demonstrates the truths of the doctrine of triune God by showing their scriptural and logical coherence without dividing Scripture and reason into separate spheres of study. Despite many in our day questioning doctrines like eternal generation, divine simplicity, and more besides, Perkins shows why these doctrines reflect biblical and theological truth. And for Perkins, no doctrine is merely true. Doctrine has an afterlife in the believer, for even in the deepest Trinitarian meditation worshipers come to know and experience the living God.

Sources for Perkins's Trinitarian Theology

Since Perkins did not produce a treatise specifically on the Trinity, one must discern his Trinitarian theology from his complete works. The two most important sources are Perkins's catechetical writings and his commentaries. His polemical works have some value, but they focus on issues like predestination or how the Church of England differs from the Church of Rome. Since the Church of Rome and the Church of England (and Reformed churches in general) agreed on the doctrine of the Trinity, there was little need for Perkins to include Trinitarian polemics in these writings. That said, his 1591 polemical work *A Golden Chain*, published in 1590 in Latin and then in 1591 in English, contains important statements of Trinitarian theology. In this work, he clearly affirms the *autotheos* of the Son, a theme that will be explored below. But perhaps the most important writing for understanding Perkins's Trinitarianism is *An Exposition of the Symbol or Creed of the Apostles* (1595).

For Perkins, "the Symbol or Creed of the Apostles...is indeed the very pith and substance of Christian religion, taught by the apostles, embraced by the ancient fathers, sealed by the blood of martyrs, used by Theodosius the Emperor as a means to end the controversies of his time, and hereupon has been called the *rule of faith*, the *key of faith*."[7] The statement, "very pith and

---

5. *Sermon on the Mount*, 1:652.

6. For example, to prove the incomprehensibility of God, Perkins begins with Exodus 33:20, 23. *Exposition of the Creed*, 5:19.

7. *Exposition of the Creed*, 5:4.

substance of Christian religion," underscores Perkins's commitment to creedal Trinitarianism. The word "religion" carries the sense of worship or piety rather than the more modern understanding of religion as a set of beliefs demarcating world religions from each other.[8]

Perkins also considers the theological implications of Scripture in his commentaries. In this regard, his commentaries on the *Sermon on the Mount* or *Exposition of Revelation 1–3* show how he united exposition with theology. The more modern division of theology and exegesis does not appear here. Perkins exposits Scripture theologically. In other words, he allows for Trinitarian reflection on Scripture, not seeing this as an imposition from a later period but a legitimate rumination that flows from Scripture. One might gain insight into why Perkins did so through his division between divine and ecclesial writings. The former refers to books of the Old and New Testament. The latter refers to various documents created by the church, including the creeds, confessions, and even writings of private persons. Of this group of writings, Perkins declares:

> Ecclesiastical writings are all other ordinary writings of the church consenting with [the] Scriptures. These may be called the word or truth of God, so far forth as their matter or substance is consenting with the written Word of God; but they cannot be called the Scripture of God, because the style and phrase of them was set down according to the pleasure of man, and therefore they are in such sort the word of God as that also they are the word of men.[9]

Ecclesial documents, including private writings of Perkins's himself, might be called the word (or truth) of God in a qualified sense. Yet one must consider an order to such things. Perkins argues that the creeds confess one and the same faith, the Apostles' Creed being the "most ancient and principal" among them.[10] Such catholic documents have the highest level of authority among ecclesial writings due to this consensus. Confessions and private writings can be more easily overturned than these creeds. All ecclesial writings, however,

---

8. Peter Harrison briefly chronicles the transformation of the meaning of "religion" from its earlier sense in Christian writings. See *The Territories of Science and Religion* (Chicago: The University of Chicago Press, 2015), 7–11.

9. *Exposition of the Creed*, 5:7.

10. *Exposition of the Creed*, 5:8. Perkins affirms an early date for the Apostles' Creed. J. N. D. Kelly notes that the Apostles' Creed is a variant of the Old Roman Creed which dates to the second century. See *Early Christian Creeds*, 3rd ed. (New York: David McKay Company, 1972), 101, 369. Statements from these creeds appears in the earlier rules of faith of the second-century fathers Tertullian (c. 155–220) and Irenaeus (c. 130–202). This means that basic elements of the Apostles' Creed date back to the earliest days of the church.

borrow their authority from Scripture, which remains the rule of faith.[11] Perkins argues particularly that the Apostles' Creed "is received as a rule of faith
among all churches to try doctrines and interpretations of Scriptures by, not
because it is a rule of itself—for that the Scripture is alone—but because it
borrows its authority from Scripture with which it agrees."[12] This expression
of *Sola Scriptura* both elevates Scripture to its rightful place while also giving
creeds their important secondary role. Given the high value that Perkins put
on ecclesial documents and in particular creedal documents like the Apostles'
Creed, it is no surprise that he will discuss the triune God in his commentaries
on Scripture. After all, the creedal documents are shaped around a confession
of the Father, Son, and Spirit. They are confessions of the triune God.

The Nature of God

Perkins vouchsafes the unity of the triune God by affirming the one nature of
the Godhead. He states that the "three are one not in person, but in nature."[13]
In his commentary on Galatians, he says, "*Nature* is a substance common to
many, as the Godhead."[14] God's oneness centers on the one nature of the Godhead. In other words, the one nature of God preserves the unity of God. By
"nature," Perkins means "a thing subsisting by itself that is common to many."
The technical language here can be understood through mundane illustrations.
Perkins notes how human nature comprises the irreducible union of body and
soul. He writes of "the substance of man, consisting of body and soul, common to all men, which we call the 'humanity' of a man" and defines it as "the
nature of man."[15] Every human person holds this nature in common. We might
put it as follows today. Paul and John are specific persons who share a human
nature. They share that nature, and they do so, as Perkins notes, as the irreducible whole of body and soul. In this example, Paul and John are individual
persons and so distinguishable from one another, even while they share human
nature. Here, Perkins follows a long line in Christian theological reasoning
about natures and persons.[16]

---

11. Perkins also calls the Creed a "rule of faith," but only insofar as it "borrows its authority
from Scripture with which it agrees." *Exposition of the Creed,* 5:8.

12. *Exposition of the Creed,* 5:8.

13. *Exposition of the Creed,* 5:24.

14. *Commentary on Galatians,* 2:246.

15. *Exposition of the Creed,* 5:24.

16. For example, see Basil of Caesarea who defines nature and person in virtually identical
ways to Perkins. "Letter 38," in *St. Basil's Letters* (New York: CUA Press, 1951), 1:84–96. For a
recent discussion on Perkins's use of the fathers, see Coleman M. Ford, "'Everywhere, Always,
by All': Williams Perkins and James Ussher on the Constructive Use of the Fathers," *Puritan
Reformed Journal* 7, no. 2 (2015): 95–111.

Perkins does not conceive of the divine nature in the exact same way as he does the human nature. He distinguishes divinity and humanity, and so characterizes the divine nature in ways appropriate to it. In the first place, the divine nature is incomprehensible. Perkins explains, "Moses, desiring to see God's face, was not permitted but to see His hinder parts [Exod. 33:20, 23]. And, therefore, no man can be able to describe God by His nature, but by His effects and properties, on this or such like manner: God is an essence spiritual, simple,[17] infinite, most holy."[18] In other words, God is unknowable except by His effects. We can trace the wonderful works of God back to Him who created them. We can apprehend God through His created media, but we cannot name or fully comprehend His nature.[19] One reason why is because the divine nature is "spiritual, simple, infinite, most holy."

Perkins defines what he means by each of these descriptions. God is spiritual because He has no body. "Neither has He the parts of the bodies of men or other creatures, but is in nature a spirit invisible, not subject to any man's senses."[20] God has no skin, veins, or bones. He is spirit and invisible unlike humans who are visible to the senses. In other words, the meaning of God's invisibility revolves around God not having a created body. Furthermore, God's simple essence "admits no manner of composition of matter or form of parts."[21] By contrast, creatures have many parts and diverse natures. Yet God, "whatsoever thing He is, He is the same by one and the same singular and indivisible essence."[22] Divine infinity refers to God's boundless existence with reference to time, beginnings, ends, and places. God has no kind of end, no limit. His holiness represents His various qualities. For this reason, holiness functions as a primary category under which other attributes fall. Perkins writes, "He alone is rightly termed 'most holy' because holiness is of the very nature of God Himself, whereas among the most excellent creatures it is otherwise."[23] As is his

---

17. God's simplicity refers to His "being absolutely free of any and all composition, not merely physical, but also logical and rational composition. Thus, God is not the sum of the divine attributes..., [rather] the attributes are understood to be identical with and inseparable from [the divine essence]." Richard A. Muller, *Dictionary of Latin and Greek Theological Terms Drawn Principally from Protestant Scholastic Theology* (Grand Rapids: Baker, 1985), 283.

18. *Exposition of the Creed*, 5:19.

19. For example, Gregory of Nazianzus (AD 330–390) wrote: "Our starting-point must be the fact that God cannot be named." *On God and Christ: The Five Theological Orations and Two Letters to Cledonius*, trans. Frederick Williams and Lionel Wickham (New York: St. Vladimir's Seminary Press, 2002), 107 (Or. 30.17)]. When Gregory says God cannot be named, he means that no one can define Him fully.

20. *Exposition of the Creed*, 5:19.

21. *Exposition of the Creed*, 5:19.

22. *Exposition of the Creed*, 5:19.

23. *Exposition of the Creed*, 5:19.

pattern, Perkins cites passages of Scripture which contribute to his theological definitions (Exod. 3:6, 14; 1 Tim. 1:17).

One might find it hard to see how Perkins's complex discussion of God's incomprehensible nature could flow directly from Scripture. But that would be to misunderstand how he sees the relationship between theology and Scripture. He does not view theology as the mere repetition of scriptural wording. In a discussion about the Spirit's procession, Perkins defends the use of this term: "The Scripture says not so much in plain terms, yet we must know that that which is gathered from thence by just consequence is no less the truth of God than that which is expressed in words."[24] The language of "just consequence" signals that Perkins has more in mind than the mere repetition of biblical language.[25] When the church interprets Scripture, it can use theological terms not found in Scripture to communicate the truth of God. In other words, terms such as "nature" and "person" not only agree with the proper sense of Scripture but are contained in Scripture. Perkins cites Scripture to show that the words "nature" and "person" appear in the text (Gal. 4:8; Heb. 1:3), but the important thing is that these terms truly describe the meaning of Scripture.[26] All of this helps to explain why Perkins privileges the creedal language and theology of Christianity since they represent scriptural truth, that is, the truth of God.

The nature of God then is one. The term "nature" vouchsafes the unity of God. To illustrate why, it is worth showing how Perkins understands the divine decree. It is eternal and belongs to God as God. There is no order in time or degree. The Father does not send the Son without the Son's consent. They inseparably, as the one God, decree all things which come to pass. "[T]he decree of the Father," argues Perkins, "is the decree of the Son and the Holy Spirit, because as they are all one in nature, so are they all one in will."[27] The divine nature is not a mere construct. It is what God is. Since the divine nature is simple (i.e., without parts), it follows that God does not have three wills. He is one nature, one will, one power. Perkins here affirms the traditional view that the will belongs to nature. Such an affirmation protects the unity of God while allowing for the Triunity of God. Since God has one will, there is one God. Thus, the will of the Father and Son is one. On the other hand, if *will* were to belong to the person of God, there would be three wills and so the unity of God would be breached. Further, if the Father even in eternity somehow willed His eternal decree without the Son, in opposition to the Son's will, or even over the

---

24. *Exposition of the Creed*, 5:308.
25. The *Westminster Confession* speaks of "good and necessary consequence." Art. 1:6.
26. *Exposition of the Creed*, 5:24.
27. *Commentary on Galatians*, 2:46.

Son's will, then the unity of God would likewise be breached. Perkins affirms the oneness of God because the term "nature" encloses within it the theological notions that preserve the unity of Godhead. The way in which the persons of God are distinguished, then, must be carefully discerned to avoid falling into tritheism.

The Persons of God

Perkins uses the word "person" to ensure that the Father, Son, and Spirit are distinguished even though they share one simple nature. Perkins here follows the teaching of Scripture. He affirms, "Scripture reveals God unto us to be one in essence and three in person, viz. the Father, the Son, and the Holy Spirit, whereof the Father is the first, the Son is the second, the Holy Spirit the third in order, though not in time or greatness."[28] More economically, he affirms that the "three are one not in person, but in nature."[29] Scripture reveals that the one God is Father, Son, and Holy Spirit. The names Father, Son, and Spirit arise directly from the biblical text. Perkins, however, follows the church's consensus on how to speak of triune persons. By person, he means "a thing or essence subsisting by itself not common to many but incommunicable—as among men, these particulars, Peter, John, Paul, are called persons."[30] In other words, Peter and Paul share humanity or human nature but what makes them a specific person is incommunicable. Peter remains Peter, and Paul remains Paul. Peter and Paul share human nature, but each person does not share their individual personness with each other. Their personness is incommunicable.

Perkins explains, "the Godhead itself" is "simply and absolutely considered; and a person is that which subsists in that Godhead, as the Father, the Son, and the Holy Spirit."[31] He continues, "A person is one and the same Godhead not absolutely considered but in relation and as it were restrained by personal or characteristical properties."[32] These personal properties follow directly from the language of Scripture. "God begetting is the Father," "God begotten" is the Son, and "God proceeding of the Father and Son" is the Holy Spirit. These personal properties of the one God indicate relations in Him. The Son relates to the Father as the begotten; the Father relates to the Son as the begetter; the Spirit relates to the Father and Son as the one proceeding from both. Perkins summarizes, "Thus, the Godhead considered with the property of fatherhood

---

28. *Sermon on the Mount*, 1:429.

29. *Sermon on the Mount*, 5:24.

30. *Exposition of the Creed*, 5:28. Perkins draws this illustration from Basil, "Letter 38" (cited above).

31. *Exposition of the Creed*, 5:24.

32. *Exposition of the Creed*, 5:24.

or begetting is the Father; and conceiving the same Godhead with the property of generation we conceive the Son; and the Godhead with the property of proceeding we conceive the Holy Spirit."[33]

These personal properties involve relations in God. The Father, as He relates to the Son, is begetter. The Son, as He relates to the Father, is begotten. The Spirit, as He relates to the Father and Son, proceeds. These relational properties specify what is incommunicable in God. The Father is not the Son or Spirit. The Son is not the Father or Spirit. The Spirit is not the Son or Father. The Father is not the Son because the Father begets the Son and the Son is begotten of the Father. This relation is declared in the very names "Father" and "Son." As we shall see Perkins argue below, the Spirit proceeds from the Father and Son as breath proceeds from the mouth. This picture arises from the name "Spirit," which in the Greek and Hebrew can be translated *breath*. This language not only uses the biblical names for the persons of God but moves one level higher. It meditates on the significance of the names "Father" and "Son." Perkins, as Christians before him, names what it is for the Father to be the Father of the Son. Fathers and sons relate to one another by begetting and being begotten. In a similar way, Perkins defines the Holy Spirit's name by His redemptive function and relation to the Father and Son. He is holy because He sanctifies the church, and He is spirit because He is spiritual and proceeds like breath proceeds from the mouth.[34] In other words, Perkins finds profound meaning even in the personal names of the one God.

In his theological exposition of the Trinity in *Exposition of the Symbol or Creed of the Apostles*, Perkins justifies his use of the language of *nature* and *person*. First, "they have been taken up by common consent in the primitive church, and that upon weighty consideration, to manifest the truth and to stop the mouths of heretics."[35] Second, "they are not so used against the proper sense of the Scriptures; nay, they are therein contained [Gal. 4:8; Heb. 1:3]."[36] The uptake in using this traditional language which accords with the sense of Scripture is as follows: "We see how it comes to pass that the three things signified by these names, Father, Son, and Holy Spirit, are each of them one and the same God."[37]

---

33. *Exposition of the Creed*, 5:24.
34. *Exposition of the Creed*, 5:305–6.
35. *Exposition of the Creed*, 5:24.
36. *Exposition of the Creed*, 5:24.
37. *Exposition of the Creed*, 5:24.

One might expect that Perkins would be content with this Trinitarian syntax, but he proceeds to wade into the waters of analogy (or comparison). He uses the pro-Nicene metaphor of light to understand the divine nature:[38]

> And this mystery may well be conceived by a comparison borrowed from light. The light of the sun, the light of the moon, and the light of the air for nature and substance are one and the same light; and yet they are three distinct lights—the light of the sun being of itself and from none, the light of the moon from the sun, and the light of the air from them both. So, the divine nature is one, and the persons are three, subsisting after a diverse manner in one and the same nature.[39]

Light radiates from the sun, reflects off the moon, and traverses through "the air," yet remains one "nature and substance." It is "the same light" that can be distinguished into "three distinct lights." Perkins uses the light in the air to illustrate the double procession of the Spirit. As the light in the air comes from both the sun and moon, so too the Spirit proceeds from both the Father and the Son. Perkins uses the light radiating from the sun and reflecting off the moon to show the Father's unoriginated life. Perkins here deftly illustrates pro-Nicene Trinitarian theology along with the doctrine of double procession.

Perkins adds further clarity by detailing "the union and the distinction of the persons."[40] By way of union, Perkins asserts that the persons are coessential or consubstantial. These traditional designations signify the essential unity of the divine persons. The Father is consubstantial with the Son; that is, the Father and Son share one substance or essence. In other words, each person shares the one Godhead. The reason why God remains *one* is because, according to Perkins, an infinite essence cannot multiply. "Now there are not three distinct Gods, but one God, because there is one God and no more in nature, considering that the thing which is infinite is but one and is not subject to multiplication."[41] This "thing" is the divine nature. Perkins argues here that the nature of the infinite God (i.e., He who is without limits) entails that He cannot be multiplied into parts. There are no parts to God—only persons. Yet each person is the one God. "They are all coequal and coeternal; all most wise, just, merciful, omnipotent by one and the same wisdom, justice, mercy, power. And because they have all one Godhead, therefore they are not only one with another but also each in [the] other—the Father in the Son, and the Son in the Father, and the Holy

---

38. The Nicene Creed, for example, speaks of the Son as being "light from light." See *Decrees of the Ecumenical Councils*, ed. Norman P. Tanner (London: Sheed & Ward, 1990), 1:5.

39. *Exposition of the Creed*, 5:24–25.

40. *Exposition of the Creed*, 5:25.

41. *Exposition of the Creed*, 5:25.

Spirit in them both."[42] We cannot and must not describe the Father as a *part* of God. Such a description is "most false because the infinite and the most simple Godhead is not subject to composition or division, but every person is whole God, subsisting not in a part but in the whole Godhead."[43] To speak of God in terms of *parts* undermines His simple nature. God has no parts or passions. He is Spirit, simple and infinite. Each person subsists in this one nature, not as parts but as subsisting persons.

It is important to realize that, for Perkins, divine infinity and simplicity ensure that the persons of God cannot be counted or multiplied as they are among humans. "Now," explains Perkins, "it is otherwise with the divine nature or Godhead, which is uncreated and infinite and therefore admits neither composition nor division but a distinction without any separation, so as the three persons subsisting in it shall not be three Gods but one and the same God."[44] Peter, John, and Paul can be counted. They are three created humans. God, however, is only one simple essence, and the three persons are one with the divine essence. In a technical move, Perkins argues that we can distinguish "in mind" personal relations in God, while affirming that the three are one in essence.[45] He denies that this results in a quaternity: the Father, the Son, the Spirit, and the Godhead. The reason is because each person subsists in the divine essence. "The Father is God or the whole Godhead, so also is the Son and the Holy Spirit."[46] Thus, the three are "distinguished and not divided."[47]

Eternal Generation and Procession

In Perkins's understanding, the Father stands in first place within the Trinity's ordering (or *taxis*).[48] This place integrates into how the Father relates to the Son and how the Father and the Son relate to the Spirit. The Father, as the principal person, eternally generates the second person of the Trinity—the Son. The Father communicates the Godhead to the Son, and the Father and Son

---

42. *Exposition of the Creed*, 5:25.
43. *Exposition of the Creed*, 5:25.
44. *Exposition of the Creed*, 5:25–26.
45. *Exposition of the Creed*, 5:27.
46. *Exposition of the Creed*, 5:27.
47. *Exposition of the Creed*, 5:27.
48. *Taxis* refers to that order among the three persons of the Trinity which is "in full harmony with their *autotheotic* status." Robert Letham, *The Holy Trinity in Scripture, History, Theology, and Worship* (rev. ed.; Phillipsburg: P&R Publishing, 2019), 301, cf. 97, 201–4, 221, 243, 468–73. That is, it is the "order without hierarchy that characterizes God's governing through Word and in Spirit." Lewis Ayres, *Augustine and the Trinity* (Cambridge: Cambridge University Press, 2010), 197.

communicate it to the Holy Spirit, the third person of the Trinity.[49] "God the Father begets His Son," writes Perkins, "by communicating to Him His whole essence or Godhead." This generation happens "before all worlds" and "in Himself." Yet this does not mean that Godhead does not beget Godhead. "The person of the Father begets the person of the Son, both which in one Godhead are really distinct."[50] Perkins's language of communication might seem to imply that the Son is not *autotheos* (that is, God of Himself), but he makes the argument clearly in his 1591 publication, *A Golden Chain*:

> Although the Son be begotten of His Father, yet nevertheless He is of and by Himself very God. For He must be considered either according to His essence or according to His filiation or sonship. In regard of His essence, He is αυτοθεος—that is, of and by Himself very God. For the deity, which is common to all the three persons, is not begotten. But as He is a person and the Son of the Father, He is not of Himself, but from another. For He is the eternal Son of His Father. And thus, He is truly said to be "very God of very God."[51]

The concluding phrase, "very God of very God," draws from the Nicene Creed and shows that Perkins aims to defend Nicene Trinitarian theology. In the surrounding context, he contrasts what is incommunicable (personality) with what is communicable (nature) to the three persons. "The incommunicable property of the Father is to be unbegotten, to be a father, and to beget."[52] The relative personal properties of God then are incommunicable. In contrast, Perkins notes, "The other two persons have the Godhead or the whole divine essence of the Father by communication—namely, the Son and the Holy Spirit."[53] In this sense, the Father is consubstantial with the Son and the Spirit through an ineffable communication of deity, one which shows that the Father, Son, and Spirit (by implication) are essentially *autotheos*.[54]

While one might wish Perkins would further elucidate how "God the Father begets His Son by communicating to Him His whole essence or Godhead," his view of the divine nature provides sufficient grounds to understand his basic meaning. In sum, "The Father is a person without beginning, from all eternity

---

49. *Exposition of the Creed*, 5:25.
50. *Exposition of the Creed*, 5:29.
51. *Exposition of the Creed*, 6:21.
52. *Golden Chain*, 6:21.
53. *Golden Chain*, 6:21.
54. For a brief discussion on this passage and the issue in general, see J. V. Fesko, *The Theology of the Westminster Standards: Historical Context and Theological Insights* (Wheaton, Ill.: Crossway, 2014), 180–81.

begetting the Son."[55] Whatever else eternal generation means, it indicates that
there is never a time when the Son is not one with the Father essentially. "In the
generation of the Son," says Perkins, "these properties must be noted: (1) He
that begets and He that is begotten are together and not one before another
in time; (2) He that begets does communicate with Him that is begotten not
some part but His whole essence; (3) the Father begot the Son not out of Himself, but within Himself."[56] Therefore, there is no temporal or ontological gap
between the Father and Son; rather, the Father and Son "communicate" the
"whole essence." The Son is coessential or consubstantial with the Father.

Eternal generation happens, as Perkins argues, "within" God Himself. It
is not an outward but inward operation, and it points to an eternal relation of
origin between the Father and the Son thereby confirming the communication
of Godhead from the Father to the Son.[57] One cannot locate this generation
within the realm of creation. When a human father begets a son, it happens
externally in time by means of physical bodies. Eternal generation describes a
reality that is mysterious yet true—the Father and the Son have always been the
Father and the Son and the one God. In distinguishing the Father and Son, one
must use the biblical logic embedded within their very names.

The Son, then, relates to the Father by eternal generation. The Father begets,
and the Son is begotten. How then does the person of the Spirit relate to the
Father and the Son? One might think that the Spirit is also eternally begotten of
the Father. But that would make the Spirit a second Son, which Scripture does
not teach. One could say that the Spirit is begotten of the Son, but that would
make the Spirit the Father's grandson and turn the Son into another Father.
Scripture denies any such relation. The Spirit must relate to the Father and
the Son in such a way as to vouchsafe the Triunity of God. The prior options
confuse the persons. The subsisting mode of Father, Son, and Spirit is incommunicable. There cannot be two Sons, two Fathers, or even a grandson. Perkins
writes, "The Son and the Holy Spirit have not a beginning of their nature or of
their Godhead from the Father, but of their person only. The person of the Son
is from the Father, and the person of the Holy Spirit is both from the Father
and from the Son. But the Godhead of all three persons is uncreate[d] and
unbegotten and proceeding from none."[58] In other words, the Spirit is from the

---

55. *Golden Chain*, 6:21. Perkins cites Hebrews 1:3 and Psalm 2:7 to prove the point.

56. *Golden Chain*, 6:21.

57. The phrase "relation of origin" describes the eternal and personal relation between the
Father and the Son. For a recent discussion of relations of origin and personal properties, see
Scott Swain, *The Trinity and the Bible: On Theological Interpretation* (Bellingham, Wash.: Lexham
Academic, 2021), 51–57.

58. *Exposition of the Creed*, 5:26.

Father and the Son, while the Son is from the Father alone, yet the three are one. The personal begetting of the Father is not Godhead producing Godhead but Father begetting the Son.

In like manner, the Spirit proceeds from the Father and the Son, while all three persons subsist in the divine nature. Perkins states, "The Holy Spirit proceeds from the Father and the Son."[59] But how does the Spirit's proceeding and the Son's begetting differ? Perkins does not know, but he is comfortable with mystery. "What may be the essential difference between proceeding and begetting, neither the Scriptures determine nor the church knows."[60] What Scripture certainly affirms is that the Father begets the Son, while the Spirit proceeds from the Father and the Son. These eternal relations name the distinguishing personal characteristics of the persons of the Godhead. They allow one to distinguish the persons in mind while affirming that God is one.

Order and Operations

The fact that the Son and the Spirit receive from the Father does not imply that the Father is greater than the Son and the Spirit. Perkins writes:

> We must know that that which the Son receives of the Father, He receives it by nature and not by grace; and He receives not a part but all that the Father has, saving the personal property. And the Holy Spirit receives from the Father and the Son by nature and not by grace. And therefore, though both the Son and the Holy Spirit receive from the Father, yet they are not inferior to Him but equal with Him.[61]

The Spirit receives from the Father everything except "the personal property," that is, the property revealed in the name, Holy Spirit. That personal property (or characteristic) is incommunicable.

This ordering in God does not imply inferiority. In his commentary on Revelation 1:6, Perkins maintains that the Father is so named according to a Trinitarian ordering and His principal role. "And the first person in the Trinity is here named above the rest not as being above them in degree or honor (for so they are equal), but because He is the first in order and the fountain of the Godhead, which is conveyed from Him to the Son and from them both to the Holy Spirit."[62] Taxis (the triune order of relations), therefore, does not imply a relation

---

59. *Exposition of the Creed*, 5:307.
60. *Golden Chain*, 6:22.
61. *Exposition of the Creed*, 5:26.
62. *Exposition of Revelation 1–3*, 4:346.

of superiority or inferiority, of greater or lesser honor. Degree and honor have no place within the ordering of the Father, the Son, and the Holy Spirit.

While Perkins admit no degrees in the order of God, he does affirm particular modes of action for each of the persons. The Father, the Son, and the Spirit operate inseparably to accomplish the one divine will. More generally, Perkins writes, "For as all the three persons subsist in one and the same divine nature or Godhead, and are not severed in will, in counsel, or in outward actions as creation, preservation, and redemption, save only that they are distinguished in the manner of working, so likewise must they be all conceived in our minds together when we pray, and none severed out though they be not named."[63] In his *Golden Chain*, Perkins defines each person's proper manner of working. Of the Father, he writes, "He is the beginning of actions because He begins every action of Himself, effecting it by the Son and the Holy Spirit."[64] Of the Son, he asserts, "His proper manner of working is to execute actions from the Father by the Holy Spirit."[65] Finally, of the Holy Spirit, he affirms, "His proper manner of working is to finish an action, effecting it as from the Father and the Son."[66] The outward acts of God flow from the Father to the Son and the Spirit; the Son executes action; and the Spirit perfects (or completes) it.

The importance of this doctrine centers on worshiping the one true God. Since His acts are inseparable, so is His worship. In his comments on the Lord's Prayer, Perkins writes:

> Some may say this prayer is a perfect platform of all prayers, and yet we are taught to direct our prayers to the Father, not to the Son or Holy Spirit. I answer, the Father, Son, and Holy Spirit are three distinct persons, yet they are not to be severed or divided, because they all subsist in one and the same Godhead or divine nature. And further, in all outward actions, as in the creation and preservation of the world and the salvation of the elect, they are not severed or divided; for they all work together—only they are distinguished in the manner of working. Now, if they be not divided in nature or operation, then they are not to be severed in worship.[67]

The outward works of the triune God are undivided: *opera trinitatis ad extra sunt indivisa.*[68] This principle means that God works are undivided and only

---

63. *Sermon on the Mount*, 1:430.

64. *Golden Chain*, 6:21.

65. *Golden Chain*, 6:22.

66. *Golden Chain*, 6:22.

67. *Exposition of the Lord's Prayer*, 5:430.

68. For a contemporary treatment of the doctrine of inseparable operations, see Adonis Vidu, *The Same God Who Works All Things: Inseparable Operations in Trinitarian Theology* (Grand Rapids: Eerdmans, 2021).

"distinguished in the manner of working." Christ entered the waters of baptism, the Spirit descended, and the Father spoke. Each accomplished the one work in distinguished manners. As the three are one, so their works are one. One must preserve this understanding for the sake of true worship. "Now, if they be not divided in nature or operation, then they are not to be severed in worship."[69]

Theological Interpretation

While Perkins does not admit any notion of inferiority or superiority into the Godhead, he affirms the commonplace that Christ is lesser according to His humanity and greater according to His divinity.[70] This theological principle, derived from Scripture, also guides his exegesis of the biblical text. Perkins adopts a partitive reading of Scripture, whereby he discerns the two natures of Christ. For example, in his commentary on Revelation, he writes: "Now Christ, as He is Mediator, is inferior to His Father and in that regard is not advanced to equal glory with His Father, though He sits with Him. So, the members of Christ, being inferior unto Him, may sit with Him in His throne, though their glory is unequal. These things for substance have been handled (Rev. 2:25–28)."[71] Perkins does not approach the text apart from knowing and affirming the reality of God in Christ. Hence, when he comes to Revelation 1:17–18, he remarks:

> In this preface, Christ is described by two notable arguments: first, [He is] "the first and the last"; secondly, He "was dead, but is alive." The meaning of them both was shown in 1:17–18, whence they are borrowed. By the first, Christ would signify that He is the ever-living God, without beginning or ending, before all creatures and after them. By the second, that He is true man and assumed man's nature to suffer death for our sins and rose again to live forever and to give to man eternal life. In this description, two points of doctrine are expressed.[72]

Here, then, Perkins interprets Scripture theologically. Since Christ is both divine and human, Scripture may use language that is more fitting to one or

---

69. *Exposition of the Lord's Prayer*, 5:430.

70. For example, based on Philippians 2:6, Augustine affirms, "In the form of a servant which he took he is the Father's inferior; in the form of God in which he existed even before he took this other he is the Father's equal." In another place, he asserts, "The Father is greater than is the form of the servant, whereas the Son is his equal in the form of God. See *The Trinity*, trans. Edmund Hill, ed. John E. Rotelle, 2nd ed. (New York: New City Press, 1991), 77–78. See discussion in Richard A. Muller, *Christ and the Decree: Christology and Predestination in Reformed Theology from Calvin to Perkins*, corrected edition, with a new preface (Grand Rapids: Baker, [1986] 2008), 142–49, 160–71.

71. *Exposition of Revelation 1–3*, 4:626.

72. *Exposition of Revelation 1–3*, 4:455.

the other. Perkins's Trinitarian theology not only leads to worship but shapes how he reads Scripture.

Conclusion

William Perkins profoundly, and yet in keeping with the tradition of the church, affirms that "one of the chiefest" doctrines of religion is "the Trinity of the persons in the unity of the Godhead," and that is "the very foundation" of religion."[73] He adds:

> This is the mystery of all mysteries to be received of us all—namely, the Trinity of the persons in the unity of the Godhead. This form of doctrine must be retained and held for these causes: (1) because by it we are able to distinguish this true God from all false gods and idols; (2) because among all other points of religion this is one of the chiefest, being the very foundation thereof.[74]

The term "religion" is a synonym for worship. Perkins's point, therefore, is that the doctrine of the Trinity supports all else. It is indeed "the mystery of all mysteries."

For Perkins, deep theological reflection complements careful biblical exegesis. While uniting the two, he never imposes his own meaning upon the text. His conviction is that Scripture is its own interpreter. If Scripture speaks of the one God in three persons, then this God has always existed. The implication is obvious: any text that speaks of God speaks of the triune God—He who is eternally the Father, the Son, and the Spirit. Perkins's theological exegesis ensures his abiding relevance for all who seek to affirm the triune God by means of the internal logic of Scripture.

---

73. *Exposition of the Creed*, 5:27.
74. *Exposition of the Creed*, 5:27.

2

The Work of Christ

Raymond A. Blacketer

R. T. Kendall accused the Elizabethan theologian William Perkins[1] of making believers' assurance of salvation dependent upon an inward examination of their good works. Kendall alleged that Perkins reverted to a focus on godly behavior that detracted from John Calvin's emphasis on Christ and His free grace.[2] Kendall's study, and the broader "Calvin against the Calvinist thesis" that it represents, have since been refuted by a considerable body of scholarship.[3]

---

1. For general introductions to the life and thought of William Perkins, see Jan Jacobus van Baarsel, *William Perkins: Eene bijdrage tot de kennis der religieuse ontwikkeling in Engeland, ten tijde van Koningin Elisabeth* (The Hague: H.P. de Swart, [1912]); Louis B. Wright, "William Perkins: Elizabethan Apostle of 'Practical Divinity,'" *The Huntington Library Quarterly* 3, no. 2 (1940), 171–96; John R. Tufft, "William Perkins, 1558–1602: His Thought and Activity" (PhD diss., University of Edinburgh, 1951); Ian Breward, "The Life and Theology of William Perkins, 1558–1602" (PhD diss., University of Manchester, 1963); idem, "The Significance of William Perkins," *The Journal of Religious History* 4 (1966–67): 113–28; Charles Munson, "William Perkins: Theologian of Transition" (PhD diss., Case Western Reserve University, 1971); Mark R. Shaw, "The Marrow of Practical Divinity: A Study in the Theology of William Perkins" (ThD diss., Westminster Theological Seminary, 1981); Paul R. Shaefer, "Protestant 'Scholasticism' at Elizabethan Cambridge: William Perkins and a Reformed Theology of the Heart," in *Protestant Scholasticism: Essays in Reassessment* ed. Carl R. Trueman and R. Scott Clark (Carlisle: Paternoster, 1999), 147–64; R. A. Blacketer, "William Perkins (1558–1602)," in Carter Lindberg, ed., *The Pietist Theologians: An Introduction to Theology in the Seventeenth and Eighteenth Centuries* (Oxford: Blackwell, 2008), 38–51; W. B. Patterson, *William Perkins and the Making of a Protestant England* (Oxford: Oxford University Press, 2014).

2. R. T. Kendall, *Calvin and English Calvinism to 1649* (Oxford: Oxford University Press, 1979). For the broader trend, see Basil Hall, "Calvin against the Calvinists," in *John Calvin*, ed. G. Duffield (Grand Rapids: Eerdmans, 1966), 19–37. Even Ian Breward, one of the more important scholars of Perkins in the twentieth century, frequently read him through the older paradigm of decline. See his "The Life and Theology of William Perkins," esp. ch. 6.

3. An important early work in the dismantling of the older paradigm is Richard A. Muller, *Christ and the Decree: Christology and Predestination in Reformed Theology from Calvin to Perkins*, corrected edition, with a new preface (Grand Rapids: Baker, [1986] 2008). On Perkins, see esp. 160–71. For a more recent review of the scholarship, see R. A. Blacketer, "The Man in the Black Hat: Theodore Beza and the Reorientation of Early Reformed Historiography," in

That older scholarly narrative deeply misunderstood both Calvin and Perkins.[4] Perkins's theology was profoundly centered on Christ.

In this chapter we review Perkins's reflections on the work of Christ. Despite some tendencies toward speculation, Perkins was profoundly focused on the work of Christ as the basis—and essentially the content—of the gospel.

Jesus Christ and His Mediatorial Office

In his *Exposition of the Creed*, the richest source of his thought on the work of Christ,[5] Perkins begins by treating the name *Jesus* and the designation *Christ*. The name *Jesus*, Perkins explains, refers to His two natures, divine and human,[6] as well as His office, and it implies that He "is both a perfect and absolute Savior, as also the [only] Savior of man, because the work of salvation is wholly and only wrought by Him, and no part thereof is reserved to any creature in heaven or in earth."[7] That is, neither sinners nor the departed saints can contribute to a sinner's salvation by their merits or half-merits, contrary to Roman Catholic teaching. In his *Problem of the Forged Catholicism*, Perkins refutes at length the practice of invoking the saints, as well as the late medieval concept of half-merits.[8] There is no other merit than that of Christ the Mediator, and thus in the *Exposition of the Creed*, Perkins claims that the church of Rome makes too much of the name of Jesus by using it in a superstitious way, yet also too little of His name when it claims a role for human merit, making Jesus but half a Savior,

---

Church and School in Early Modern Protestantism: Studies in Honor of Richard A. Muller on the Maturation of a Theological Tradition, ed. Jordan J. Ballor, David S. Sytsma, and Jason Zuidema (Leiden: Brill, 2013), 227–41. Andrew S. Ballitch demonstrates that Perkins does, in fact, point believers to Christ. "'Not to Behold Faith, But the Object of Faith': The Effect of William Perkins's Doctrine of the Atonement on his Preaching of Assurance," *Themelios*, 40, no. 3 (2015): 445–58.

4. See Richard A. Muller, "*Fides* and *Cognitio* in Relation to the Problem of Intellect and Will in the Theology of John Calvin," *Calvin Theological Journal* 25, no. 2 (1990): 207–24.

5. *Exposition of the Creed*, 5:1–416. It is the closest equivalent to a system among Perkins's publications, as he himself appears to acknowledge in his opening comments in *Commentary on Hebrews 11*, 3:5. The creedal order allows Perkins to expound more fully on subjects such as theology proper, the work of Christ, the believer's faith in Christ and union with Christ, and the church. As usual, Perkins also applies the doctrines practically in the form of duties and consolations.

6. On the person of Christ in Perkins, see Andrew S. Ballitch, "God the Son in the Theology of William Perkins," *Puritan Reformed Journal* 9, no. 2 (2017): 147–64.

7. *Exposition of the Creed*, 5:98.

8. By way of example, see *Problem of the Forged Catholicism*, 7:260–70, 279–82. Originally published in Latin in 1604, Perkins here employs his considerable knowledge of the church fathers to argue that the Protestant churches, and not the teachings of the Roman church, best represent the earliest and thus superior thought of the church fathers. Calvin made a similar argument in his *Institutes*, especially in the prefatory letter to King Francis I, see *Joannis Calvini Opera Selecta*, ed. Peter Barth, Wilhelm Niesel, and Dora Scheuner (Munich: Christian Kaiser Verlag, 1926–74), cited as *OS*, 3:17–22.

and invoking the aid of saints, "especially of the Virgin Mary, whom they call 'the queen of heaven,' 'the mother of mercy,' [thereby] requesting of her that 'by the authority of a mother, she would command her Son.'"[9]

Perkins understands the title "Christ" to mean that, as the Mediator, Jesus is anointed in both His human and divine natures to the threefold office of prophet, priest, and king.[10] Perkins, like many other Reformed theologians including Calvin, here echoes the patristic idea of the threefold office to exposit Christ's work as the Mediator. While Calvin did not invent this schema,[11] his use of the pattern in the final, 1559 edition of his *Institutes of the Christian Religion* and in the Geneva Catechism of 1542/45[12] was widely adopted in the Reformed tradition and beyond, making its way into Reformed systems and confessional documents, as well as reemerging in Lutheran dogmatics and even Roman Catholic thought.[13]

In addition to this consecration to His mediatorial office, Christ's anointing also refers to "the pouring out of the fullness of the Spirit of grace into the manhood of Christ," that is, those special gifts, including the Holy Spirit, with which Jesus was endowed in order to fulfill His mission.[14] As a benefit of this anointing, moreover, believers share in that unction and are thereby consecrated to the prophetic, priestly, and royal office, as well as receiving the gift of the Holy Spirit.

Redemption for the Elect

Perkins, in his typical Ramist fashion,[15] proceeds to lay out the work of redemption in terms of whom Jesus saves, by what means, and from what. Perkins is very clear that Christ died intentionally and exclusively for the elect.

---

9. *Exposition of the Creed*, 5:99.

10. *Exposition of the Creed*, 5:103–4.

11. See John Frederick Jansen, *Calvin's Doctrine of the Work of Christ* (London: James Clark, 1956); Klauspeter Blaser, *Calvins Lehre von den drei Ämtern Chrsti*, Theologische Studien, 105 ([Zurich]: EVZ Verlag [1970]), esp. 4 for patristic uses.

12. *OS* 3:471–81 (*Institutes*, 2:15); 2:79–81 (Catechism, cap. 5–6).

13. Robert S. Franks, *A History of the Doctrine of the Work of Christ in its Ecclesiastical Development* (London: Hodder and Stoughton, [1918]), 2:1–6. On the development of the threefold office in Reformed orthodoxy, see Heinrich Heppe, *Reformed Dogmatics Set Out and Illustrated from the Sources*, rev. and ed. Ernst Bizer; trans. G. T. Thomson (London: George Allen & Unwin, 1950), 452–87.

14. *Exposition of the Creed*, 5:104.

15. On Perkins's use of Peter Ramus's pedagogical and rhetorical method, see Donald K. McKim, "The Functions of Ramism in William Perkins's Theology," *Sixteenth Century Journal* 16 (1985): 503–17; idem, *Ramism in William Perkins' Theology* (New York and Bern: Peter Lang, 1987).

He considers the first point, the extent and object of redemption,[16] to be crucial in preserving the sovereignty of God in salvation so that Christ does not
only make salvation available, but fully effects salvation for the elect. Perkins
emphatically denies that "Christ is a Savior of all and every man; for if that were
true, then Christ should make satisfaction to God's justice for all and every
man's sins." Were that the case, Perkins concludes, all persons would be saved.
He teaches the doctrine of particular redemption in a number of his writings,
including *A Golden Chain*, where he opposes a novel and erroneous doctrine:

> There is a certain universal or general election whereby God without any
> either restraint or exception of persons has decreed to redeem by Christ
> and to reconcile to Himself all mankind wholly, fallen in Adam, yea every
> singular person, as well the reprobate as the elect.[17]

In fact, the purpose of *A Golden Chain* was largely to refute those whom he calls
"the new Pelagians," specifically the French theologian Peter Baro (1534–1599)
at Cambridge. Baro had been personally ordained by John Calvin in Geneva,
but his views on salvation apparently changed, so much so that his teachings
anticipated those of Jacob Arminius. Another English divine, William Barrett
(fl. 1595), was also attacking the doctrines of Geneva. The Lambeth articles
(1595) were adopted in response to these teachings, only to be suppressed
by the Queen.[18] In earlier editions of the work, Perkins names two Lutheran
theologians, Jacob Andreae (1528–1590) and Niels Hemmingsen (or Nicholas Hemmingius, 1513–1600)—these men who were on opposite sides in the

---

16. The literature on the extent of redemption is extensive. See R. A. Blacketer, "Blaming
Beza: The Development of Definite Atonement in the Reformed Tradition," in *From Heaven
He Came and Sought Her: Definite Atonement in Historical, Biblical, Theological, and Pastoral
Perspective*, ed. David Gibson and Jonathan Gibson, (Wheaton: Crossway, 2013), 121–41, and
the literature cited there. See also Michael J. Lynch, *John Davenant's Hypothetical Universalism: A
Defense of Catholic and Reformed Orthodoxy* (New York: Oxford University Press, 2021).

17. *Golden Chain*, 6:249. First published in Latin as *Armilla Aurea* in 1590, this treatise is a
basic outline of the order of salvation. Perkins intends to refute views of salvation that misconstrue
God's eternal saving plan and its outworking in history. Not merely a treatise on predestination,
Perkins intends for readers to grow in assurance by understanding God's salvation in Christ as
applied by the Spirit. See Richard A. Muller, "Perkins' *A Golden Chain*: Predestinarian System or
Schematized *Ordo Salutis*?" *Sixteenth Century Journal* 9, no. 1 (1978): 69–81; Patterson, *William
Perkins*, 69–76.

18. See Dewey D. Wallace, *Puritans and Predestination: Grace in English Protestant Theology,
1525–1695* (Chapel Hill: University of North Carolina Press, 1982), 66–68, 72–73; Patterson,
William Perkins, 70–72, 78–80; and Joel R. Beeke and Greg A. Salazar in the preface to Perkins,
Works, 6:xvii–xx.

conflict between Gnesio-Lutherans and Philippists, but who both taught a doctrine of universal grace.[19]

Perkins was determined to prove that the Reformed doctrine of predestination as he understood it, including the specific scope of Christ's redemption and the particularity of grace, was biblical and had broad support not only among numerous Protestant divines but also among the church fathers and medieval theologians, and to that end he wrote his *Treatise on the Manner and Order of Predestination*.[20] This work turned out to be particularly important in the history of Reformed doctrine, given that Jacob Arminius found the teaching highly objectionable. Arminius wrote his own treatise refuting it[21] and sought out Franciscus Junius in order to conduct an epistolary debate on predestinarian teachings.[22] Thomas Tuke, the translator of Perkins's treatise, identifies its target as "some ubiquitaries," that is, Lutherans, whom Perkins had faulted for teaching, among other things, "that the reprobate may be converted and saved," that "Christ died for the reprobates, and that it is the purpose and will of God simply that all men without exception should be saved."[23] In terms of the traditional maxim of Peter Lombard, that Christ's satisfaction was sufficient for all but effective for the elect,[24] Perkins appears to have understood this sufficiency in terms of what John Davenant (1572–1641), a member of the English delegation to the Synod of Dordt, would later refer to as a "mere

---

19. *Armilla Aurea*, 2nd ed. (Cambridge: J. Legatt, 1591), cap. 52, fol. T8v°.

20. It was first published in Latin in 1598. It demonstrates Perkins's full scholastic abilities. He makes extensive use of the church fathers and references a broad range of Reformed theologians in defending his view that Christ died exclusively for the elect and refuting the claim that election or reprobation are based on foreknowledge of human faith or unbelief, merit or demerit, as well as the claim that true believers can fall away to the extent that they lose their salvation.

21. Jacob Arminius, *Examen modestum libelli, quem D. Gulielmus Perkinsus...edidit...de praedestinationis modo et ordine*, in idem, *Opera theologica* (Leiden: Godefridus Basson, 1629), 621–807; translated in *The Works of James Arminius*, trans. James Nichols and William Nichols (1825–75; repr., Grand Rapids: Baker, 1986), 3:249–84.

22. Jacob Arminius, *Amica cum Francisco Junia de praedestinatione per litteras habita collatio*, in *Opera*, 445–619; *Works of James Arminius*, 3:1–248, and on this work, see Richard A. Muller, "Arminius's 'Conference' with Junius and the Protestant Reception of Molina's *Concordia*," in *Beyond Dordt and De Auxiliis: The Dynamics of Protestant and Catholic Soteriology in the Sixteenth and Seventeenth Centuries*, eds. Jordan Ballor, Matthew Gaetano, and David Sytsma (Leiden: Brill, 2019), 103–26.

23. *Manner and Order of Predestination*, 6:277, 351.

24. Peter Lombard, *Sententiae in IV libris Distinctae*, 3:20:5:1, ed. Ignatius Brady (Grottaferrata: Editiones Collegii S. Bonaventurae ad Claras Aquas, 1971–1981), 2:128; idem, *The Sentences*, trans. Giulio Silano (Toronto: Pontifical Institute of Mediaeval Studies, 2007–2010), 3:86.

sufficiency" as opposed to the "ordained sufficiency" that Davenant affirmed.[25] In other words, Perkins affirmed that Christ "paid the price of redemption (λύτρον)" that in itself was of sufficient value to pay for the sins of the entire world of sinners, or even a thousand such worlds.[26] But unlike Davenant, he did not describe this sufficiency as "a general intention or ordination by the death of Christ concerning the salvation of each and every human being under this condition, if they should believe."[27] It is decisive for Perkins that Christ in His priestly office only intercedes for the elect, and that "the Son does not sacrifice for those for whom He does not pray, because to make intercession and to sacrifice are conjoined."[28]

Perkins was aware that some were troubled due to what he considers to be misunderstandings about the doctrine of the so-called "Calvinists," and in this treatise he answers objections. He even asserts, "I do willingly acknowledge and teach universal redemption and grace, so far as it is possible by the Word."[29] Thus, Perkins affirms that "we do acknowledge with glad minds that Christ died for all (the Scripture averring so much); but we utterly deny that He died for all and every one alike in respect of God, or as well for the damned as elect, and that effectually on God's part."[30] Like Calvin and numerous other Reformed thinkers, Perkins interprets the universal statements of Scripture to mean all the elect, or persons chosen from all nations or all classes of people.[31] Drawing on Augustine, he also recommends that believers adopt an attitude of charity with respect to the salvation of others, given that they are unable to discern between the elect and the reprobate.[32] While he accepts in principle the distinction between God's antecedent and consequent will,[33] he denies its suitability for arguing a universal divine will to save all, and he provides numerous objections to it, including that it implies a weakness in or frustration of God's will. If it is objected that this will is conditional upon a sinner's belief, it then

---

25. See Lynch, *John Davenant's Hypothetical Universalism*, 59 and n. 85–88. See also Ballitch, "Not to Behold Faith," 450–51.

26. *Manner and Order of Predestination*, 6:311–12.

27. John Davenant, *Sententia de Gallicana controversia*, in *Dissertationes duae: Prima de morte Christi, quatenus ad omnes extendatur* etc. (Cambridge: Roger Daniels, 1650), fol. Ii [5]v° (note g), translated in Lynch, *John Davenant's Hypothetical Universalism*, 19.

28. *Manner and Order of Predestination*, 6:312.

29. *Manner and Order of Predestination*, 6:304.

30. *Manner and Order of Predestination*, 6:339.

31. *Manner and Order of Predestination*, 6:341–44.

32. *Manner and Order of Predestination*, 6:344.

33. See Richard A. Muller, *Dictionary of Latin and Greek Theological Terms: Drawn Principally from Protestant Scholastic Theology*, 2nd ed. (Grand Rapids: Baker Academic, 2017), cited as *DLGTT*, s.v. *voluntas Dei*.

makes the primary cause, God's will, dependent upon secondary causes, the will of sinners.

Perkins, moreover, because of sin's enslaving effects on the will, denies that sinners can simply choose to believe.[34] Thus, it is not enough for salvation to be made available; it must be made effective. The extent of Christ's redemption, then, is identical with the number of the elect, for whom it is intended. Perkins here draws on Prosper of Aquitaine, the *Hypomnesticon* (a work also by Prosper but misattributed to Augustine), Thomas Aquinas, and Hugh of Saint Victor.[35] Later in the work, he claims that if God intends every individual to be saved, when in fact they are not, then "sin, Satan, death, and hell should be more mighty than Christ the Redeemer, and (as Augustine says), *vitia humano vincitur Deus*—God is overcome by man's sin."[36] He rejects the idea of a universal supernatural grace available to all, enabling persons to believe if they will, because sin imprisons the will. As Augustine points out, God must enable a sinner to believe.[37]

The Nature of Redemption

As Perkins takes up the details of Christ's work, he asks Anselm of Canterbury's classic question: Why did the Son of God become man? Perkins's answers reveal affinities with those of Anselm. First, Perkins replies, the justice of God requires that "in that nature in which God was offended, in the same should a satisfaction be made to God for sin." Thus, the Son had to take on Adam's nature to make satisfaction for Adam's sin, the guilt of which is shared by all his descendants. Secondly, the law that was binding on Adam and all humanity remained unfulfilled. So, Christ's incarnation was necessary so that "in man's nature He might fulfill all righteousness, which the law does exact at our hands." Third, since there is no forgiveness without the shedding of blood, the immortal Son's assumption of a mortal human nature was necessary, "that in man's nature He might die and fully satisfy God's justice for man's offence." Finally, the nature of the office of Mediator makes the incarnation necessary:

> He that must make reconciliation between God and man must be such a one as may make request or speak both to God and man. For a mediator

---

34. *Manner and Order of Predestination*, 6:345.
35. *Manner and Order of Predestination*, 6:346–47.
36. *Manner and Order of Predestination*, 6:353.
37. *Manner and Order of Predestination*, 6:353–54. Perkins incorrectly cites Augustine *De natura et gratia contra Pelagium*, 5; the correct reference is *De gratia Christi et peccato originali*, 1:14:15, in J.-P. Migne, ed., *Patrologiae cursus completus, series Latina* (Paris: Vives, 1844–1865), cited as *PL* 44:368.

is as it were a middle person, making intercession between two other persons—the one offended; the other offending. Therefore, it is necessary that Christ should not only be God to speak unto the Father for us and to present our prayers unto Him, but also man, that God might speak to us, and we to God by Christ.[38]

Under the creedal statement that Christ *suffered under Pontius Pilate,* Perkins addresses Christ's states of humiliation and exaltation. The former he defines as "the condition of Christ the Mediator in which He abased Himself even to the death of the cross, that by that means He might perform the office of a priest in making satisfaction to the justice of His Father." This state of humiliation is not limited to Christ's human nature; in a Perkinsian theme, the divine nature is also humiliated in a sense, in that "the Godhead lay hid from the first moment of the incarnation to the time of His resurrection, without any great manifestation of His power and majesty therein."[39]

Perkins examines the passion of Christ according to seven points, the first four corresponding to traditional Aristotelian fourfold causality. (1) The efficient cause of the passion is "the decree and providence of God," and as Peter says in Acts 2:23, Christ was "delivered by the determinate counsel and foreknowledge of God." Perkins emphasizes that there was no cause in human beings, because they are morally disabled by sin; the efficient cause is solely God's "will and good pleasure."[40] (2) The material cause is the curse of the law, as a result of which Christ endured temptation, disgrace and slanders, many sorrows and causes of grief, and finally, sustaining the wrath of God against sin. (3) The formal cause is the satisfaction that Christ makes to the Father by suffering on behalf of humanity's sin. Perkins adds that "we must conceive it as a propitiation or a means satisfactory to God's justice." Consequently, it is a "most damnable and wicked" opinion of Rome that Christ's passion is insufficient and must be supplemented by works of satisfaction, either those of sinners or of departed saints. (4) The final cause, the goal of the passion, is to "more fully manifest His justice and mercy than He did in the creation, and that is the reconciliation between God and man." Perkins here also emphasizes the "active obedience of Christ in fulfilling the law," because he deems it necessary that both Christ's passive and active obedience must be imputed to the sinner in order to effect salvation. This was a doctrine that developed after the time of the second generation reformers like Melanchthon and Calvin, an emphasis that removes any need for meritorious human obedience in salvation, but one

---

38. *Exposition of the Creed,* 5:121.
39. *Exposition of the Creed,* 5:137.
40. *Exposition of the Creed,* 5:138–39.

that was not at first universally accepted.[41] "Now the passion of Christ considered apart from His legal obedience only takes away the guilt and punishment, frees man from death, and makes Him of a sinner to be no sinner," Perkins asserts; thus, for a sinner to be "fully reconciled to God and accepted as righteous to life everlasting, the legal obedience of Christ must also be imputed."[42]

Perkins adds further distinctions to Christ's passion. (5) As for its duration, it lasted from Christ's birth to His resurrection, but especially concerns the time of His final suffering on the cross.[43] (6) The person who suffered is the very Son of God. Here Perkins answers two questions. First, how can it be just to punish the most righteous person who ever lived, and especially for the sake of "grievous sinners"? Yet Christ is no private person, Perkins observes, but is to be considered "as one in the eternal counsel of God set apart to be a public surety or pledge for us to suffer and perform those things which we in our own persons should have suffered and performed." Here Perkins emphasizes the federally representative and substitutionary nature of Christ's redemptive work, where He stands in the place (or "room," in Perkins's Elizabethan English) of sinners, a phrase that one frequently finds throughout his writings.[44] The second question is how a short and temporary death can free a sinner from eternal death and damnation. Perkins explains that, while only the human nature of Christ can suffer, the passion is attributed to "the whole person of Christ, God and man." He explains, "from the dignity of the person which suffered arises the dignity and excellency of the passion, whereby it is made in value and price to countervail everlasting damnation. For when as the Son of God suffered the curse for a short time, it is more than if all men and angels had suffered the same forever." (7) There is a twofold difference between Christ's passion and the suffering of the martyrs. First, Christ's suffering, Perkins observes, was a cursed punishment, while the martyrs were not cursed by God but only chastised or made to endure trials. Second, Christ's passion was meritorious due both to His office as Mediator who serves as the surety in the covenant of grace and to the special nature of His person. But because the martyrs suffered as private persons, their suffering has nothing to do with us and the idea that they have amassed some "treasure of merit" as Rome teaches is "nothing else but a sense-

---

41. On this doctrine, see Muller, *DLGTT*, s.v. *obedientia Christi*; and in more historical detail, see Heber Carlos de Campos, *Doctrine in Development: Johannes Piscator and Debates over Christ's Active Obedience* (Grand Rapids: Reformation Heritage, 2017).

42. *Exposition of the Creed*, 5:139. See Perkins on the active imputation of Christ's righteousness in *Golden Chain*, 6:181–85, and *Commentary on Hebrews 11*, 3:113–14.

43. Perkins details this suffering at length in *Golden Chain*, 6:57–59.

44. In *Exposition of the Creed* alone we find it numerous times. See 5:143, 156, 170–71, 185, 188, 195, 238, 274, 334, 399.

less dotage of man's brain." As for the idea that Christ obtained merit so that the saints could also obtain merit for others, Perkins finds this ridiculous, "as if they should say the Son of God became Jesus to make everyone Jesus."[45]

After considering the passion itself, Perkins takes up the phrase "under Pontius Pilate," which is significant for Christ's work in various ways. First, because Pilate was the governor of the Jews at the time, Christ's trial is the fulfillment of numerous prophecies regarding the Jews. More significantly, however, and more astounding, is that "Christ, the Son of God, King of heaven and earth, was arraigned at the bar of an earthly judge and there condemned." Again, Perkins emphasizes, Christ's arraignment before Pilate is not that of a private person, but as the one who represents sinful humanity in a covenantal or federal way. Humanity, then, was "arraigned before God" in Christ, and, moreover, this arraignment occurred publicly, in the sight of the whole world, and in unwitting fulfillment of God's eternal plan.[46]

Perkins goes into further detail about this arraignment, analyzing it in terms of Christ's apprehension, accusation, and condemnation. Notably, Perkins reflects on Christ's preparation to be apprehended in the garden of Gethsemane. Even this detail is important to the work of Christ, because, as Perkins exposits it, Jesus deliberately chose that place so that His enemies could easily find Him. And so "it is manifest that Christ yielded Himself to death willingly and not of constraint; and unless His sufferings had been voluntary on His part, they could never have been a satisfaction to God's justice for our sins."[47] In connection with this, Perkins answers the question of whether it is permissible to flee danger or persecution. It is permissible, Perkins counsels, if one is not strong enough to bear the cross, if such flight serves God's glory and the good of one's neighbor, and if it is in accord with one's calling; a serving magistrate or pastor may not flee unless there is a release from their charge.

A notable speculation on Perkins's part arises as he proceeds to consider Christ's prayer in the garden. He considers the question of how Jesus, knowing His Father's plan and the purpose of His own coming into the world, could ask to avoid the cup of suffering, and do so without sinning, which is quite a reasonable question. Perkins replies that this petition arises "only of a weakness or infirmity in Christ's manhood without sin." When Christ made this request, "the whole wrath of God and the very dolors [sorrows] and pangs of hell seized upon Him," which caused "the senses and powers of His mind" to be stunned, so that they were "wholly bent to relieve nature in His agony."

---

45. *Exposition of the Creed*, 5:140.
46. *Exposition of the Creed*, 5:143.
47. *Exposition of the Creed*, 5:145.

Perkins further explains this as a mental disturbance in Jesus, according to His human nature, caused by an external source, namely, "the apprehension of God's anger." With rather bold speculation, Perkins claims that this perception of divine wrath did not take away Christ's understanding or memory to the extent that He "forgot His Father's will, but only stopped and stayed the act of reasoning and remembering for a little time." Further, to the objection that Christ's will and that of the Father were completely contrary, Perkins responds, "Christ's will as He is man and the will of His Father in this agony were not contrary but only diverse, and that without any contradiction or contrariety."[48] This is a traditional theological distinction that goes back to Augustine.[49] Perkins illustrates: A minister may charitably will the salvation of everyone in the congregation whereas the Lord in His eternal counsel does not necessarily will the same.[50] After much more consideration of Christ before Pilate, Perkins concludes that the purpose of Christ's condemnation, "though not in Pilate's will, yet in God's eternal counsel—was that He might be the cause of absolution at the bar of God's justice unto all those whatsoever they are which shall come to life eternal."[51]

Proceeding to Christ's execution, burial, and descent into hell, Perkins notes a twofold significance in the fact that He was crucified. First, it fulfills Old Testament types of Christ's sacrifice, such as Moses's bronze serpent, but more importantly, it assures us that Christ submitted to the law and its curse in the place of sinners, bearing God's wrath upon sin.[52] Characteristically, Perkins identifies many more details of the crucifixion in which he finds both theological meaning, practical import, and even polemical ammunition (against Roman crucifixes, for example). His treatment of Christ's forsakenness is remarkable as well. Perkins asserts that "Christ's manhood was forsaken," not in a severing of the incarnation, but in that "the Godhead of Christ, and so the Godhead of the Father did not show forth His power in the manhood but did as it were lie asleep for a time, that the manhood might suffer."[53] Perkins seems to have derived this idea from Irenaeus, whom he cites in *A Golden Chain*: "The Word rested that the human nature might be

---

48. *Exposition of the Creed*, 5:147.

49. Augustine, *Enchiridion*, 101, PL, 40:279. Western theologians frequently take up Augustine's example, e.g., Thomas Aquinas, *Summa Theologiae* Ia-IIae Q.19 art. 10; Calvin, *Institutes*, 1:18:3.

50. *Exposition of the Creed*, 5:148.

51. *Exposition of the Creed*, 5:175.

52. *Exposition of the Creed*, 5:182.

53. *Exposition of the Creed*, 5:189; cf. Perkins's discussion of Christ's exaltation, 5:236.

crucified and dead."[54] Notably, Perkins says, Christ's "manhood seemed to be forsaken."[55] And yet Perkins seems to imply that it is more the feeling of being forsaken than the Father actually turning His back, so to speak, on the Son, or even on the Son's human nature. For Christ calls out, "My God, my God," exhibiting trust that He is not, in fact, forsaken or hated by the Father. Perkins, moreover, draws a lesson from this, that faith continues even when feelings of confidence or assurance are absent.[56]

Nonetheless, Perkins teaches that Christ suffered both the first and, in a certain sense, the second death, that is, physical death as separation of the soul from the body, and the second death as separation of both body and soul from God. This, again, is a phenomenon that Perkins describes in terms of Christ's feeling or experience: "He did in soul apprehend the wrath of God due to man's sin." But Perkins makes it clear that Christ was not "wholly and every way to be severed from all favor of God," and He was not "forsaken of God more than in His own apprehension or feeling. For in the very midst of His sufferings the Father was well pleased with Him."[57]

It is on the cross that Christ performs important aspects of His priestly office, though not all of them. He offers His manhood as a propitiatory sacrifice, though He is priest in both His divinity and humanity, and He fulfills the Old Testament types of both the Aaronic priesthood and that of Melchizedek. His sacrifice is once for all, contrary to the repeated sacrifice of the Roman mass. But His priesthood also includes Christ's ongoing intercession for believers, that God will accept His sacrifice, as well as His role as teacher of doctrine, something that one might have expected under the office of prophet. His sacrifice purges believers of sin, justifies them before God, relieves their consciences from "dead works" (Heb. 6:1), and makes them free to enter heaven.[58] Notably, unlike Peter Lombard, who, in his maxim about the sufficiency and efficiency of the price Christ paid, identified the cross as the altar, Perkins asserts that Christ is the priest, the sacrifice, and the altar. Specifically, Christ's divinity is the altar.[59] He bases this conclusion on Matthew 23:19, where Jesus says the altar sanctifies the sacrifice. Thus, the divinity of Christ both sets apart

---

54. *Golden Chain*, 6:58; Irenaeus, *Against Heresies*, 3.19.3; *Libros quinque adversus haereses*, ed. W. W. Harvey (Cambridge: The University Press, 1857), 2:104. See Ballitch, "God the Son," 151, 154.

55. *Exposition of the Creed*, 5:189.

56. *Exposition of the Creed*, 5:190.

57. *Exposition of the Creed*, 5:196–97.

58. *Exposition of the Creed*, 5:202–7.

59. *Exposition of the Creed*, 5:207.

His manhood to be the sacrifice for the sins of believers and gives His death a merit and worth beyond that of any other man.

After treating Christ's victory on the cross and His burial, Perkins goes on to discuss the creed's statement about Christ's descent into hell. Perkins is not at all confident about this assertion, and the first thing he notes is that some (Pierre Viret and Desiderius Erasmus) had argued the phrase was a later addition to the creed.[60] He assumes that the words have "crept into the text," but he acknowledges that they have been hallowed by long use. He considers four major interpretations of the *descensus*. First, it refers to the descent of Christ's soul to the place of the damned. Perkins rejects this theory for lack of biblical warrant and the fact that Jesus tells the thief that he will be with Him in paradise, as well as other reasons that Perkins adduces at length.[61] Second, it refers to Christ being buried, but Perkins rejects this as pointlessly superfluous. Third, it means that on the cross Christ "felt and suffered the pangs of hell and the full wrath of God seizing upon His soul."[62] Perkins considers this the usual interpretation, and he considers it a true statement but not the best interpretation of the creed, since that meaning should already be assumed under the terms "crucified, died, and was buried." Instead, Perkins affirms a fourth interpretation, that "when He was dead and buried, He was held captive in the grave and lay in bondage under death for the space of three days." This has the added aesthetic benefit, perhaps a result of Perkins's love for symmetrical Ramist analysis,[63] that Christ's humiliation would then have three stages, death, burial, and the period of captivity in the grave, to correspond with the three stages of Christ's exaltation: resurrection, ascension, and present session.[64]

The Exaltation of Christ

The exaltation of Christ is the gradual awakening, so to speak, of the divinity that was mostly dormant during Jesus's humiliation; Christ's divinity becomes increasingly evident.[65] Here Perkins allows himself a remarkable latitude

---

60. See Pierre Viret, *Exposition familière faicte par dialogue sur le symbole des apostres*, rev. ed. (Geneva: J. Girard, 1546), 118 (indicated in *Exposition of the Creed*, 5:229 n. 249 as "P. Viretin. Symb."); Desiderius Erasmus, *Colloquies, Inquisitio de fide*, in *Collected Works of Erasmus* (Toronto: University of Toronto Press, 1974), 39:426.

61. *Exposition of the Creed*, 5:230–33.

62. *Exposition of the Creed*, 5:233.

63. See Lori Anne Ferrell, "Transfiguring Theology: William Perkins and Calvinist Aesthetics," in *John Foxe and his World*, ed. Christopher Highly and John N. King (Aldershot: Ashgate, 2002), 160–79.

64. *Exposition of the Creed*, 5:234.

65. *Exposition of the Creed*, 5:236.

for speculation. He imagines Christ's glorified body to be free of the scars of crucifixion, though they remain temporarily as a witness to the disciples and especially Thomas, and he presumes that glorified bodies can levitate, based on the ascension. Nevertheless, His body remains a real body and thus retains the properties of such, contrary to those who would, for example, make His flesh omnipresent.[66]

In discussing the resurrection, Perkins notes that Christ rises not as a private but as a public person; that is, He represents all believers. It is a vicarious resurrection, such that believers today have in a sense already been raised. A notable feature of Perkins's doctrine of the resurrection is his repeated assertion that Christ raised Himself from the dead by His own power, that of His divine nature, despite considerable biblical ambiguity about the agency of the resurrection.[67] Why does Perkins cite the gospel of John to that effect (2:19, 10:18), yet make no mention of the far greater number of passages that indicate the agency of God generally (usually understood to be the Father), the Father specifically, or, in a few cases, the Holy Spirit?[68] One possible answer is the distant threat of the Socinians, the radical sect centered in Poland that revived ancient Arian teachings and denied the divinity of Christ, though this would not become a significant feature of polemics in England until three decades after Perkins's death.[69]

Christ ascends into heaven by His own powers: a combination of Christ's divine power and the new power of His glorified body. Here polemics are again necessary. Perkins emphasizes that Christ really ascends bodily to heaven; thus, His physical body is not present on earth, contrary to both Roman and Lutheran eucharistic and Christological doctrine. Yes, Christ keeps His promise to remain with His church always, but that promise is fulfilled by the presence of His Spirit.[70] This polemic returns when Perkins considers Christ's session at the Father's right hand; Christ as He is man, and as the Mediator, is inferior to the Father, Perkins contends. The creature is always inferior to the Creator; accordingly, there is no communication of divine attributes to Christ's human nature as the proponents of Christ's ubiquity contended.[71]

---

66. *Exposition of the Creed*, 5:237–38, 246–47.

67. *Exposition of the Creed*, 5:238, 240, 251–52, 255, 400. See *Golden Chain*, 6:62.

68. On this tendency among Reformed theologians, see Heppe, *Reformed Dogmatics*, 498.

69. See Sarah Mortimer, *Reason and Religion in the English Revolution: The Challenge of Socinianism* (Cambridge: Cambridge University Press, 2010).

70. *Exposition of the Creed*, 5:260.

71. *Exposition of the Creed*, 5:272.

Conclusion

If space allowed, we could say far more about Perkins's exposition of the work of Christ and His future work of returning to judge the living and the dead. We have largely overlooked Perkins's extensive sections on the application of these doctrines. Nonetheless, this brief overview is sufficient to provide a window into this most popular and bestselling of Reformed theologians of his day. Through the panes we see a Perkins who is profoundly biblical, sensitively pastoral and practical, one who is critically respectful of the patristic and medieval theological inheritance. Immovably focused on Christ—not only incarnate in history but as the eternal Son of God—Perkins seeks to produce a truly Reformed catholic theology.

3

Sin, Grace, and Free Will

Matthew N. Payne

William Perkins's account of sin, grace, and free will go to the heart of his theological and pastoral agenda, both literally and figuratively. His views on these themes are drawn principally from biblical, Augustinian, and Reformed sources, and fit within the mainstream of international Reformed theology in the early modern period.[1] Perkins was a particularly notable case of an English theologian who read and imbibed the thought of a wide range of European theologians, including Calvin, Beza, Vermigli, Zanchius, Ursinus, Musculus, and others.[2] Indeed, works such as Calvin's *Institutes*, Bullinger's *Decades*, and the commonplace volumes of Vermigli and Musculus were well known among Perkins's contemporaries, and Perkins was more widely read than most, as attested both by his published works and reputation among his contemporaries.[3] While Perkins made remarkably broad use of patristic and medieval theological writings, Augustine (354–430), and to a lesser extent Bernard of Clairvaux (1090–1153), appear as particularly prominent influences with respect to these themes.

Recent scholarship has emphasized that Perkins was a conformist theologian within the established English church.[4] As such, he developed his

---

1. Richard A. Muller, *Grace and Freedom: William Perkins and the Early Modern Reformed Understanding of Free Choice and Divine Grace* (Oxford: Oxford University Press, 2020). Cf. Stephen Hampton, "Sin, Grace, and Free Choice in Post-Reformation Reformed Theology," in *The Oxford Handbook of Early Modern Theology, 1600–1800*, eds. Ulrich L. Lehner, Richard A. Muller, A. G. Roeber (Oxford: Oxford University Press, 2016), 228–41.

2. Muller, *Grace and Freedom*, 7, 14–16.

3. Fuller reports that Perkins "had a rare felicity in speedy reading of books, and as it were but turning them over would give an exact account of all considerables therein…perusing books so speedily, one would think he read nothing; so accurately, one would think he read all." Thomas Fuller, *The Holy State* (Cambridge: Roger Daniel, 1642), 91. The inventory taken of Perkins's possessions upon his death reveals that he owned one of the larger book collections in Cambridge (Cambridge University Library, Archives, VCCt Inventories folder 6).

4. W. B. Patterson, *William Perkins and the Making of a Protestant England* (Oxford: Oxford University Press, 2014), esp. 40–63.

theological views within the bounds of the confessional standard of the English church, the Thirty-Nine Articles of Religion (1563, 1571), even while he elaborated upon its teaching, both theologically and practically.[5] Indeed, in the midst of theological controversy, Perkins's Cambridge colleagues would claim that his account of predestinarian grace was merely that of the English confession.[6] Such protestations notwithstanding, it is more accurate to recognize that the English confession allowed a broader range of Reformed theological views than those of Perkins and his circle, not least on matters relating to sin and grace.[7] It is at this point that the Puritan character of Perkins's work becomes important as a means to distinguish it among late-Elizabethan English Reformed theologies. A large part of what distinguishes Perkins's account of predestinarian grace from that of other English conformist predestinarians, such as Richard Hooker and Archbishop John Whitgift, is his distinctly Puritan practical divinity. Whitgift's thought came to expression in quietistic, and even fatalistic, maintenance of social and ecclesiastical order: so long as the means of grace remained available, he reasoned, God could be expected to be at work.[8] Hooker also emphasized the priority of ecclesiastical and liturgical order, in his case by producing an expansive and highly sophisticated theological defense of the ecclesiastical *status quo*.[9]

---

5. In the early modern period, the English (or "Anglican") Church was Reformed, and its confession was recognized as such in the international Reformed community. See Stephen Hampton, "Confessional Identity," in *Reformation and Identity, c. 1520–1662*, in *The Oxford History of Anglicanism*, ed. Anthony Milton (Oxford: Oxford University Press, 2017), 1:210–27; Donald John MacLean, *"Ours Is a True Church of God": William Perkins and the Reformed Doctrine of the Church*. St Antholin Lecture, 2018 (London: The Latimer Trust, 2019).

6. H. C. Porter, *Reformation and Reaction in Tudor Cambridge* (Cambridge: Cambridge University Press, 1958), 322. Perkins himself claimed that his double predestinarian theology was "the doctrine of the Church of England." *Exposition of the Creed*, 5:355.

7. Hampton, "Confessional Identity," 217–19. Jay Collier's recent work moves the discussion forward on the foundation of Tyacke's "Calvinist consensus" by beginning to delineate the significantly different views on predestinarian grace that existed within that broad consensus. Jay T. Collier, *Debating Perseverance: The Augustinian Heritage in Post-Reformation England* (Oxford: Oxford University Press, 2018); cf. Nicholas Tyacke, *Anti-Calvinists: The Rise of English Arminianism c. 1590–1640* (Oxford: Clarendon Press, 1987). Such diversity reflected the Reformed tradition more broadly. See Richard A. Muller, "Diversity in the Reformed Tradition: A Historiographical Introduction," in *Drawn into Controversie: Reformed Theological Diversity and Debates within Seventeenth-Century British Puritanism*, Reformed Historical Theology 17, ed. Herman J. Selderhuis (Göttingen: Vandenhoeck & Ruprecht, 2011), 1–30.

8. Peter Lake, *Anglicans and Puritans? Presbyterianism and English Conformist Thought from Whitgift to Hooker* (London: Allen & Unwin, 1988), 37–42.

9. Hooker's great work, *Of the Laws of Ecclesiastical Polity*, was released in several parts during and after his lifetime (Bks. I–IV, 1593; Bk. V, 1597; Bks.VI & VIII, 1648; Bk. VII, 1662). On Hooker's Reformed doctrines of sin and grace, see Randall Ingalls, "Sin and Grace," in *A Companion to Richard Hooker*, Brill's Companions to the Christian Tradition 8 (Leiden: Brill, 2008), 151–83. For comparisons between Hooker and Perkins, see W. B. Patterson, "Richard

In contrast, Perkins's theology of sin and grace came to expression in zealous evangelistic concern for all of England, powerful preaching, pastoral training, tireless pastoral engagement with individual seekers, and intensely rigorous and introspective piety. Perkins happily operated within existing ecclesiastical arrangements while maintaining a quietly unenthusiastic stance toward them.[10] For Perkins, the practical implications of understanding sin and grace aright made matters of ecclesiastical polity so relatively unimportant that he barely ever mentioned them. What truly mattered was that English people would know themselves as sinners and would know Christ as full of grace. Such differences of emphasis, temperament, and priority often proved as significant as formal theological differences and were a substantial part of what tended to delineate theologians into distinguishable factions.[11]

Perkins's practical divinity brought the life of godliness to the forefront of theological and practical concern, combining Reformed predestinarian soteriology with an intensely practical "how to" approach to matters of faith, conscience, and Christian conduct.[12] Whereas many clergy excelled as either pastoral practitioners or theologians, Perkins excelled at both, establishing himself as a preeminent Reformed theologian and as a celebrated practical instructor, whether by preaching, pastoral counseling, or publishing. The

---

Hooker and William Perkins: Elizabethan Adversaries or Allies?" in *Richard Hooker and Reformed Orthodoxy*, eds. W. B. Littlejohn and S. N. Kindred-Barnes, Reformed Historical Theology 40 (Göttingen: Vandenhoeck & Ruprecht, 2017), 61–71; Bryan Spinks, *Two Faces of Elizabethan Anglican Theology: Sacraments and Salvation in the Thought of William Perkins and Richard Hooker*, Drew University Studies in Liturgy 9 (Lanham: Scarecrow Press, 1999).

10. This is the essence of what Lake describes as "moderate puritanism." Peter Lake, *Moderate Puritans and the Elizabethan Church* (Cambridge: Cambridge University Press, 1982). Perkins's lack of enthusiasm for the ecclesiastical particulars of the Elizabethan settlement modifies Patterson's claim that he was an "apologist" for the England Church. Patterson, *William Perkins*, 40–63. It is more accurate to say that he promoted magisterial Reformed Christianity in general. Cf. *Exposition of the Creed*, 5:376–84.

11. On these differences, see especially Peter Lake, "'Puritans' and 'Anglicans' in the History of the Post-Reformation English Church," in *Reformation and Identity, c. 1520–1662*, in *The Oxford History of Anglicanism*, ed. Anthony Milton (Oxford: Oxford University Press, 2017), 1:352–79; Peter McCullough, "Avant-Garde Conformity in the 1590s," in *Reformation and Identity, c. 1520–1662*, in *Oxford History of Anglicanism*, 1:380–94.

12. On practical divinity, see Michael P. Winship, "Weak Christians, Backsliders, and Carnal Gospelers: Assurance of Salvation and the Pastoral Origins of Puritan Practical Divinity in the 1580s," *Church History* 70, no. 3 (2001): 462–81; Kenneth Parker and Eric J. Carlson, *"Practical Divinity": The Works and Life of Revd Richard Greenham* (Aldershot: Ashgate, 1998), 87–119; David D. Hall, *Puritanism: A Transatlantic History* (Princeton: Princeton University Press, 2019), 109–43; Lake, *Moderate Puritans*, 116–68; Charles E. Hambrick-Stowe, "Practical Divinity and Spirituality," in *The Cambridge Companion to Puritanism*, ed. John Coffey; (Cambridge: Cambridge University Press, 2008), 191–205.

scholarly sophistication of Perkins's thought must not lead us to overlook the fact that virtually all his work retains an essentially practical orientation. Even his most scholastic wrangling over proper theological distinctions is ultimately directed toward establishing a stable theological foundation upon which sinners might experience the "blessed life" of grace that arises from a true knowledge of God, and that without hindrance from false and misleading theologies.[13]

Perkins's Axioms Relating to Sin and Grace

Before progressing, it will prove helpful to the reader to lay out several axioms of Perkins's thought upon which his accounts of sin and grace are built.

The Creator-Creation Distinction and Causality

Fundamental to Christian theology is the distinction between God and all else, the Creator and His creation. Upon this foundational distinction Perkins constructed his theology of grace, and of divine and human action. With respect to causality—a major concern in Perkins's thought—this foundational doctrine came to expression in the distinction between transcendent divine causation (primary causality) and created causes including human wills (secondary causality).[14] God is simple, eternal, and transcendent, and thus His will is one eternal act, though it comes to expression in creation in a multitude of secondary causes, unfolding in "degrees" toward His decreed ends.[15]

The importance of the transcendence of primary causality with respect to secondary causes is difficult to exaggerate. In popular understanding, divine and created causes are typically pictured as mutually exclusive explanations for events acting in competition with one another. Imagery of God as a kind of divine puppet master is commonplace in the modern imagination, particularly in pejorative portrayals of Calvinism. Indeed, the popular modern notion of a "God of the gaps" with respect to knowledge of the natural world assumes that primary and secondary causality are competing explanations of events. The idea is that divine causality is ruled out as an explanation of something to the extent to which we can offer purely natural explanations for it, and thus with every degree of increase in scientific knowledge, there is a corresponding degree to which God's action and presence are exorcised from the universe. Yet Perkins, along with the Christian tradition broadly, emphasized that God's

---

13. *Golden Chain*, 6:11.

14. Perkins typically refers to "second causes." *Sermon on the Mount*, 1:308; 384; *Commentary on Galatians*, 2:173; 364, 375; *Exposition of Jude*, 4:51; *Exposition of the Creed*, 5:45–46, 360; *Golden Chain*, 6:24–25; *Manner and Order of Predestination*, 6:303, 330–36, 345, 352, 430; *Prognostication*, 9:417; *Three Books on Cases of Conscience*, 8:241–42.

15. *Golden Chain*, 6:47, 170–89, 212–13, 242–47.

will is transcendent, and thus occupies a noncompetitive relationship to created causality.[16] Indeed, primary causality is the metaphysical substructure
upon which created causes are established, sustained, and enabled to function
according to their own inherent natures. Thus, Perkins's strong emphasis on
God's comprehensive determination of all history and human destiny[17] does
not undermine the contingencies inherent in creation:

> The first and principal cause, howbeit in itself it be necessary, yet it does
> not take away freedom of will in election or the nature and property of
> second causes, but only brings them into a certain order. That is, it directs
> them to the determinate end, whereupon the effects and events of things
> are contingent or necessary, as the nature of the second cause is.[18]

While God's will imposes a comprehensive determining necessity on all things,
it is a transcendently imposed necessity. "This kind of necessity takes not away
the contingency and liberty of second causes, but rather establishes and confirms it."[19] In this way, primary causality determines "that the agency of second
causes shall be according to their condition, so as natural causes shall work
naturally; free causes, freely; necessary causes, necessarily; contingent causes,
in contingent and variable sort."[20]

In sum, God's eternal decree both transcendently imposes a comprehensive necessity upon creation and establishes that created beings will genuinely
operate as what they are, with their own inherent causal integrity. In this, as
recent research has emphasized, Perkins's views on necessity and contingency
fit within the mainstream of early modern Reformed orthodoxy.[21]

---

16. Carter highlights the centrality of this notion to the broader Christian tradition,
critiquing modern "theistic personalism," a distinctly modern notion that treats God as a person
in the same sense as us (rather than analogically), and thus operating in the same manner as
us in creation: "If one takes a theistic personalist position, then one is automatically driven in
an Arminian direction in which God's acts and our acts are on the same plane and therefore in
direct opposition. The more God acts, the less we do; the more we act, the less God does. It is a
zero-sum game: both actors are beings within the universe in competition with each other. In the
Great Tradition (not just Calvinism), God operates on an entirely different plane than creatures
do." Craig A. Carter, *Interpreting Scripture with the Great Tradition: Recovering the Genius of
Premodern Exegesis* (Grand Rapids: Baker Books, 2018), 54–56.

17. "There is nothing in the world that comes to pass either universally or particularly
without the eternal and unchangeable decree of God." *Exposition of the Creed*, 5:332.

18. *Golden Chain*, 6:24.

19. *Manner and Order of Predestination*, 6:334.

20. *God's Free Grace*, 6:430. For further discussion of necessity, see *Manner and Order of
Predestination*, 6:332–38.

21. See Willem J. van Asselt, J. Martin Bac, and Roelf T. te Velde (eds.), *Reformed Thought on
Freedom: The Concept of Free Choice in the History of Early-Modern Reformed Theology* (Grand

As we shall see, many of Perkins's central contentions regarding grace and soteriological causality flow out of this understanding of the Creator-creature distinction. First, it is the reason that Perkins relentlessly contends that God's decree must be the sovereign first cause of all things, completely unconditioned by human actions, including foreseen ones. To hold otherwise is to transgress the Creator-creature distinction by presenting the creature as having a causal effect upon God the first cause, which is among the most fundamental metaphysical and theological errors a theologian can make.[22]

Second, the Creator-creature distinction corresponds to that between grace and nature. In short, nature has no power to even desire, much less seek, supernatural grace. The power of salvation must come entirely from the other side, with God supernaturally empowering natural man to seek and to know Him: grace perfecting nature.[23] Perkins was not only opposed to theologies that explicitly compromised the monergism of grace, but also to theologies that treat grace as a universally available commodity, thus for all practical purposes transforming grace into nature.

Free Choice and the Conditions of Nature

Perkins held that at the level of secondary causality, human wills are contingent and possess genuine freedom of choice, even while operating under the necessity of God's decree as primary cause. Thus, human choices are not determined by any inherent necessity (which would contradict the very notion of choice) though they are determined by the transcendent necessity of God's decree. Perkins illustrates this principle by describing people going to a church service: "Before they come they had all freedom and liberty in themselves to come or not to come," and yet unbeknownst to them they came according to God's providence, "and in that respect necessarily."[24]

Richard Muller's recent study on Perkins's views of grace and free will represents not only a significant contribution to Perkins scholarship but is also part of an ongoing debate on how to characterize the relationship between divine sovereignty and human free choice in early modern Reformed thought.[25] Paul

---

Rapids: Baker, 2010), 30–47; Richard A. Muller, *Divine Will and Human Choice: Freedom, Contingency, and Necessity in Early Modern Reformed Thought* (Grand Rapids: Baker, 2017), 181–324; Muller, *Grace and Freedom*, 155–81.

22. *Manner and Order of Predestination*, 6:352–53, 361–62; *Exposition of the Creed*, 5:357–58; *Golden Chain*, 6:48.

23. *Sermon on the Mount*, 1:494; *Commentary on Galatians*, 2:47, 120; *Exposition of Jude*, 4:186; *Exposition of the Creed*, 5:11; *Manner and Order of Predestination*, 6:349, 373; *God's Free Grace*, 6:387, 426; *Grain of Mustard Seed*, 8:647. See also Muller, *Grace and Freedom*, 127–28, 193.

24. *Exposition of the Creed*, 5:45, 86.

25. Muller, *Grace and Freedom*.

Helm (and others) have argued that early modern Reformed theology is fundamentally *compatibilist*, asserting both determinism and human moral agency.[26]
In contrast, Muller argues that this is anachronistic, and he seeks to frame
these matters in the terms in which early modern thinkers understood them.[27]
Muller (and others) have argued that the early modern Reformed understanding of human free choice entails genuine alternativity rather than an inherent
determination to one effect as compatibilism holds.[28] Simply stated, to say that
human beings make genuinely free choices means that they could have chosen otherwise. This is what fundamentally distinguishes human willing from
bare animal instinct. In Perkins's words: "The liberty of will stands in double
power. The first is when it wills anything of its own self to be apt and able to
nill the same, and so on the contrary, and it is called in schools 'the liberty of
contradiction.'"[29]

While Helm's framing of these issues may be more intuitive to many modern
readers (compatibilism, after all, is built upon philosophical categories native to
our own intellectual milieu), at the level of historical description Muller's account
is convincing. The difference may be illustrated with reference to Perkins's critique of astrological prediction. One of the foundations of Perkins's critique is
that astrology assumes a deterministic account of secondary causality, whereby
sufficient knowledge of physical causes might theoretically enable one to predict
the future. In contrast, Perkins portrays creation as a complex web of intersect-
ing and overlapping secondary causes, each acting in accordance with their own
inherent natures.[30] The nature of human agency, even within this cosmological

---

26. Helm defines compatibilism as follows: "Some determinate states of affairs are consistent
with praise or blame. Freedom and responsibility are consistent with determinism." Paul Helm,
Reforming Free Will: A Conversation on the History of Reformed Views (Carlisle: Mentor, 2020),
239. See also Paul Helm, "'Structural Indifference' and Compatibilism in Reformed Orthodoxy,"
Journal of Reformed Theology 5 (2011): 184–205; Michael Patrick Preciado, *A Reformed View
of Freedom: The Compatibility of Guidance Control and Reformed Theology* (Eugene: Pickwick
Publications, 2019); James N. Anderson and Paul Manata, "Determined to Come Most Freely:
Some Challenges for Libertarian Calvinism," *Journal of Reformed Theology* 11 (2017): 272–97.

27. See Muller, *Divine Will and Human Choice*; Muller, "Goading the Determinists: Thomas
Goad (1576–1638) on Necessity, Contingency and God's Eternal Decree," *Mid-America Journal
of Theology* 26 (2016): 59–75.

28. Muller, *Grace and Freedom*, 1–6, 45–68, 94; idem, *Divine Will and Human Choice*,
46–79, 311–24. Helm argues that contingency with respect to human agency is properly
understood as "spontaneous choice" determined to one effect. *Reforming Free Will*, 188, 227.
A key difference occurs at the level of terminology. Early modern authors treated the language
of "determine" abstractly as "to render something definite," whereas moderns tend to read it in
causal terms. See Muller, *Grace and Freedom*, 162–64.

29. *God's Free Grace*, 6:397. See discussion in Muller, *Grace and Freedom*, 115–16.

30. Perkins, *Prognostication*, 9:416–18, 420–22, 426, 430–31.

setting of diverse causes and influences, remains one of nondetermined free choice.[31] Here Perkins does not reason as a compatibilist might, contending for the compatibility of human free agency with a deterministic universe, rather he held that these notions were strictly *incompatible*.

However, Perkins should not be understood as propounding a kind of libertarian account of free will wherein human free choice consists in an arbitrary and unhindered range of choices unshackled from any kind of determination.[32] Firstly, human choices are always made in accordance with God's determining decree. A key contributor to the debate about free will is compatibilism's tendency to conflate primary and secondary causality, supplanting the distinction with an overarching determinism.[33] It then forces all views into a narrow set of mutually exclusive options: one is either a determinist or a libertarian with no third option,[34] and without specifying whether the determinism under consideration belongs to primary or secondary causality.[35] Perkins's

---

31. *Prognostication*, 9:422, 429–30.

32. Helm mistakenly characterizes Muller as holding to nondeterminism or a form of libertarianism. *Reforming Free Will*, 14, 15, 19, 22, 35. See Muller, *Divine Will and Human Choice*, 29.

33. Muller has highlighted this problem as follows. "Arguably, the modern understandings of both compatibilism and libertarianism operate without a significant distinction between primary and secondary causality, without a clear understanding of divine concurrence, and without the assumption, intrinsic to the notion of an ontologically and causally two-tiered universe, that divine and human causality are, taken together, the necessary and sufficient conditions for free acts of the human will.... [These ideas] yielded a highly nuanced view of necessity, contingency, and freedom." Muller, *Divine Will and Human Choice*, 324.

34. Helm's recent volume, *Reforming Free Will* (2021), exemplifies the problem of forcing historical theological figures into a set of predetermined philosophical categories: one is either compatibilist or libertarian (non-determinist) with no third way (239). Freedom either denotes freedom from compulsion or pure alternativity with no middle way (227). Helm's analysis does not consider whether the determinism under discussion belongs to primary or secondary causality, a consideration which radically impacts the possible positions one might take. Although Helm discusses the distinction, he does not appear to recognize its significance (166–67, 180–88). Cf. Muller, *Grace and Freedom*, 165–66. Analysis is thus hamstrung from the start by ill-fitting analytical categories. It is true that much of early modern Reformed thought has a significant degree of compatibility with compatibilism (as Muller recognizes in *Divine Will and Human Choice*, 295, 322–24). However, (contra Helm) it does not follow that this distinctly modern position is the native conceptual framework within which early modern thought is best understood. The points at which it hinders rather than promotes historical understanding, such as those highlighted above, adequately testify to its shortcomings.

35. From one perspective, Muller and Helm approach these issues from competing historical points of reference, Muller reading through late-medieval categories, and Helm arguing that the Protestant Reformers tacitly used modern categories. A significant aspect of this debate has therefore hinged on the historical "moment" when Reformed thought allegedly shifted on the issue of determinism. Muller contends that Jonathan Edwards (1703–1758) represents a departure from Reformed Orthodoxy on freedom, in large part by conflating primary and

discussion characteristically keeps this distinction clear: "The same action may be both necessary and contingent: necessary, in regard of the highest cause, the counsel of God; not necessary but contingent, in respect of the second causes, as among the rest, the will of man."[36]

Second, for Perkins, human free choice is always exercised according to the properties of human nature. As was standard among the Reformed orthodox, Perkins discussed anthropology at two levels: substance and accidents.[37] First, he described the substance of human personhood according to the common premodern anthropology. As such, he made significant use of faculty psychology, according to which the human soul possesses the faculties of the mind (which contains conscience and memory), the will, and the affections. The workings of these inward faculties dictate the acts of the body.[38] Such is the anthropological map upon which Perkins laid out the effects of sin and grace in the human person.

---

secondary causality such that human willing is deterministic at the level of secondary causality. Richard A. Muller, "Jonathan Edwards and the Absence of Free Choice: A Parting of Ways in the Reformed Tradition," *Jonathan Edwards Studies* 1, no. 1 (2011): 15, 21. Cf. idem, "Jonathan Edwards and Francis Turretin on Necessity, Contingency, and Freedom of Will. In Response to Paul Helm," *Jonathan Edwards Studies* 4, no. 3 (2014): 266–85; idem, "Neither Libertarian nor Compatibilist: In Response to Paul Helm," *Journal of Reformed Theology* 13 (2019), 267–86. See also Philip John Fisk, *Jonathan Edwards's Turn from the Classic-Reformed Tradition of Freedom of the Will*, New Directions in Jonathan Edwards Studies 2 (Göttingen: Vandenhoeck & Ruprecht, 2016). In response, Helm has set out to demonstrate that Edwards's compatibilism was shared by earlier Reformed theologians. Paul Helm, "A Different Kind of Calvinism? Edwardsianism Compared with Older Forms of Reformed Thought," in *After Jonathan Edwards: The Courses of the New England Theology*, eds. Oliver D. Crisp and Douglas A. Sweeney (Oxford: Oxford University Press, 2012), 91–104; idem, "Jonathan Edwards and the Parting of the Ways?" *Jonathan Edwards Studies* 4, no. 1 (2014): 42–60; idem, "Turretin and Edwards Once More," *Jonathan Edwards Studies* 4, no. 3 (2014): 286–96; idem, "Francis Turretin and Jonathan Edwards on Compatibilism," *Journal of Reformed Theology* 12 (2018): 335–55; idem, *Reforming Free Will*, 105–59; idem, "Francis Turretin and Jonathan Edwards on Contingency and Necessity," in *Learning from the Past: Essays on Reception, Catholicity and Dialogue in Honour of Anthony N. S. Lane*, eds. Jon Balserak and Richard Snoddy (London: Bloomsbury T & T Clark, 2015), 163–78. Cf. "Reformed Thought on Freedom: Some Further Thoughts," *Journal of Reformed Theology* 4 (2010): 184–206.

36. *Exposition of the Creed*, 5:46.

37. Perkins's account of free will follows this structure, first discussing the will and subsequently its accidents according to the four states. *God's Free Grace*, 6:405–28. Cf. Muller, *Grace and Freedom*, 45–154. Cf. *Commentary on Hebrews 11*, 3:407–8; *Exposition of the Creed*, 5:89; *Golden Chain*, 6:37. Cf. van Asselt, *Reformed Thought on Freedom*, 43–46. On faculty psychology generally, see Paul Helm, *Human Nature from Calvin to Edwards* (Grand Rapids: Reformation Heritage Books, 2018), 79–210; Perry Miller, *The New England Mind: The Seventeenth Century* (Harvard: Harvard University Press, 1983), 239–79.

38. *Golden Chain*, 6:37–40, 187–89; *Discourse of Conscience*, 8:7–9.

Second, for Perkins, the range of possible choices available to the human will is determined by the accidental properties of one's nature, as determined by one's state as either created, fallen, redeemed, or glorified.[39] This description of the four states of man was seminally outlined by Augustine, and was used by Perkins and other Reformed theologians to distinguish the potential choices available to sinners and saints.[40] He therefore paid close attention to the effects of sin and grace on the faculties.[41]

Finally, Perkins's account of free will insists that a sufficient explanation of human acts involves the alignment of primary and secondary causes (*concursus*) wherein divine causality retains priority as the providential basis of creaturely action.[42] As such, Perkins characteristically describes God's determination and governance of humanity in the language of subtle orchestration—"orders," "arranges," "inclines," and the like[43]—not denoting control or manipulation, but rather God's absolute sovereignty over secondary causes such that they retain their inherent properties and potentialities without coercion.

Covenant Theology

Perkins's covenant theology set the priorities for his theology of sin and grace. Man was created for a covenantal relationship with God wherein each party would mutually fulfill their promises to the other. Man's promise of allegiance to God, expressed in the covenant of works, calls him to perfect obedience to God's moral law.[44] By sinning man transgressed that covenant and lost the ability to fulfill its demands. In Christ God fulfilled the covenantal conditions in man's place, fundamentally transforming man's position in the covenant into

---

39. *God's Free Grace*, 6:405–28; *Combat of the Flesh and Spirit*, 9:179–80. See discussion in Muller, *Grace and Freedom*, 97–154.

40. Augustine, *Enchiridion*, ch. 118; idem, *On Rebuke and Grace*, ch. 33. Perkins also made use of Bernard's exposition of this framework in the latter's *On Grace and Free Will*. Muller, *Grace and Freedom*, 42, 97, 127. See further Han-Luen Kantzer Komline, *Augustine on the Will: A Theological Account* (Oxford: Oxford University Press, 2019).

41. *Golden Chain*, 6:37–40, 187–89; *Treatise Whether a Man*, 8:483–88. See also Matthew N. Payne, "William Perkins's Doctrines of Faith and Assurance through the Lens of Early-Modern Faculty Psychology," *Westminster Theological Journal* 83 (2021): 317–36.

42. *God's Free Grace*, 6:428–30. See discussion in Muller, *Grace and Freedom*, 145–46, 155–72. Helm questions how Muller's account of free will with genuine alternativity can make God's decree correspond to the actualities of human decisions except by sheer coincidence. *Reforming Free Will*, 189.

43. *Manner and Order of Predestination*, 6:334; *God's Free Grace*, 6:396–97, 430; *Golden Chain*, 6:24; *Exposition of the Creed*, 5:86; *Exposition of Revelation 1–3*, 4:314.

44. *Golden Chain*, 6:65–66.

that of a recipient.[45] Nevertheless, the two-sided shape of covenantal thought structures Perkins's theology of grace in at least two ways.[46]

First, the covenant of grace is intended to produce godly and obedient people. To that end, the progressive renewal of human agency toward full obedience to God's law sits in the foreground of Perkins's thought, wherein God works in man that he might live out his side of the covenantal relationship even while God fulfills it in him and for him. This is the underlying rationale for the strongly voluntaristic language pervading Perkins's work: the Christian must "labor," "strive," "endeavour," "groan," and so on.[47] The rigorous tone of Perkinsian piety is based on his conviction that God is graciously at work by His Spirit to renew human agency for the obedience which He has sought in humanity from the very dawn of creation.[48] Thus, the Decalogue remains central to Christian moral instruction for the regenerate "for it guides them to new obedience in the whole course of their life."[49]

Second, the covenant of grace exacts conditions of man, namely faith and repentance, however these conditions are dramatically tempered by grace. While Perkins asserts that Christians must strive for faith and repentance, he also insists that God imputes whatever deficiency exists in the faith and repentance of the regenerate.[50] Perkins's account of the "mustard seed" of faith describes how the least genuine desire after Christ is, by its very nature, a work of supernatural grace, and testifies to God's present acceptance of that seeker, and His urging them onward to further growth.[51]

---

45. *Golden Chain*, 6:153–55.

46. On the mutuality of the covenant in Perkins, see Woolsey, *Unity and Continuity*, 472–89. Woolsey observes that "the strong unilateral strain in Perkins's ethical teaching did not minimize the bilateral tone" (488).

47. See *Golden Chain*, 6:178–79; *God's Free Grace*, 6:427. Exhortations of this sort pervade virtually all of Perkins's writings.

48. See Woolsey, *Unity and Continuity*, 467–72.

49. This is known as "the third use of the law." *Golden Chain*, 6:152. Perkins's exposition of the Decalogue is found in *Golden Chain*, 6:67–150.

50. As Perkins repeatedly stated, God "accepts the will for the deed." *Sermon on the Mount*, 1:275, 432, 552; *Commentary on Galatians*, 2:121; *Commentary on Hebrews 11*, 3:222–23; *Exposition of Revelation 1–3*, 4:557–58; *God's Free Grace*, 6:424–25; *Reformed Catholic*, 7:122–23; *Three Books on Cases of Conscience*, 8:165, 210; *Treatise Whether a Man*, 8:590; *Case of Conscience*, 8:601, 638; *Grain of Mustard Seed*, 8:648, 650; *Nature and Practice of Repentance*, 9:163. Perkins derived this notion from John Bradford. *Case of Conscience*, 8:638; *Grain of Mustard Seed*, 8:650. See also Payne, "Faith and Assurance," 328.

51. See *Grain of Mustard Seed*, 8:639–58; *Golden Chain*, 6:178–79; *Exposition of the Creed*, 5:14–16; *Foundation of Christian Religion*, 5:502.

Perkins's Inwardness and Introspection

One of the distinctives of Perkins's theology is its inward, introspective character, and the central place he gives to the role of conscience.[52] The conscience is "of a divine nature," and functions as the judging presence of God within man, variously approving or disapproving his actions, and serving as the instrument by which he may know his estate before God and in relationship to others.[53] Thus *A Case of Conscience* (1592) identifies the issue of Christian assurance as the greatest issue confronting the conscience, and his enormous pastoral manual *The Whole Treatise of the Cases of Conscience* (1606) resolves questions of conscience relating to man's status before God (book 1), his worship of God (book 2), and his relationship toward others (book 3).[54]

Perkins's introspective emphasis becomes particularly clear by way of contrast. Calvin's *Institutes of the Christian Religion* famously begins with the claim that true wisdom consists of two parts, "the knowledge of God and of ourselves."[55] Perkins's *A Golden Chain* (1592) begins with an echo of Calvin, though with his own distinctly introspective emphasis: "Blessed life arises from the knowledge of God.... And therefore it arises likewise from the knowledge of ourselves, because we know God *by looking into ourselves*."[56]

Perkins is not here advocating a kind of mysticism in which divine knowledge wells up within. Indeed, he was emphatically devoted to the exclusive authority and sufficiency of Scripture for divine knowledge, as attested by his devotion to expository Bible teaching, and his cessationist stance on ecstatic prophesy.[57] Rather, Perkins's point is that the experience of knowing God is inseparable from the process of introspective self-examination, whereby one observes the workings of sin and grace in one's own soul. Likewise true worship begins with "experimental knowledge" both of the vile depths of sinful nature and of "what we are by grace."[58] Throughout his works, Perkins maintains a stark contrast between a merely outward or superficial Christian profession,

---

52. See further Baird Tipson, *Inward Baptism: The Theological Origins of Evangelicalism* (Oxford: Oxford University Press), 79–109.

53. *Discourse of Conscience*, 8:7–9, 86–94; *Exposition of the Creed*, 5:83.

54. *Case of Conscience*, 8:595–638; *Three Books on Cases of Conscience*, 8:95–440; *Combat between Christ and the Devil*, 1:87.

55. Calvin, *Institutes*, 1:1:1.

56. *Golden Chain*, 6:11 (emphasis added).

57. *Art of Prophesying*, 10:289–90; *Damned Art of Witchcraft*, 9:396; *Commentary on Galatians*, 2:39–42. On Perkins's approach to Scripture, see Andrew S. Ballitch, *The Gloss and the Text: William Perkins on Interpreting Scripture with Scripture* (Bellingham: Lexham Press, 2020).

58. *Warning against Idolatry*, 7:476.

which can be feigned, and the inward experience of grace, which cannot.[59] Indeed, a central priority of Perkins's ministry was that more people might move from bare outward profession toward seeing and feeling the depths of the sin within their souls, in order that they might subsequently likewise see and feel God's regenerating grace within. People must "descend" into and "ransack" their own hearts by the law and gospel if they are to proceed on the journey toward knowing and experiencing God's grace.[60]

A striking example of Perkins's introspective emphasis is his *Exhortation to Repentance*, originally a pair of sermons preached at Stourbridge Fair, Cambridge, in 1593, in which Perkins explains "the manner how men in repentance are to search themselves."[61] The sermon describes introspective self-examination for sin using a range of vivid images to portray the vastness of sin within and the rigorous intent one must have to expose it.[62] To that end, he expressed his threefold doctrine of sin (outlined below) into three "rules" for self-examination.[63] Perkins emphasizes that while people like to keep close account of the deeds of others, the internal nature of sin means that exposing its true depths is something that all must do for themselves, each person having an exclusive inward-facing window within them through which they might observe the state of their own soul before God.[64]

The Polemical Context of Perkins's Account of Sin and Grace

Perkins regarded his *A Golden Chain* as the definitive account of his theology,[65] and thus it presents a fitting starting point for investigating most of his doctrines. This is particularly so in relation to the doctrines of sin and grace since the work is structured according to the Reformed *ordo salutis* (order of salvation), and thus treats sin and grace as among its central concerns.[66] Perkins's

---

59. *Exposition of the Creed*, 5:220; *Golden Chain*, 6:174; *Treatise Whether a Man*, 8:57–59, 451–64; *Grain of Mustard Seed*, 8:645; *Damned Art of Witchcraft*, 9:389–90; *God's Free Grace*, 6:408.

60. *Sermon on the Mount*, 1:271–72, 530, 718; *Exposition of Revelation 1–3*, 4:397; *Exposition of the Creed*, 5:277; *Treatise Whether a Man*, 8:469.

61. *Exhortation to Repentance*, 9:79 (titlepage).

62. *Exhortation to Repentance*, 9:90–94.

63. *Exhortation to Repentance*, 9:96–104.

64. *Exhortation to Repentance*, 9:94–96, 104–5.

65. Muller's observation that this is not a "body of divinity" or a systematic theology notwithstanding, we must allow Perkins to define his own work, somewhat idiosyncratic though it may appear. In the diagram at the beginning of the work, he frames it as his account of the "sacred science of theology" and ends the work with "thus much theology" (2:265). *Golden Chain*, 6:7, 265. See Muller, "Perkins's *A Golden Chain*: Predestinarian System or Schematized Ordo Salutis?" *Sixteenth Century Journal* 9, no. 1 (1978), 80–81; idem, *Grace and Freedom*, 26–29.

66. *Golden Chain*, 6:32–46, 153–55, 172–202.

double-predestinarian framework is well-known, especially as represented in the chart appended to the work.[67] It sets out a soteriological vision for the eternal destinies of elect and reprobate alike, and their paths to their respective ends, all grounded in God's "decree and eternal counsel," which itself has no cause besides God's own "will and pleasure."[68] Perkins was deeply committed to the notion that, for grace to be grace, God's predestinating will must be entirely unconditioned by anything outside God Himself.

The preface to *A Golden Chain* introduces the main theological alternatives to Perkins's account of grace, namely *Pelagianism* (both in its ancient and contemporary forms), *Lutheranism*, and *Roman Catholicism*, which Perkins describes as "semi-Pelagian."[69] While Perkins's theology underwent no substantial changes during his career, polemical necessity led him to formulate and articulate his position with a greater degree of scholarly sophistication in several of his later works.

Pelagianism

First, Perkins distinguished between "new" and "old" Pelagians. Pelagius (c. 360–420) taught that humanity was capable of faith and good works without the enabling of divine grace. Perkins mainly took his understanding of Pelagianism from Augustine, Pelagius's most significant opponent.[70] The identity of Perkins's "new Pelagians" is more elusive, partly because he nowhere specifies the target of his critique. Moreover, classical Pelagianism was heterodox by measure of England's Reformed confessional standard, which asserted that God's prevenient and cooperating grace were necessary for the performance

---

67. *Golden Chain*, 6:9.

68. *Golden Chain*, 6:5.

69. *Golden Chain*, 6:5. This polemical framing was not present in the first Latin edition. *Armilla Aurea*, 1590. The preface appeared in 1591, as did the chapter critiquing Roman Catholic soteriology (6:219–41). The chapter critiquing Lutheran soteriology appeared in the 1592 revision (6:248–57). The editor of *Manner and Order of Predestination*, Thomas Tuke, rehearses Perkins's taxonomy in his dedication (6:277).

70. Perkins made regular reference to Augustine's key works on grace, including *On Rebuke and Grace, Treatise on the Gift of Perseverance, Of Predestination and Grace, On Nature and Grace, On the Spirit and the Letter, On Grace and Free Will*, as well as a range of more general works, significantly including *City of God, Enchiridion*, and *Tractates on the Gospel of John*. Many of Augustine's most important works on grace can be found in *Nicene and Post-Nicene Fathers, Volume 5: Augustine: Anti-Pelagian Writings, First Series*, ed. Philip Schaff (Peabody, Mass.: Hendrickson Publishers, 1994). For discussions of Perkins's use of Augustine, see Donald K. McKim, "Perkins, William (1558–1602)," in *The Oxford Guide to the Historical Reception of Augustine*, ed. Karla Pollman (Oxford: Oxford University Press, 2013), 3:1517–19; Muller, *Grace and Freedom*, 7–8, 67–8, 111–12, 161–62, 190; David M. Barbee, "A Reformed Catholike: William Perkins's Use of the Church Fathers" (PhD diss., University of Pennsylvania, 2013), 204–59.

of faith and good works, and that works prior to conversion are displeasing to God.[71] In short, to straightforwardly profess Pelagianism in England was to be a heretic. Perkins's concern was that a new, subversive form of Pelagianism was emerging among confessing Protestant theologians which effectively amounted to the old Pelagian error of negating the necessity of God's particular redeeming grace for salvation. While Perkins does not engage this position directly in *A Golden Chain*, it was the target of sustained critique in his *Exposition of the Creed* (1595) and *Manner and Order of Predestination* (1598).[72] The Pelagian "new frame or platform" which Perkins critiques represents the synthesis of his own extensive reading of contemporary Protestant theologians.[73]

New Pelagians, Perkins asserts, hold that God's predestination was determined by His foresight of who would receive grace by the power of their natural human free will.[74] Their theological work-around to this conclusion (under the guise of orthodoxy) was to assert that prevenient grace is universal, placing all of humanity in a position to choose or reject salvation by grace.[75] In so doing

---

71. The Thirty-Nine Articles of Religion, articles 10, 13.

72. *Exposition of the Creed*, 5:355–65; *Manner and Order of Predestination*, 6:351–81; *God's Free Grace*, 6:412–15.

73. Perkins identifies the "platform" with new Pelagianism in *Manner and Order of Predestination*, 6:376. While much research remains to be done, the identities of some of these theologians can be ascertained by the connection between Perkins's critique of this position and the Cambridge predestinarian dispute of 1595, from which emerged the Lambeth Articles, a brief set of theological distinctions intended to clarify the teaching of the Thirty-Nine Articles of Religion on predestination (art. 17). Key "Pelagians" included Cambridge's own Lady Margaret Professor of Divinity, Peter Baro (1534–1599), and John Overall (1559–1619) who was appointed Regius Professor of Divinity in the wake of these disputes. See further Mark R. Shaw, "William Perkins and the New Pelagians: Another look at the Cambridge Predestination Controversy of the 1590s," *Westminster Theological Journal* 58, no. 2 (1996): 267–301; Porter, *Reformation and Reaction*, 277–413; David Hoyle, *Reformation and Religious Identity in Cambridge, 1590–1644* (Cambridge: Cambridge University Press, 2004), 41–95; Collier, *Debating Perseverance*, 20–58; Seán Hughes, "The Problem of 'Calvinism': English theologies of predestination c. 1580–1630," in *Belief and Practice in Reformation England: A Tribute to Patrick Collinson from his Students*, ed. Susan Wabuda and Caroline Litzenberger (Aldershot: Ashgate, 1998), 241.

74. *Golden Chain*, 6:5; *Manner and Order of Predestination*, 6:277. More fundamentally, this difference in soteriology is grounded in different doctrines of God. For Perkins, God sovereignly chooses objects of his love or hatred; therefore, His grace is particular. *Golden Chain*, 6:16, 47. The "platform" presents God as simply "infinite love, goodness, and mercy itself," and therefore grace is essentially the indiscriminate overflow of these attributes toward creation, expressed in indefinite and universal election, redemption, and calling. *Exposition of the Creed*, 5:355–56.

75. *Sermon on the Mount*, 1:196, 420–22, 572, 639, 662–63, 707; *Commentary on Galatians*, 2:201, 204; *Commentary on Hebrews 1–11*, 3:250, 332–33; *Exposition of Jude*, 4:261–62; *Exposition of Revelation 1–3*, 4:449, 452–53, 503, 553; *Exposition of the Creed*, 5:298–99, 329–30, 334–35, 355–56, 360–65, 395; *Golden Chain*, 6:248–54, 256–57; *Manner and Order of Predestination*, 6:304, 310–11, 341–51, 353–60, 372–78; *Three Books on Cases of Conscience*, 8:164–65.

they de facto "turn grace into nature,"[76] undermining Protestant soteriology at a fundamental level.[77]

Lutheranism

Perkins's first major polemical engagement with alternative Protestant accounts of predestinarian grace came with the second revision of *A Golden Chain* (1592), in which he added a chapter "concerning the new devised doctrine of predestination taught by some new and late divines" in Germany, which reflected engagement with the Formula of Concord (1577) and Lutheran theologians such as Jakob Andreae, Niels Hemmingsen, and Samuel Huber.[78] Perkins describes this position in essentially infralapsarian and single-predestinarian terms, arguing that it rightly maintains sovereign grace with respect to election (and thus Perkins insists that Lutheran churches are true churches, though they differ with the Reformed on important points),[79] yet that it erroneously bases reprobation upon foreseen human response, thus subjecting primary causality

---

76. *Manner and Order of Predestination*, 6:378. Citing Peter Martyr Vermigli, *Loci Communes*, class 3, ch. 1. See *Exposition of the Creed*, 5:365.

77. To call this position "Arminian" is anachronistic, though there are similarities. See Richard A. Muller, "Grace, Election, and Contingent Choice: Arminius' Gambit and the Reformed Response," in *The Grace of God and the Bondage of the Will*, ed. Thomas Schreiner and Bruce Ware (Grand Rapids: Baker, 1995), 2:251–78. When Perkins died in 1602, Jacob Arminius (1560–1609) was still a pastor at Amsterdam working out his personal theological convictions; however, it is noteworthy that one of Arminius's landmark works (*Examen Modestum*, 1612) was a critique of Perkins's *Manner and Order*. While Arminius's work only appeared in print after both men had died, both works played a significant role in the lead-up to the Synod of Dort (1618–19). For an English translation of Arminius's treatise, see Jacob Arminius, "An Examination of the Treatise of William Perkins concerning the Order and Mode of Predestination," in *The Works of James Arminius*, trans. James Nichols and William Nichols (London: Longman, Rees, Orme, Brown, & Green, 1875), 3:249–525. Nevertheless, while there were no "Arminians" in Perkins's day, many of the churchmen who Perkins would label as "Pelagian" would embrace Arminianism when it emerged in the early seventeen century. See Tyacke, *Anti-Calvinists*.

78. *Golden Chain*, 6:248–57. In *The Formula of Concord* (1577), see especially the articles on original sin (art. 1), free will (art. 2), and election (art. 11), which argues strongly for single predestination and equally strongly against active reprobation. See further Joel R. Beeke, *Debated Issues in Sovereign Predestination: Early Lutheran Predestination, Calvinian Reprobation, and Variations in Genevan Lapsarianism*, Reformed Historical Theology 42 (Göttingen: Vandenhoeck & Ruprecht, 2017), 47–54, 75–76. The excerpt from Beza appended to *A Golden Chain* (6:267–72) came from a published version of Beza's debate with Jakob Andreae at the Colloquy of Montbéliard (1586). See discussion in Beeke, *Debated Issues*, 37–45. See also Dewey D. Wallace, *Puritans and Predestination: Grace in English Protestant Theology 1525–1695* (Chapel Hill: University of North Carolina Press, 1982), 73; Hughes, "The Problem of Calvinism," 237–38; Muller, *Grace and Freedom*, 29.

79. *Exposition of the Creed*, 5:379, 382–83; *Exposition of Jude*, 4:245. Note that Perkins describes Lutherans as holding to both a particular and a universal election. *Golden Chain*, 6:248–49; *Exposition of the Creed*, 5:379.

to the contingencies of secondary causes.[80] Further, it falls prey to some of the universalizing tendencies of the Pelagians, though less egregiously. It is, there-fore, unsurprising that Perkins did not maintain a clear distinction between the "Lutheran" and "New Pelagian" positions in subsequent works; his main concerns about the soteriology emerging from Germany increasingly found more pronounced expression in the emerging Pelagian "platform" whose voice and influence was only growing in England.[81]

Roman Catholicism

As with Protestants generally, Perkins's primary theological opponent through-out his career was Roman Catholicism. *A Golden Chain* included a chapter critiquing Roman Catholic soteriology from its second Latin edition (1591).[82] Perkins made substantial critique of the Roman Catholic doctrines of sin and grace in several major treatises, most notably in his *A Reformed Catholic* (1597) and *God's Free Grace and Man's Free Will* (1601).[83] He also made Roman Cathol-icism a regular point of contrast and critique throughout his sermons, not least on these themes.[84]

Perkins's engagement with Roman Catholic theology is lengthy due to the complexity of the issues. In brief, we might summarize his concerns under the "semi-Pelagian" categorization. Roman Catholicism's deficient account of the effects of original sin lead it to posit that human response to the gospel is by a combination of natural human willing and divine grace, rather than by the

---

80. *Golden Chain*, 6:5. For a comparison of the early modern Reformed and Lutheran approaches to election, see Robert Kolb and Carl R. Trueman, *Between Wittenberg and Geneva: Lutheran and Reformed Theology in Conversation* (Grand Rapids: Baker, 2017), 87–115.

81. Note the overlap in Perkins's critiques of the Lutherans (*Golden Chain*, 6:248–57) and the Pelagians (*Manner and Order of Predestination*, 6:351–81). The key difference is that the Lutherans held to a form of sovereign election, where this is dropped in the latter scheme. The connection between various members of these groups is reflected in the correspondence between Cambridge Lady Margaret Professor of Divinity, Peter Baro (doubtlessly one of Perkins's "new Pelagians") and the Danish Lutheran, Niels Hemmingsen. See Hoyle, *Reformation and Religious Identity*, 81, 86. Perkins makes a positive use of Hemmingsen elsewhere. *Art of Prophesying*, 10:356.

82. *Golden Chain*, 6:219–41.

83. *Reformed Catholic*, 7:13–24, 51–63, 105–10; *God's Free Grace*, 6:387–90, 410–12. See *Problem of the Forged Catholicism* for Perkins's engagement with patristic thought in connection to Roman Catholicism on free will (7:242–47), concupiscence (7:248–49), venial sin (7:249–51), merit (7:279–82), and penance (7:338–43). Muller notes that *Reformed Catholic* and *God's Free Grace* contain Perkins's most detailed accounts of grace and free choice. *Grace and Freedom*, 17, 31, 47–51. The latter work was especially set against the theology of the eminent Roman Catholic theologian, Robert Bellarmine.

84. See *Sermon on the Mount*, 1:239, 471, 689–90; *Commentary on Galatians*, 2:116, 153–54, 167–68, 224, 303, 326, 337, 370; *Commentary on Hebrews 11*, 3:16, 40–41; *Exposition of Jude*, 4:64, 73, 91, 213, 254, 259–60.

sovereign enabling grace of God alone. This aligns with the Roman Catholic conflation of justification and sanctification which turns salvation into a meritorious work. As a result, they teach a false optimism about the possibility of attaining perfection in this life alongside such a feeble view of divine grace that even the elect might apostatize and be eternally condemned.[85] Such theology is "no better to be accounted of than as a gallows set up for the torture and massacre of men's consciences."[86]

Perkins's Doctrine of Sin

Perkins's account of sin is decidedly Augustinian and Reformed in content and emphasis and echoes the discussion of sin and its effects in the Thirty-Nine Articles of Religion.[87] Sin in all its aspects flows from the original transgression of Adam. Perkins distinguishes sin into three parts: original guilt, original corruption, and actual sin.[88]

Original Guilt

All of Adam's descendants share in his original transgression and consequent guilt.[89] Perkins does not settle on a single theory of how Adam's guilt and corruption is transmitted to his descendants, but canvasses two. The first approximates federal headship, whereby Adam was a "public person" whose estate is shared with his descendants whom he represents. The second focuses on the seminal presence of Adam's descendants in him and makes use of contagion imagery to convey the notion that a corrupted humanity can only produce corrupted offspring.[90] However, Perkins expresses disinterest in identifying the precise mechanism by which Adam's descendants participate in his guilt, preferring to focus on its factuality and its desperate need of a solution.[91]

Original Corruption

Throughout his writings Perkins emphasizes the presence and effects of original corruption in all people. As with Protestants generally, Perkins holds an Augustinian account of concupiscence—the "flesh"—referring to the

---

85. *Golden Chain*, 6:5, 220–41; *Reformed Catholic*, 7:15–16, 21–22, 34–36, 58, 107.

86. *Golden Chain*, 6:223.

87. *The Thirty-Nine Articles of Religion*, articles 9–16. The broad contours of Perkins's doctrine of sin are found in *Golden Chain*, 6:32–46.

88. *Golden Chain*, 6:36; *Exhortation to Repentance*, 9:96–104; *Exposition of the Creed*, 5:82–94.

89. *Golden Chain*, 6:36.

90. *Golden Chain*, 6:36; *Exposition of the Creed*, 5:89–91. See further Muller, *Grace and Freedom*, 109–10, 122.

91. *Exposition of the Creed*, 5:90.

inordinate inward disposition and desire to sin.[92] Concupiscence is the first motion toward actual sin. Not only is concupiscence explicitly prohibited by the tenth commandment,[93] but the full application of the commandments applies them all to the desires of the heart,[94] thereby exposing one's sinful estate before God.[95] Thus Perkins made concupiscence a focal point for the establishment of personal guilt. While he acknowledged the goodness of outward civil conduct, he warned that many congratulate themselves for their civility and equate it to good standing before God, which only further blinds them to the sea of corruption within.[96] Mere civility must not be mistaken for regenerating grace; only the latter transforms the heart.

Sin is a privative notion, meaning that at an ontological level sin does not exist as such. Sin itself is not a "thing," a part of God's creation; rather "sin" describes a defect, lack, or distortion in creation.[97] Sin parasitically thrives upon created being's potential for change, particularly upon the potentiality of human wills to choose badly. Thus, under the corruption of sin, the human will suffers loss with respect to created goodness: "though liberty of nature remain, yet liberty of grace—that is, to will well—is lost, extinguished, abolished by the fall of Adam."[98]

Sin corrupts the faculties, not the substance of human nature, leading Perkins to describe the specific corrupting effects upon the mind, conscience, will,

---

92. *Commentary on Galatians*, 2:172, 223–24, 360, 368–69; *Exposition of Jude*, 4:211–15; *Golden Chain*, 6:149–50, 165, 199–200; *Manner and Order of Predestination*, 6:369; *Reformed Catholic*, 7:20–24; *Problem of the Forged Catholicism*, 7:248–49; *Discourse of Conscience*, 8:121, 128–29; *Whether a Man*, 8:493–94; *Case of Conscience*, 8:603, 632; *Combat of Flesh and Spirit*, 9:179.

93. *Golden Chain*, 6:149–50; *Sermon on the Mount*, 1:255–56, 684; *Exposition of Revelation 1–3*, 4:485; *Exposition of the Creed*, 5:89; *Golden Chain*, 6:228; *Problem of the Forged Catholicism*, 7:409; *Whether a Man*, 8:552. This is in accordance with the Protestant assertion "that concupiscence and lust hath of itself the nature of sin," rather than simply being potential for sin. The Thirty-Nine Articles of Religion, art. 9.

94. *Golden Chain*, 6:125, 129.

95. *Golden Chain*, 6:151.

96. "Civil life without grace in Christ is nothing else in God's sight but a beautiful abomination." *Nature and Practice of Repentance*, 9:139. See *Sermon on the Mount*, 1:180–81, 235, 543, 578, 659, 688–89, 699–700, 714, 723; *Commentary on Galatians*, 2:26; *Commentary on Hebrews 11*, 3:110–12, 176, 324; *Exposition of Jude* 4:30–31, 87, 131, 158–59, 222, 476; *God's Free Grace*, 6:408–9; *Reformed Catholic*, 7:13–19, 36–37; *Treatise on Whether a Man*, 8:586; *Grain of Mustard Seed*, 8:652; *True Gain*, 9:33; *Exhortation to Repentance*, 9:97–98, 100, 108–9; *Man's Imagination*, 9:197, 220, 234; *How to Live Well*, 10:20.

97. *Golden Chain*, 6:32; *Manner and Order of Predestination*, 6:329, 406–7. See Muller, *Grace and Freedom*, 113–14.

98. *God's Free Grace*, 6:410. See also Muller, *Grace and Freedom*, 120–24.

affections, and body.[99] Perkins's view of sin amounts to what has come to be called the doctrine of *total depravity*, that is, that sin infects the entire person, and that the degree of this corruption is limited only by God's grace.

Alongside Perkins's account of inward corruption, he frequently mentions Satan, who takes full advantage of the weakness of fallen human nature to tempt humanity, even from within.[100] The world likewise tempts from without, these three elements—flesh, devil, world—powerfully coalescing to draw people into sin.[101] Temptation can also be a positive act of God whereby He trains and proves the devotion of His people;[102] however, even the regenerate cannot escape struggling with temptation to sin in this life,[103] especially when facing their own death.[104]

Actual Sin

The corrupting effects of sin in the faculties of the soul come to expression in sinful actions performed by the instrument of the body. Perkins systematically lays out how actual sins come about in four degrees, progressing from temptation in the mind, to consent of the will, to execution by means of bodily action, and finally to becoming a habit of action.[105] Sin and grace alike "tend to a perfection" and thus the practice of sinning tends to grow to dominate the life.[106] This anatomy of concupiscence, temptation, and sin provides the road map for Perkins's account of spiritual combat (below).

---

99. *Golden Chain*, 6:37–40, 194, 196, 199; *Exposition of the Creed*, 5:89–90, 142. See also Payne, "Faith and Assurance," 326.

100. *Combat between Christ and the Devil*, 1:87, 97, 141; *Sermon on the Mount*, 1:346–48, 479–86; *Exposition of the Creed*, 5:142; *Exposition of the Lord's Prayer* 5:459–62; *Exhortation to Repentance*, 9:100–101; *Damned Art of Witchcraft*, 9:315–16. See also Harman Bhogal, "Miracles, Cessationism, and Demonic Possession: The Darrell Controversy and the Parameters of Preternature in Early Modern English Demonology," *Preternature* 4, no. 2 (2015): 152–80.

101. *Commentary on Galatians* 2:73, 85; *Commentary on Hebrews 11*, 3:12, 379–80; *Exposition of Revelation 1–3*, 4:436; *Three Books on Cases of Conscience*, 8:161–62, 176–218; *Exhortation to Repentance*, 9:96.

102. *Commentary on Hebrews 11*, 3:224–37; *Exposition of the Creed*, 5:281–82; *Exposition of the Lord's Prayer*, 5:460–61; *Three Books on Cases of Conscience*, 8:161, 170–75; *Treatise Whether a Man*, 8:582–94; *Exhortation to Repentance*, 9:103–4.

103. *Treatise Tending unto a Declaration*, 8:493–502; *Man's Imagination*, 9:249–50; *Art of Prophesying*, 10:340–42.

104. *Salve for a Sick Man*, 10:411–12, 430, 458.

105. *Golden Chain*, 6:42–43; *Sermon on the Mount*, 1:481; *Manner and Order of Predestination*, 6:369–70; *Three Books on Cases of Conscience*, 8:134–35, 331. Perkins bases this progression on James 1:14–15.

106. *Exhortation to Repentance*, 9:99.

The Consequences of Sin

The ultimate consequence for sin is God's eschatological judgment and just condemnation of the sinner into hell.[107] Yet sin also has a myriad of effects on the present life. The practice of sin distresses the conscience, hardens sinners, and leads to the withdrawal of God's grace and presence.[108] Making a practice of sin leads to spiritual ruin.

Furthermore, God presently acts in judgment against unrepentant and sinful nations. Disease, natural disasters, and bad harvests are manifestations of God's judgment upon sinners and discipline of His children.[109] Most terrifying was the prospect that England might be so hard-hearted in its response to the gospel that God would withdraw its availability from among them entirely.[110] Theologically, Perkins roots this in covenant theology whereby Old Testament Israel lost its land and covenant privileges through unbelief. In Perkins's day, the instrument of God's potential judgment on England seemed likely to be invasion by foreign Roman Catholic powers. England's recent history of swift, tumultuous changes in religious policy made this seem very plausible, lending further urgency to the call to repent.[111]

Perkins's Doctrine of Grace

While sin is universal, grace is both universal and particular. For Perkins, grace denotes God's generous and loving disposition toward sinners, and any work of God's Spirit whereby He enables human agency with respect to goodness,

---

107. *Golden Chain*, 6:257–61; *Exhortation to Repentance*, 9:101.

108. *Exposition of the Creed*, 5:76–77, 283–85; *Golden Chain*, 6:38, 71–73, 243–47; *Manner and Order of Predestination*, 6:317, 330–32; *God's Free Grace*, 6:430–31, 441; *Treatise Whether a Man*, 8:499–501, 582–83.

109. *Combat between Christ and the Devil*, 1:132, 141, 161; *Sermon on the Mount*, 1:301, 326, 354, 385, 440, 538, 579; *Commentary on Hebrews 11*, 3:84–86; *Exposition of Revelation 1–3*, 5:526–29, 535, 585; *Exposition of the Creed*, 5:63; *God's Free Grace*, 6:435; *End of the World*, 6:469–70; *Reformed Catholic*, 7:62; *Warning against Idolatry*, 7:465; *Three Books on Cases of Conscience*, 8:202, 311; *Exhortation to Repentance*, 9:111–19; *Nature and Practice of Repentance*, 9:125, 159; *Man's Imagination*, 9:226–27, 244; *Government of the Tongue*, 9:269; *Damned Art of Witchcraft*, 9:392; *Prognostication*, 9:414–15, 429; *How to Live Well*, 10:22; *Vocations*, 10:47; *Christian Equity*, 10:394–95.

110. *Exhortation to Repentance*, 9:109–19.

111. Henry VIII (r. 1509–1547) separated from Rome in 1534 but preserved an uncomfortable mix of Protestant and Roman Catholic doctrines in England. Under Edward VI (r. 1547–1553) England enjoyed a zealous and progressively reforming Reformed Protestantism. Mary I (r. 1553–1558) attempted a full-scale reversion of English religion to Roman Catholicism. Elizabeth I (r. 1558–1603), under whose reign Perkins lived, instituted a stable moderate Protestantism which promulgated the theological convictions of Edward's reform, though without that regime's progressive reformist intent.

restrains it with respect to evil, or (most especially) regenerates His elect people to be gradually conformed to the image of Christ.

God's Gracious Disposition toward Sinners in Christ

In Christ God demonstrates His gracious and loving disposition toward sinners, uniting them to Christ along with all His benefits. Perkins firmly held to the Protestant emphasis on free justification by faith alone and believed that this doctrine was so central as to constitute sufficient grounds to warrant separation from Rome.[112] By the gospel, God graciously invites sinners to come to Christ and to freely receive salvation. Perkins emphasized that the evangelical promises (that is, "whosoever will believe") "are indefinite and do exclude no man, unless peradventure any man do exclude himself."[113] Thus Perkins urged all people to make introspective use of law and gospel to expose sin and, God willing, to come to Christ by His gracious enabling.[114]

Natural Grace, Common Grace, and Natural Liberty

Perkins describes God's ongoing activity as the sustainer of His creation in terms of grace. Natural grace describes the Godward aspect of created human nature, especially the image of God, now marred by the fall.[115] Only supernatural renewing grace can recreate and restore the image of God in man.[116] Nevertheless, God's common grace is experienced by all sinners in varying degrees, both restraining vice and enabling civil virtue. This upholds the notion that God is the source of all goodness in creation, while clearly distinguishing the experience of saving and regenerating graces (which are particular) from natural and common grace (which are universal).[117]

---

112. *Reformed Catholic*, 7:36; *Golden Chain*, 6:181–85.

113. *Golden Chain*, 6:197. See *Exposition of the Creed*, 5:340; *God's Free Grace*, 6:427; *True Gain*, 9:61. Underlying Perkins doctrine of the invitation is the distinction between the will of God's good pleasure and His signifying will. *God's Free Grace*, 6:397–404.

114. *Golden Chain*, 6:174–79; *Exposition of the Creed*, 5:13–15; *Foundation of Christian Religion*, 5:501–02; *Three Books on Cases of Conscience*, 8:141–42; *Treatise Whether a Man*, 8:467–78.

115. *Manner and Order of Predestination*, 6:349.

116. *Exposition of the Creed*, 5:64–66, 71, 90, 113, 118, 248, 291, 370; *Golden Chain*, 6:27, 37; *Grain of Mustard Seed*, 8:645–46.

117. An Augustinian conception of common grace was likewise employed by earlier Reformers, including Calvin, Bullinger, Musculus, and Vermigli, all of whom sought to guard its use against Pelagian errors. See further J. Mark Beach, "The Idea of a 'General Grace of God' in some Sixteenth-Century Reformed Theologians other than Calvin," in *Church and School in Early Modern Protestantism: Studies in Honor of Richard A. Muller on the Maturation of a Theological Tradition*, Studies in the History of Christian Traditions 170, ed. Jordan J. Ballor, David S. Sytsma, and Jason Zuidema (Leiden: Brill, 2013), 97–109.

Perkins's expansive account of the insatiable corruption of indwelling sin would not accord with experience were it not for his account of God's common grace restraining the concupiscent affections of sinners. Perkins emphasizes that all are equally sinful by nature—none is "of better nature than others"—and thus differences in comparative levels of outward sinfulness ultimately come down to differing degrees of God's gracious restraint at work in a person.[118] Common grace accounts for how many pagans have been virtuous even without knowledge of law and gospel. In the case of Christian societies, the virtuous effects of common grace are often mistaken for Christian conversion. In both cases, the experience of common grace increases one's culpability on the day of judgment.[119] By means of common grace, man retains his free will with respect to natural objects of choice, and thus possesses free choice in civil and ecclesiastical matters, though these acts remain polluted by original corruption.[120]

Regenerating Grace

Perkins's account of regenerating grace can be summarized in three logically sequential degrees which move one from the estate of sin to that of grace-enabled perseverance unto glory. The first is a monergistic act of God whereby He renews the agency of the sinner to be capable of responding to the gospel. The second is a synergism of divine and human action, wherein God's grace sustains, renovates, and empowers human agency such that the regenerate person actively employs their renewed faculties to apprehend and apply Christ to themselves by faith and to live obediently.[121] These two steps together constitute what Perkins refers to as "first grace."[122] "Second grace" is merely God's preservation of the first, whereby the elect persevere in faith unto glory.[123]

---

118. *Exposition of the Creed*, 5:91–92, 310–11; *Golden Chain*, 6:37; *Manner and Order of Predestination*, 6:348–49; *Nature and Practice of Repentance*, 9:140. Thus, even Perkins's account of common grace is ultimately particularistic.

119. *Grain of Mustard Seed*, 8:645.

120. *God's Free Grace*, 6:408–9; *Man's Imagination*, 9:234; *Sermon on the Mount*, 1:402; *Exposition of Jude*, 4:219–20. See discussion in Muller, *Grace and Freedom*, 98–99; 111, 115–19, 186–87.

121. See Muller, *Grace and Freedom*, 132–35.

122. The dynamic of initial monergistic enabling grace and subsequent synergistic divine-enabled human agency is common to the Reformed tradition, and expressed in the Thirty-Nine Articles of Religion, article 10: "We have no power to do good works pleasant and acceptable to God, without the grace of God by Christ preventing [i.e., enabling] us, that we may have a good will, and working with us, when we have that good will." More specifically, the article describes prevenient grace and cooperating grace. Perkins often appealed to Philippians 1:6 and 2:12–13 as support.

123. *Sermon on the Mount*, 1:546, 712; *Commentary on Hebrews 11*, 3:297; *Exposition of Jude*, 4:38; *Exposition of Revelation 1–3*, 4:434; *Exposition of the Creed*, 5:85; *Manner and Order of Predestination*, 6:317, 366–69, 372; *Reformed Catholic*, 7:40; *Three Books on Cases of Conscience*,

Perkins's emphasis on the necessity of supernatural confirmation of the will in perseverance follows from his emphasis on the will's mutability and power of alternative choice. It also exposes the inadequacy of the New Pelagians' universal prevenient grace for salvation by highlighting the need for enabling grace for conversion and perseverance.[124] God's grace preserves His people from the fickleness of their own wills unto glorification. In sum, the monergistic-then-synergistic first grace along with the confirming second grace corresponds to the distance represented on Perkins's *ordo salutis* from effectual calling to glorification, and it describes God's supernatural activity in the believer by which He ensures the links in the "golden chain" are truly unbreakable.[125]

Perkins did not restrict himself to one rigid taxonomy of the kinds of regenerating grace, rather he varied in his terminology and degree of detail as context required. For example, in *God's Free Grace and Man's Free Will*, when discussing God's liberation of the will in redemption, Perkins distinguishes prevenient grace (producing new desire), working grace (producing the act of well-willing: faith, repentance, obedience), and coworking grace (giving the deed to the will).[126] His most extensive taxonomy of renewing graces comes in his *Manner and Order of Predestination*, and it is fivefold.[127] First, prevenient ("preventing") grace produces desire for supernatural grace. Second, preparing grace enables the sinner to consent to God's offer of grace. Third, operating grace describes God's renewal of human faculties such that human agency might be employed to enact the consent previously enabled. Fourth, cooperating grace is God's continuance in the third in order that renewed human agency may persist in producing faith and obedience over time.[128] Fifth, conserving grace describes the grace of perseverance.[129]

8:142. While this meaning is primary, Perkins uses the term "second grace" in several ways, referring to broad divine confirmation of previous grace received or to the grace wherein God gives man a regenerate will and deed in addition to the regenerate power (i.e., operating grace). *Commentary on Hebrews 11*, 3:297; *Exposition of Jude*, 4:38, 228; *Commentary on Galatians*, 2:22, 57, 364–65; *God's Free Grace*, 6:422, 425.

124. See *Manner and Order of Predestination*, 6:372.

125. See *Golden Chain*, 6:9. Recipients of the first grace are infallibly promised the second. *Exposition of Revelation 1–3*, 4:434.

126. *God's Free Grace*, 6:424.

127. Perkins, *Manner and Order of Predestination*, 6:373–74. Perkins describes this as the fruit of his reading Augustine's *On Grace and Free Will* (ch. 17). This fivefold account of the actualizations of grace would become standard among Protestant Scholastics. See Richard A. Muller, *Dictionary of Latin and Greek Theological Terms Drawn Principally from Protestant Scholastic Theology* (Grand Rapids: Baker, 1985), 129–30.

128. "Being first turned by grace, we then can move and turn ourselves." *Commentary on Galatians*, 2:56.

129. See *Commentary on Galatians*, 2:364.

Whatever the variances in expression or delineation, Perkins's theological account of grace remains recognizably the same, moving from initial divine monergism to ongoing divine-human synergism undergirded by God's confirming and preserving grace. In practice this theology emphasizes the notion that grace produces rigorous effort in the regenerate believer since grace restores nature, renewing human faculties for active faith and obedience:

> It will be said that faith, repentance, and the rest are all gifts of God. I answer, there is no virtue or gift of God in us without our wills; and in every good act God's grace and man's will concur—God's grace as the principal cause; man's will renewed as the instrument of God. And therefore, in all good things industry and labor and invocation on our part is required.[130]

Nonelect Experiences of Renewing Grace

We have seen that all people experience God's natural, common, and restraining grace, however Perkins also held that many reprobate people had genuine, though decidedly partial, experiences of regenerating grace too. Many reprobates experience an "ineffectual calling" and "temporary faith."[131] Perkins made this a focal point of his practical divinity, describing "how far" reprobates may experience Christian religion, and "how far…beyond" that the elect could be expected to go.[132] Perkins's account of the elect's and reprobate's qualitatively different experiences of regenerating grace is grounded in biblical passages such as Mark 4:1–20 and Hebrews 5:11–6:12, and is perhaps best summarized in his illustration of a banquet. The reprobate see, smell, and even taste the food, but do not eat or digest it, whereas the elect "truly eat, digest, and are nourished by Christ unto everlasting life."[133] There is some likeness here to the Reformed doctrine of right reception of Christ in the sacrament, wherein the regenerate recipient of the bread does "feed on [Christ] in thine heart by faith with thanksgiving."[134] Perkins's warning is that many reprobates come into startlingly close contact to regenerating grace, while never truly partaking of it.

---

130. *God's Free Grace*, 6:427; *Commentary on Galatians*, 2:22.

131. *Golden Chain*, 6:243–45; *Exposition of the Creed*, 5:9–11; *Exposition of Revelation 1–3*, 4:433.

132. This is the focus of the first two tracts in *Treatise Whether a Man*, 8:451–64, 465–507. The fifth tract critiques Roman Catholicism in these terms, arguing that even reprobates may successfully perform its religion, thus revealing its spiritual bankruptcy (8:558–66).

133. *Treatise Whether a Man*, 8:456. See *Golden Chain*, 6:244–45; *Exposition of the Creed*, 5:9–11.

134. "The order for the administration of the Lord's Supper, or Holy Communion," *The Book of Common Prayer* (1559). This was the official liturgy of the Elizabethan Established Church, and Perkins would have been familiar with it from infancy.

This serves as a warning against complacency, calling the seeker to take every opportunity to "turn his temporary faith (if he finds it in himself) into a true saving faith."[135] In keeping with this kind of direct instruction, Perkins sought to train preachers to apply doctrine in their sermons with sensitivity to the variety of experiences of sin and grace present among their hearers.[136]

Eschatological Grace

Perkins dedicates relatively little space to describing eschatological grace, noting the inadequacy of man to "open the nature" of this subject in detail.[137] The life of eternal blessedness in God's kingdom is the great goal of God's work of grace in his elect, to His everlasting glory.[138] In terms of human agency, this eternal blessedness largely consists in the liberation of the will from the possibility of sinning, and a state of freedom in choosing between righteous options forever.[139] Regenerate man seeks to live the "blessed life" of grace before God in the present while awaiting the day when He will do so in full.

Sin, Grace, and God's Sovereignty

Since God executes His sovereign decree in history through both good and evil secondary causes, Reformed theology has long had to account for how God is not culpable for human sin, and especially for how He does not bear blame for the fall of Adam. We have seen that Perkins not only asserts that there is a concurrence between divine and creaturely activity in creaturely acts, but that he asserts the priority of divine action.[140] However, it does not follow that God is the agent of evil acts. Perkins distinguishes between those good things straightforwardly willed by God (His "operation") and evil actions willed by evil agents by means of God's "operative permission."[141] Thus, "God sustains nature and not the sin of nature; and therefore He only sustains will as will and not as it is corrupt or sinful will."[142] This distinction is grounded not only in the inherent goodness of God, but also in the privative nature of evil. It is metaphysically impossible for God to "will" evil since it is not a "thing" in His creation, but

---

135. *Treatise Whether a Man*, 8:585. See also Payne, "Faith and Assurance," 328–29, 333.

136. *Art of Prophesying*, 10:334–43.

137. *Exposition of the Creed*, 5:406.

138. *Golden Chain*, 6:216–18; *Exposition of the Creed*, 5:406–16.

139. *God's Free Grace*, 6:421, 428. See Muller, *Grace and Freedom*, 153–54.

140. For example, see *God's Free Grace*, 6:429–30. Perkins advocates something akin to the Thomistic concept of physical premotion (*praemotio physica*) regarding the priority of the divine will in its concurrence with secondary causes, enabling the being-created acts. See Muller, *Grace and Freedom*, 145–46, 155–58, 183–84.

141. *Golden Chain*, 6:24; *Exposition of the Creed*, 5:75–76; *Art of Prophesying*, 10:315.

142. *God's Free Grace*, 6:429.

rather a deprivation or distortion in created things.[143] Thus, all events occur according to God's decree, but at the level of secondary causality God's involvement in evil is one of "forsaking the second cause in working evil" inasmuch as it is evil, willing it inasmuch as it is good, and in all cases directing it toward the fulfilment of His own righteous ends.[144]

Not only does God permit secondary causes to act sinfully, but He withholds or withdraws the grace necessary to impede such acts. Yet, Perkins emphasizes that man still sins contingently according to the dictates of his own will rather than by any inherent necessity.[145] The archetypal example is the fall of Adam. On the one hand Adam fell according to the eternal decree of God and would have persevered in righteousness had God added the second grace of perseverance to the first. However, Adam fell according to the dictates of his own contingent free will and was thus responsible for his sin.[146]

With respect to reprobation, Perkins insists that God is just to condemn the reprobate, though He sovereignly decreed their destruction. While God's sovereign decree is not conditioned by any foreseen response, He does not condemn any apart from the presence of damnable sin in them, for that would be unjust: "No man is absolutely ordained to hell or destruction but for his sin."[147] Thus, while the ultimate cause of reprobation is ultimately found in God's sovereign decree, the immediate and inherent cause of condemnation is sin.[148]

Christian Warfare: Sin vs. Grace

Regeneration and sinful corruption are not mutually exclusive states, rather the elect must await glorification to be freed from the effects of concupiscence.[149] Thus, the introduction of regenerating grace into the sinner initiates an internal combat and struggle against inherent sin and unbelief (and conversely, *for* obedience and faith) that is the focal point of the Christian life.[150] Perkins typically describes this conflict as between the flesh and the renewed spirit of the

---

143. *Manner and Order of Predestination*, 6:329, 338; *Exposition of Jude*, 4:52. See also Muller, *Grace and Freedom*, 166–72.

144. *Golden Chain*, 6:24–25; *Manner and Order of Predestination*, 6:330–32; *Exposition of the Creed*, 5:77–78; *God's Free Grace*, 6:429.

145. *Manner and Order of Predestination*, 6:328, 338; *God's Free Grace*, 6:430–31.

146. *Manner and Order of Predestination*, 6:306–7, 328; *Exposition of the Creed*, 5:84–87; *Exposition of the Lord's Prayer*, 5:461. See also Muller, *Grace and Freedom*, 104–8, 162.

147. *Manner and Order of Predestination*, 6:216.

148. *Golden Chain*, 6:242; *Manner and Order of Predestination*, 6:315–21.

149. *The Thirty-Nine Articles of Religion*, art. 9.

150. *Three Books on Cases of Conscience*, 8:142.

Christian,[151] or as between Satan and the Christian.[152] The "how to" character
of Perkins's practical divinity is particularly evident in his approach to spiritual
warfare. For example, in his *A Golden Chain*, Perkins lays out the key spiritual assaults that the Christian ought to expect with respect to each step of the
ordo salutis, describing in practical terms how Christians are to resist those
temptations, and what remedies they should make use of when they fail.[153]
Throughout his sermons Perkins highlights spiritual dangers that God's people
face, as well as the helps, graces, preservatives, and remedies offered by God for
times of temptation or falling into sin.

One's success or failure in the face of temptation has large consequences.
On the one hand, victories over temptations bring greater "experience of God's
love in Christ and so increase of peace of conscience and love in the Holy
Spirit."[154] Such experiences constitute the pathway that leads toward the fulness
of Christian assurance.[155] On the other hand, sin has its own inherent tendency
toward fullness. While Christians inevitably fall into sin periodically, they do
not do so with full consent of their wills, and they recover themselves by repentance.[156] In contrast, for sin to become a "habit" of action (the fourth degree
of sin, above) is incompatible with regeneration, and amounts to apostasy.[157]
Thus, Christians must watch closely for the creeping influence of temptation
and sin in their lives, and energetically apply themselves to their own sanctification. The Christian's goal is ever the cultivation and maintenance of a good
conscience, that is, a well-grounded, assured, self-knowledge of oneself before
God and others.

God's Invitation and the Availability of Grace

Perkins's primary application of predestinarian grace was that all people must
seek out God's grace in Christ by the means that He has made available in their
midst. They must never assume their exclusion from salvation whilst there is

---

151. *Combat of the Flesh and Spirit*, 9:169–80; *Commentary on Galatians*, 2:356–82.

152. *Treatise Whether a Man*, 8:558–66; *Golden Chain*, 6:192–93. See *Combat between Christ and the Devil*, 1:71–165.

153. *Golden Chain*, 6:194–202. See *Treatise Whether a Man*, 8:493–502.

154. *Foundation of Christian Religion*, 5:504.

155. *Foundation of Christian Religion*, 5:502; *Golden Chain*, 6:179; *Exposition of the Creed*, 5:16–17.

156. *Sermon on the Mount*, 1:481–82; *Commentary on Galatians*, 2:137, 362; *Exposition of Jude*, 4:170, 214; *Exposition of Revelation 1–3*, 4:431; *Manner and Order of Predestination*, 6:289, 369–70; *God's Free Grace*, 6:427; *Discourse of Conscience*, 8:72; *Treatise Whether a Man*, 8:489; *Case of Conscience*, 8:605; *Combat of Flesh and Spirit*, 9:177–78.

157. *Manner and Order of Predestination*, 6:369–70.

present opportunity to receive it.[158] This was undergirded by Perkins's doctrine of God's *providentially available invitation*, namely that God makes the gospel and the means of grace available to particular peoples and nations: "Where God erects the ministry of His word, He signifies thereby that His pleasure is to gather men to salvation."[159]

Perkins emphasized that the gospel has not been heard in every age and nation; indeed, it is only by God's great kindness that it has been so freely preached in England during Elizabeth's reign. God's provision of the means of grace to a nation ought to urge people to make earnest and diligent use of them, lest God judge that nation for its lack of fruit and remove His gospel from among them.[160] The availability of the gospel in England testified that the English people were called, indeed obligated, to repentance and faith in Christ.[161]

Furthermore, Perkins treated God's grace—even sovereign saving grace—as fleetingly accessible to all through the creaturely means which He has made available. Natural man is unable to seek spiritual things without the enabling of supernatural grace, however the means of grace are themselves natural objects signifying supernatural realities, at least to those given eyes to see. Natural free will is sufficient to receive the bread and wine of the Lord's Supper, or to listen to a sermon, yet only through supernatural grace does one receive Christ Himself by faith by those means.[162] In short, even unregenerate man may make choice of the means of grace, bringing him into contact with the very instruments through which God bestows eternal life upon his elect.[163] Perkins was eager to instruct people in how to make profitable (i.e., spiritual) use of sermons, sacraments, and traditional catechetical materials: the Apostles' Creed, Lord's Prayer, and Decalogue.[164] Thus, throughout Perkins's work there is a sense that, while one might begin with a mere natural will performing the outward duties of religion, the very process of striving to make use of those means may lead one to earnestly seek God, and to only retrospectively recognize that

---

158. *Golden Chain*, 6:262–63; *Exposition of the Creed*, 5:343.

159. *God's Free Grace*, 6:403. Perkins's discussion of extent of the gospel invitation is not to be confused with his views on the extent of the atonement.

160. *Commentary on Galatians*, 2:29, 59, 73–74, 153–56, 337, 346; *Commentary on Hebrews 11*, 3:104; *Exposition of Jude*, 4:92, 101, 242, 248; *Exposition of Revelation 1–3*, 4:444; *Exposition of the Creed*, 5:9–10, 39, 347–48; *God's Free Grace*, 6:392, 403–4, 436, 438–39, 441; *Warning against Idolatry*, 7:413; *Exhortation to Repentance*, 9:105–22; *Golden Chain*, 6:154–55, 256–57.

161. *Exposition of the Creed*, 5:21–22; *God's Free Grace*, 6:412–13, 438.

162. *Reformed Catholic*, 7:85–86, 134–38; *Exposition of the Creed*, 5:343. See the Thirty-Nine Articles of Religion, art. 28.

163. *Commentary on Hebrews 11*, 3:176; *God's Free Grace*, 6:408–9, 421; *Exhortation to Repentance*, 9:108; *Art of Prophesying*, 10:290.

164. *Foundation of Christian Religion*, 5:481, 484–85.

supernatural grace had begun working within. This is likewise the logic of Perkins's approach to the second use of the law: the natural and regenerate man
alike may make introspective use of the law to expose and condemn their sin.
But whereas the natural man despairs of his state and proceeds no further, the
grace-enabled man finds a merciful Savior and ultimately comes to faith and
full assurance in Him.[165] In both cases the application is the same: all must
seek Christ through the means which He has established, for in the very act
of seeking God in this way, a man may discover the minutest "mustard seed"
beginnings of regenerating grace within, urging him to press on all the more.
In the final analysis, Perkins called on all people to regard themselves and one
another not only as sinners, but as potential objects of God's mercy in Christ,
and thus to seek His saving grace through the means which He has established
while it may be found.

---

165. *Three Books on Cases of Conscience*, 8:141–42. The second use of the law refers to its
exposing and condemning of sin.

4

The Order of Salvation
J. V. Fesko

In the preface to *A Golden Chain*, William Perkins observes that there are four different opinions regarding the order of God's predestination.[1] The Pelagians claim that God bases His predestination upon the foreseen faith of man, which means that human choice comes first in the order of causes. A second opinion among Lutheran theologians is that God foresaw that people would reject offered grace and so He determined to choose some to salvation out of His mere mercy without respect to their faith or good works. In this case, human rejection of God's grace plays a causal role in determining the scope of God's electing grace. The third view comes from semi-Pelagian Roman Catholics (Papists), who contend that predestination rests partially upon foreseen preparations and meritorious works and partially upon God's mercy. Such a view gives divine grace and human action equal causal power in divine election. The fourth and final opinion maintains that the sole cause of God's predestination is His mercy in Christ, and that God's eternal counsel does not have any cause but His own will and pleasure. The cause of predestination thus lies solely in God. Perkins rejects the first three views and defends the last. Although not initially included with the first English published edition of his *Golden Chain*, Perkins later integrated a table that diagrammed the order of the causes of salvation and damnation, what he called an *ocular catechism*, by which a reader could perceive both the chief points of religion and their order.[2] In his table Perkins presents an order of the different elements of salvation that moves from God's election to effectual calling, justification, sanctification, glorification, and

---

1. *Golden Chain*, 6:5.
2. The 1591 Latin edition of Perkins's work includes the table, but the chart does not appear in the English translations of 1591 or 1592. It does appear in the 1597 edition. See William Perkins, *Armilla Aurea, id est, Theologiae Descriptio* (Cambridge: John Legate, 1591); idem, *A Golden Chaine, or the Description of Theology* (London: Edward Alde, 1591); idem, *A Golden Chaine, or the Description of Theology* (Cambridge: John Legate, 1597).

eternal life. There is a causal connection of some sort between these different elements of salvation that spring from the fount of divine election.

What Perkins believed was pedestrian and mundane has been described as a betrayal of the theology of the Reformation by some. William B. Evans, for example, has characterized John Calvin's (1509–1564) soteriology of union with Christ as the garden and the supposed innovation of the *ordo salutis* ("order of salvation") as the fall. Rather than conceive of salvation in terms of a holistic application of redemption through union with Christ, Reformed Orthodox theologians claimed that justification is a logically and temporally prior act to sanctification.[3] They did not maintain Calvin's dynamic formulation of union with Christ; Reformed Orthodox theologians instead looked to the *ordo*. The *ordo salutis* "vitiated" Reformed theology and compromised the relationship between justification and sanctification.[4] Evans's historiographical and theological claims raise several questions. What is the *ordo salutis*? Do advocates of the *ordo salutis* posit both a logical and temporal sequence of redemptive acts to effect a sinner's salvation? As an early orthodox Reformed theologian, does Perkins affirm salvation by union with Christ or the *ordo salutis*? A *prima facie* reading of Perkins's *A Golden Chain* might lead readers to the conclusion that Perkins affirms the *ordo salutis* as a causal, temporal, sequential chain of redemptive acts that bring about a sinner's salvation. In other words, Perkins formulates his soteriology around the *ordo salutis* rather than union with Christ. But first impressions can be misleading.

This chapter defends the thesis that Perkins affirms both union with Christ and the *ordo salutis*. This simple thesis, however, requires an important caveat; namely, the question of the *ordo salutis* does not hinge on the absence or presence of the specific term but rather the use of the concept. In other words, the thesis that Perkins affirms the *ordo salutis* is not a question of whether Perkins uses the term—he does not. Rather, does Perkins present an ordered understanding of union with Christ? The answer to this question is, yes. Perkins argues for an ordered doctrine of union with Christ by using a common medieval distinction, namely, the *ordo naturae* ("order of nature"). This chapter proves the thesis that Perkins affirms both union with Christ and the *ordo salutis* by first examining the state of the question. What have historians claimed about the *ordo salutis* as it relates to early modern Reformed theology generally, and specifically, what have they said about Perkins and the *ordo*? Second, the chapter explores the medieval background to Perkins's soteriology, namely,

---

3. William B. Evans, *Imputation and Impartation: Union with Christ in American Reformed Theology* (Carlisle, England: Paternoster, 2008), 37.

4. Evans, *Imputation and Impartation*, 265.

the concept of the *ordo naturae* and how it functions. Third, the chapter examines Perkins's soteriology that he presents in his *A Golden Chain* and how he employs the *ordo naturae* to order union with Christ. Fourth, and finally, the chapter concludes with summary observations about Perkins' understanding of the *ordo salutis* and union with Christ.

State of the Question

In the twentieth century, many historians and theologians have engaged the doctrine of the *ordo salutis* from both historical and theological perspectives. There are a number of theologians who have rejected the *ordo salutis* on exegetical and theological grounds, but their views are beyond the scope of the historical question of Perkins's use of the concept.[5] As a matter of historical theology there are three main schools of thought: (1) those who argue that the *ordo salutis* is a corruption of Calvin's doctrine of union with Christ; (2) those who believe that the concept is a development of eighteenth-century Lutheran pietist theologians, though some Reformed theologians substantively express the concerns of the *ordo salutis*; and (3) those who recognize the late provenance of the term but argue that early modern Reformed theologians employ the concept. As noted above, William Evans is among the first group, those who pit Calvin against the later tradition and union with Christ against the *ordo salutis*. In addition to Evans, other representatives include Reinhold Seeberg (1859–1935), Karl Barth (1886–1968), Charles Partee, and T. F. Torrance (1913–2007).[6]

The second group argues that the term *ordo salutis* originated among Lutheran pietist theologians, a claim that goes back to Barth. He argued that pietist theologians conceived of the application of salvation as a temporal sequence of spiritual awakenings, movements, and actions.[7] Otto Weber (1902–1966) repeats this idea but adds that Reformed theologian Daniel Wyttenbach (1746–1820) employed the term.[8] These same claims appear in Wolfhart

---

5. For engagement with theological critics, see J. V. Fesko, "Romans 8:29–30 and the Question of the *Ordo Salutis*," *Journal of Reformed Theology* 8 (2014): 35–60.

6. Reinhold Seeberg, "*Ordo Salutis*," in *The New Schaff-Herzog Encyclopedia of Religious Knowledge*, ed. Samuel Macauley Jackson (New York, N.Y.: Funk and Wagnalls Co., 1910), 8:252–53; Karl Barth, *Church Dogmatics*, ed. G. W. Bromiley and T. F. Torrance (Edinburgh: T & T Clark, 1958), IV/2:502; Charles Partee, "Calvin's Central Dogma Again," *The Sixteenth Century Journal* 18, no. 2 (1987): 191–99; idem, *The Theology of John Calvin* (Louisville, Ky.: Westminster John Knox Press, 2008), 3; T. F. Torrance, *Scottish Theology: From John Knox to John McLeod Campbell* (Edinburgh: T & T Clark, 1996), 128–29.

7. Barth, *Church Dogmatics*, IV/2:502.

8. Otto Weber, *Foundations for Dogmatics*, trans. Darrel Guder (Grand Rapids: Eerdmans, 1983), 2:336, n. 68.

Pannenberg (1928–2014), Richard B. Gaffin Jr., and Sinclair Ferguson. But unlike Weber and Pannenberg, Gaffin and Ferguson recognize a substantive similarity between the *ordo salutis* and early modern Reformed soteriologies, such as in the theology of Heinrich Bullinger (1504–1575), Martin Luther (1483–1546), Calvin, and subsequent Reformed orthodox theologians.[9] At the same time, Gaffin tries to separate Calvin's soteriology from later developments: Calvin was more concerned with union with Christ whereas later Reformed theologians were more concerned about the order of received benefits.[10]

The third group recognizes that the term *ordo salutis* is of late provenance as a *terminus technicus* but that the concept is present among early modern Reformed theologians, not just among the early, high, or late orthodox theologians.[11] In an essay on the topic, Richard A. Muller refutes the common claim that Reformed theologians deduced their systems of theology from the doctrine of predestination.[12] Critical historians and theologians held up Perkins's table or ocular catechism as a smoking gun because the chart begins with God and the decree from which all other salvific benefits flow. Critics also based their argument on the subtitle of Perkins's work: "The Description of Theology." The assumption was that Perkins's table represented his system of theology.[13] Muller, however, demonstrates that Perkins's table is a schematized presentation of the *ordo salutis*, not a system of theology. Perkins simply traces the causes of salvation and damnation, which originate in the divine decree.[14] In his subsequent research on Perkins and the *ordo salutis*, Muller notes that Perkins and other early orthodox theologians promote both union with Christ and the "degrees or steps" of salvation. In a footnote, Muller acknowledges that he previously loosely referred to Perkins's ordering of the causes of salvation as an *ordo salutis* but in his more recent work refrains because the term is

---

9. Wolfhart Pannenberg, *Systematic Theology* (Grand Rapids: Eerdmans, 1993), 3:228–29n, 422–30; Richard B. Gaffin Jr., "Biblical Theology and the Westminster Standards," *Westminster Theological Journal* 65, no. 2 (2003): 165–79; Sinclair Ferguson, "*Ordo Salutis*," in *New Dictionary of Theology*, ed. Sinclair Ferguson, David Wright, and J. I. Packer (Downers Grove, Ill.: IVP Academic, 1988), 480–81.

10. Gaffin, "Biblical Theology and the Westminster Standards," 172–73, 177.

11. J. V. Fesko, *Beyond Calvin: Union with Christ and Justification in Early Modern Reformed Theology, 1517–1700* (Göttingen: Vandenhoeck & Ruprecht, 2012), 76–102.

12. Richard A. Muller, "Perkins' *A Golden Chaine*: Predestinarian System of Schematized Ordo Salutis?" *Sixteenth Century Journal* 9, no. 1 (1978): 69–81. See also, idem, *Christ and the Decree: Christology and Predestination in Reformed Theology from Calvin to Perkins* (1986; Grand Rapids: Baker Academic, 2008), 129–74.

13. See R. T. Kendall, *Calvin and English Calvinism to 1649* (Eugene, Ore.: Wipf & Stock, 1997), 51–78; Basil Hall, "Calvin against the Calvinists," in *John Calvin*, ed. G. E. Duffield (Appleford, England: Sutton Courtney Press, 1966), 19–37, esp. 29–30.

14. Muller, "Perkins' *A Golden Chaine*," 79.

not common to early modern Reformed theology.[15] Recent historical research confirms Muller's unwillingness to label Perkins's ordered understanding of salvation as an *ordo salutis* given its Lutheran eighteenth-century provenance.[16] Nevertheless, the impropriety of the term as a matter of careful historiography does not negate the fact that Perkins affirms both union with Christ and an ordered understanding of the causes of salvation. In short, Perkins affirms an ordered union. Muller explains that, even though the term *ordo salutis* is absent from early modern Reformed works, the most common way of referring to the *ordo* was by the *armilla aurea* or *catena aurea* ("golden chain"), which was based directly on the exegesis of Romans 8:28–30.[17]

Medieval Background

Before we proceed to examine Perkins's ordered union, we must first establish the medieval background of a common early modern concept that enabled theologians to explain the relationship between the different aspects of union with Christ, namely, the *ordo naturae*. In medieval debates about the relationship between the divine decree and future contingents, Thomas Aquinas (1224–1275) and Boethius (d. 524) posited God's relationship to history as surveying all moments, past, present, and future as all equally present. Everything is an eternal present to God, as time is an artifact of human, not divine, agency. John Duns Scotus (c. 1265/66–1308) on the other hand, argued that in a first instant of nature (*instantes naturae*) God knows creation through His will in a single act of knowing and willing that is His present time. In a second instant of nature God surveys all possibilities of a contingent temporal future, and in a third instant God establishes creation as the actuality of the temporal present. No past exists for God because His decree stands logically prior to the creation. God therefore knows and wills events in the creation in a logical order that is the reverse of the temporal flow of time.[18] In order to explain the relationship between God's eternal decree and future contingents, Scotus therefore posits nontemporal, logical, instants. In other words, Scotus delineated the solitary

---

15. Richard A. Muller, *Calvin and the Reformed Tradition: On the Work of Christ and the Order of Salvation* (Grand Rapids: Baker Academic, 2012), 229, n. 136.

16. Markus Mattias, "Ordo salutis—Zur Geschichte eines dogmatischen Begriffs," *Zeitschrift für Kirchengeschichte* 115 (2004): 318–46.

17. Richard A. Muller, *Dictionary of Latin and Greek Theological Terms: Drawn Principally from Protestant Scholastic Theology*, 2nd ed. (1986; Grand Rapids: Baker Academic, 2017), s. v. *ordo salutis*, 250–51.

18. Hester Goodenough Gelber, *It Could Have Been Otherwise: Contingency and Necessity in Dominican Theology at Oxford, 1300–1350* (Leiden: Brill, 2004), 132.

decree of God in terms of logical or structural moments that are rationally, or logically, rather than temporally ordered.[19]

While this medieval distinction originated with Duns Scotus, it later became pedestrian among early modern theologians. Reformed theologians later referred to the idea behind *instantes naturae* by another term, namely, *ordo naturae*.[20] Another interchangeable term is *in signo rationis*, "in the relation of reason," that is, a purely rational relationship. So, a theologian can speak of God's singular decree as a series of decrees, degrees, or steps, that are distinct and logically ordered according to their rational priority, although they are not temporally distinguished.[21] For example, in his discussion of the decree of election, Thomas Goodwin (1600–1680) quotes John Davenant (1572–1641): "God's deputation or ordaining men to death is not to be conceived as that which was performed in the same *signo rationis* (or instant according to reason) in which God's non-electing them was appointed, but in another, after which such a non-elected person, finally persevering in a state of sin, was foreseen."[22] Goodwin also employs the term *ordo naturae* to the same effect when he discusses the order and priority of the eternal decree(s). He explains that election of the Son as the federal head of the elect, was "in order of nature to be supposed before our election, though coexistent together from eternity."[23] Both the medieval background and early modern Reformed use of the concept of nontemporal rational moments (*instantes naturae, in signo rationis*, or especially *ordo naturae*), set the stage for understanding Perkins's ordered union.

---

19. Muller, *Dictionary*, s. v. *instantes naturae*, 173–74.

20. Richard A. Muller, *Grace and Freedom: William Perkins and the Early Modern Reformed Understanding of Free Choice and Divine Grace* (Oxford: Oxford University Press, 2020), 147. See also idem, *Divine Will and Human Choice: Freedom, Contingency, and Necessity in Early Modern Reformed Thought* (Grand Rapids: Baker Academic, 2017), 151, 167.

21. Muller, *Dictionary*, s. v. *in signo rationis*, 168.

22. Thomas Goodwin, *A Discourse of Election*, in *The Works of Thomas Goodwin* (Edinburgh: James Nichol, 1864), 9:91.

23. Thomas Goodwin, *An Exposition of the First Chapter of the Epistle to the Ephesians*, in *Works of Thomas Goodwin* (Edinburgh: James Nichol, 1861), 1:72. Other Reformed theologians employ the *ordo naturae* distinction. See John Flavel, *The Method of Grace in the Gospel-Redemption*, in *The Whole Works of the Rev. Mr. John Flavel* (London: J. Mathews, 1799), 2:98; William Ames, *The Marrow of Theology*, trans. John Dykstra Eusden (Grand Rapids: Baker, 1968), 1.2.5; John Owen, *Justification by Faith through the Imputation of the Righteousness of Christ, Explained, Confirmed, and Vindicated* (London: R. Boulster, 1677), 162; Patrick Gillespie, *The Ark of the Covenant Opened* (London: Tho. Parkhurst, 1677), 54–55, 79–80, 376; Francis Roberts, *Medulla Bibliorum: The Mysterie and Marrow of the Bible* (London: George Calvert, 1657), 1477; Jonathan Edwards, *A Careful and Strict Enquiry into the Modern Prevailing Notions of That Freedom of Will* (Glasgow: David Niven, 1790), 53.

Perkins's Golden Chain

We come full circle to Perkins's *A Golden Chain* and the main thrust of the work, namely, to defend the Reformed view of predestination in contrast to Pelagian, Lutheran, and Roman Catholic views. In his assessment, Perkins believed there was a different order of causes that informed each view. There are two features that we must observe about Perkins's soteriology: (1) he saw redemption in terms of union with Christ; and (2) believers receive union with Christ in terms of a series of nontemporal, rational, steps, or degrees.

Union with Christ

The easiest way to observe Perkins's soteriology is to examine his table or ocular catechism.[24] In the lower left-hand corner of the table, the legend explains that the black line traces the causes of damnation and the white line traces the causes of salvation: the table places salvation on the left and damnation on the right. The immediate tendency might be to isolate the left side and observe the golden chain of salvation, which appears as seven individual circles: the decree of election, the love of God to the elect in Christ, effectual calling, justification, sanctification, glorification, and eternal life. The impression one might get is that salvation is a set of separate blessings detached from one another and given that the first circle begins with the decree and the last circle ends with eternal life, some might erroneously assume that the series of circles are temporally distinct. On the other hand, we must read Perkins's table by also noting the center column of circles that features the person and work of Christ: Mediator of the elect, holiness of manhood, fulfilling of the law, death, burial, state in the grave, resurrection, ascension, royal session at the Father's right hand, and intercession. Every link the golden chain of salvation has lines that connect to the center column. In other words, every element of salvation connects to union with Christ.

Beyond Perkins's table, he presents reasoned exegetical and theological argumentation to show that union with Christ lies at the heart of salvation. Perkins explains that there are three types of union: a union of nature, such as the union between Father, Son, and Holy Spirit, a union of person, such as the union between body and soul, and the spiritual union whereby Christ and the redeemed are united together. Regarding the third union, Perkins writes: "The benefits which we receive by this mystical union are manifold, for it is the ground of the conveyance of all grace."[25] Perkins then elaborates the nature of the union and the manifold benefits believers receive in their justification and

---

24. See also Fesko, *Beyond Calvin*, 251–68, esp. 255–58.
25. *Exposition of the Creed*, 5:368.

sanctification: "For there is a most near and straight union between Christ and all that believe in Him. And in this union Christ with all His benefits according to the tenor of the covenant of grace is made ours really, and therefore we may stand just before God by His righteousness."[26] At the same time, union with Christ is the fountain and spring of the believer's sanctification, "whereby we die to sin and are renewed in righteousness and holiness."[27] Perkins's emphasis on the doctrine of union with Christ has not been lost on historians. Heinrich Heppe (1820–79), for example, has observed in his *History of Pietism* that the Christian's life had to be directly connected to the crucified Christ and possess Him by union and communion with Christ.[28]

An Ordered Union

Given Perkins's commitment to union with Christ, why does he insist that there are steps, or degrees, of this union, and why do these steps unfold in a prioritized order? It is important to recall that the specific issue at stake in *A Golden Chain* is the different order of causes in predestination according to Pelagian, Roman Catholic, and Lutheran views. Do humans save themselves by their own effort? Is salvation a combination of God's grace and human effort? Or does God save sinners by His grace? The place of a believer's works in salvation is a matter of order and priority. Do the believer's works come first, and then God justifies him? Do these works in some sense come after justification because the legal verdict rests on the obedience of Christ? Perkins answers these questions based upon exegetical and theological warrants. When he explains the believer's union with Christ, or the golden chain, he identifies four degrees: effectual calling, justification, sanctification, and glorification.[29] Each of these is an element of union with Christ. Effectual calling, for example, is the beginning of the "union or conjunction which is the engrafting of such as are to be saved into Christ."[30] God justifies sinners because righteousness is in Christ as in a subject, and "because by means of the forenamed union Christ with all His benefits is made ours."[31] The means of the believer's mortification is the death

---

26. *Exposition of the Creed*, 5:369–70.

27. *Exposition of the Creed*, 5:370.

28. Heinrich Heppe, *Geschichte des Pietismus und der Mystik in der Reformirten Kirche* (Leiden: Brill, 1879), 224–26; Muller, *Christ and the Decree*, 131–32. For the prominence of union with Christ in English early modern Reformed theology, see R. Tudur Jones, "Union with Christ: the Existential Nerve of Puritan Piety," *Tyndale Bulletin* 41 no. 2 (1990): 186–208; Joel R. Beeke and Mark Jones, *A Puritan Theology: Doctrine for Life* (Grand Rapids: Reformation Heritage Books, 2012), 481–90.

29. *Golden Chain*, 6:172, 181, 186, 212.

30. *Golden Chain*, 6:172.

31. *Golden Chain*, 6:183.

and burial of Christ, and the means of the believer's vivification is derived from Christ's resurrection.[32] The believer's glorification finds both its power and goal in the Son of God.[33] Each degree is an aspect of union with Christ. But why does Perkins describe these aspects of the believer's union as "degrees"?

Perkins writes of the degrees of union with Christ because this is how the apostle Paul describes it. Reformation era exegesis of Romans 8:28–30 made this text the *sedes doctrinae* for the golden chain as early as 1527 by Ulrich Zwingli (1484–1531) and later by Peter Martyr Vermigli (1499–1562). Reformed exegetes recognized that Paul employed a *sorites*, a tool of Greek rhetoric where an argument proceeds by means of a series of steps or degrees.[34] The argument commonly runs as follows: A, and if A, then B; and if B, then C, and if C, then D. In other words, each step, degree, or link in the argument logically rests upon the previous step. If any step or link in the chain is eliminated, then the argument fails—the chain breaks. Thus, Paul writes, "For whom he did foreknow, he also did predestinate [A] to be conformed to the image of his Son, that he might be the firstborn among many brethren. Moreover whom he did predestinate [A], them he also called [B]: and whom he called [B], them he also justified [C]: and whom he justified [C], them he also glorified [D]" (Rom. 8:29–30). Numerous Reformed exegetes explain these verses in this manner, including Conrad Pelikan (1478–1556), Calvin, Bullinger, Wolfgang Musculus (1497–1563), Andreas Hyperius (1511–64), Vermigli, Theodore Beza (1519–1605), Caspar Olevianus (1536–1587), Johannes Piscator (1546–1625), Giovanni Diodati (1576–1649), Daniel Featly (1582–1645), and the Westminster divines.[35] Thus, Perkins distinguishes between the aspects of union with Christ by degrees because this is how Paul explains the chain of salvation.

At the same time, these degrees have a specific order because this is how the apostle Paul explicates union with Christ and because, though each degree is a part of union with Christ, they individually have different functions and relationships to each other. To explain the priorities and relationships between the different degrees of union with Christ, Perkins resorts to the *ordo naturae*. Looking to Perkins's table, he conceives of the causes of salvation that begin with election, which causes effectual calling, justification, sanctification, and glorification. Election and glorification are obviously temporal poles of salvation, as predestination occurs before the foundation of the world and

---

32. *Golden Chain*, 6:186.

33. *Golden Chain*, 6:212.

34. Muller, *Calvin and the Reformed Tradition*, 168; Fesko, "Question of the *Ordo Salutis*," 41–57, esp. 46–47, 51–53.

35. Muller, *Calvin and the Reformed Tradition*, 167–68; *Annotations upon all the Books of the Old and New Testament* (London: Evan Tyler, 1657), comm. Rom. 8:28–30.

glorification occurs at the conclusion of history at the return of Christ. But in between these temporal poles are effectual calling, justification, and sanctification, which Perkins explains according to their prioritized relationships. In his table, in the column of circles in between the degrees of union and the person and work of Christ, he places faith as a subset of effectual calling. He explains that there are certain things that precede and succeed faith in the *ordo naturae*. In terms of observable phenomenon of repentance, "It does first manifest itself, yet regarding the order of nature, it follows both faith and sanctification."[36] The only way a person can repent of his sin is if he possesses faith in Christ; moreover, repentance is a fruit of the believer's sanctification. In the order of causes of salvation, repentance, therefore, does not precede but succeeds faith.

Perkins makes similar observations regarding the relationship between faith, pardon, and conversion. "Faith," says he, "goes before conversion in order of nature, yet in the order of teaching and practice, they are both together."[37] Concerning faith and pardon, he adds, "The giving and the receiving of pardon and faith are both at one moment of time. For when God gives the pardon of sin, at the same instant He causes men to receive the same pardon by faith. For order of nature, faith goes before the receiving of the pardon (because faith is given to them that are to be engrafted into Christ, and pardon to them that are in Christ."[38] Perkins makes several claims that challenge criticisms of the *ordo salutis*. Regarding conversion and pardon, he clearly states that they occur at the same time—pardon and faith occur "at the same instant."[39] Correlatively, Perkins also speaks of pardon and faith as constituent elements of the believer's union with Christ. Union with Christ has an order of causes but it is not a temporally sequenced reception of blessings; nevertheless, the different elements of union with Christ relate to one another in specific ways. How can a person receive the forgiveness of sins unless he first believes in the promise of the gospel? There is a rational relationship between faith and pardon that requires that faith takes priority to pardon, and though they are both received in the same instant, in their rational relationship (in the *ordo naturae*), faith comes before pardon.

The rational relationship between the elements of union with Christ is not merely a matter of logical precision. The relative order of the different elements separates Roman Catholic, Lutheran, and Pelagian soteriologies from the biblical view. Perkins, for example, identifies an error with the Roman Catholic

---

36. *Golden Chain*, 6:190.
37. *Commentary on Galatians*, 2:25.
38. *Commentary on Galatians*, 2:213.
39. See also *God's Free Grace*, 6:420, 424.

doctrine of justification: "They make faith which justifies, to go before justification itself, both for order of nature, as also for time; whereas by the Word of God, at the very instant when any man believes, first, he is then justified and sanctified, for he that believes, eats and drinks the body and blood of Christ, and is already passed from death to life."[40] In other words, the Tridentine teaching on justification argues that faith itself justifies—people receive justifying faith in their baptism through the infusion of grace—and thus in the order of nature goes before justification.[41] Faith is not an instrumental but material cause of justification. Justifying faith also goes before justification in the order of time because God does not declare a person righteous until they are truly just at their second, or final, justification. Faith must work through love to achieve this final justification.[42]

Once again, the order of nature assists Perkins in delineating the difference between biblical and Roman Catholic soteriology. Like Trent, Perkins affirms that faith works through love and that a believer will produce good works, but the relative order of faith to these aspects of soteriology is key. In his commentary on Galatians, for example, Perkins explains what Paul means when he writes: "For in Jesus Christ neither circumcision availeth any thing, nor uncircumcision; but faith which worketh by love" (Gal. 5:6). Perkins avers that Roman Catholic theologians believe faith and love are joint causes of justification based upon this verse, but if this were true, it would overturn Paul's entire argument in Galatians.[43] This is the point of Paul's statement: "Christ is become of no effect unto you, whosoever of you are justified by the law" (Gal. 5:4). If God justifies sinners by their obedience to the law, then there is no need for Christ (Rom. 3:21; 2 Cor. 5:21). Faith and love do not work together to justify a person. Rather, faith and love are the two hands of the soul: "Faith is a hand that lays hold of Christ, and it does (as it were) pull Him and His benefits into our souls. But love is a hand of another kind, for it serves not to receive in, but to give out the good it has and to communicate itself unto others."[44] Believers, therefore, receive both faith and love through union with Christ, but: "Love in order of nature follows justification, and therefore it does not justify. For first of all faith lays hold on Christ. Then follows justification. Upon justification follows sanctification, and

---

40. *Reformed Catholic*, 7:42–43.

41. Council of Trent, "Session VI, 13 January 1547," VIII, X, in Philip Schaff, *The Creeds of Christendom: With a History and Critical Notes* (1931; Grand Rapids: Baker Books, 1990), 2:97–100.

42. *Golden Chain*, 6:222.

43. *Commentary on Galatians*, 2:333.

44. *Commentary on Galatians*, 2:333.

love is a part of sanctification."[45] Perkins blankets this sequence under a rational not temporal order; apart from observing the proper biblical rational order one can fall into the errors of Roman Catholic soteriology.

Perkins applies this same pattern of analysis to the place of good works in contrast to Roman Catholic views. Trent claims that God justifies sinners initially in their baptism and then finally by faith working through love: there is an initial and final justification. Perkins counters this claim by arguing that a person must be fully justified before he can do a good work. He affirms that justification is not partial, as with Rome, but complete the moment of its reception. There are no degrees of justification. Rome, on the other hand, claims there are degrees of justification. Why are there no degrees of justification? A sinner cannot please God until he is justified, therefore good works cannot be a meritorious cause of justification, which is what Rome believes "both for time and order of nature."[46] Instead, Perkins explains: "In a word, whereas they make two distinct justifications, we acknowledge that there be degrees of sanctification. Yet so as justification is only one, standing in remission of sins, and God's acceptation of us to life everlasting by Christ; and this justification has no degrees but is perfect at the very first."[47] So, Perkins admits that believers produce good works, but these works are the fruit of their sanctification, not the cause of their justification. Why? Among other biblical, exegetical, and theological reasons, "Good works do by order of nature follow man's justification and his absolution from sins."[48]

Conclusion

The missing element in much of the criticism against the *ordo salutis* is a close reading of primary sources to see how early modern Reformed theologians explain union with Christ. Reading Perkins on soteriology shows that he affirmed an ordered union on exegetical and theological grounds. He summarizes his view in this manner:

> There are four special works of grace in every child of God: union with Christ, adoption, justification, and conversion. And these four are wrought all at one instant, so as for order of time neither goes before nor after [the] other. And yet, in regard of order of nature, union with Christ, justification, and adoption, go before the inward conversion of a sinner, it being the fruit and effect of them all. Upon this it follows necessarily that

---

45. *Commentary on Galatians*, 2:333. See also *Exposition of Jude*, 4:231.
46. *Reformed Catholic*, 7:48.
47. *Reformed Catholic*, 7:48.
48. *Golden Chain*, 6:234.

a sinner, in the very first act of his conversion, is justified, adopted, and incorporated into the mystical body of Christ.[49]

The medieval distinction of *instantes naturae*, also known as *in signo rationis* or as the *ordo naturae*, gave theologians like Perkins a heuristic device to explain how the various blessings of union with Christ relate to each other. By distinguishing the order of time from nature, Perkins preserves both the unity of union with Christ, something that occurs in an instant, but also maintains the distinct nature of the individual blessings of effectual calling, justification, adoption, and sanctification. Union with Christ and an ordered salvation are not antithetical concepts just as forests and trees are not contradictory ideas. The *ordo naturae* enabled Perkins to distinguish between biblical and unbiblical soteriologies and arguably rests in the links of Paul's golden chain in Romans 8:28–30.

---

49. *Grain of Mustard Seed*, 8:644.

5

The Experience of Salvation
Joel R. Beeke

Contemporary scholars have called William Perkins (1558–1602) the "father of Puritanism."[1] They have classed Perkins with Calvin and Beza as third in "the trinity of the orthodox."[2] Perkins was the first theologian to be more widely published in England than Calvin, and the first English Protestant theologian to have a major impact in the British Isles, on the European continent, and in North America. Many Puritan scholars marvel that Perkins's rare works have been largely unavailable until the recent printing of his *Works* in ten volumes.[3]

---

1. Puritanism has been variously defined. I use the term "Puritans" here of those who desired to reform and purify the Church of England and were concerned about living a godly life consonant with the Reformed doctrines of grace. As J. I. Packer writes, "Puritanism was an evangelical holiness movement seeking to implement its vision of spiritual renewal, national and personal, in the church, the state, and the home; in education, evangelism, and economics; in individual discipleship and devotion, and in pastoral care and competence…. It was Perkins, quite specifically, who established Puritanism in this mould" *(An Anglican to Remember—William Perkins: Puritan Popularizer,* St. Antholin's Lectureship Charity Lecture [1996], 1–2). In a more recent seminal study on Perkins, William B. Patterson denies that Perkins should be linked to the Puritan movement at all (*William Perkins and the Making of a Protestant England* [Oxford: Oxford University Press, 2014], 64–89); for a concise refutation of that view, see Joel R. Beeke and Greg A. Salazar, "Preface," *The Works of William Perkins, Volume 6* (Grand Rapids: Reformation Heritage Books, 2018), xv. For a most helpful work that grapples with what a Puritan is, see Randall J. Pederson, *Unity in Diversity: English Puritans and the Puritan Reformation, 1603–1689* (Boston: Brill, 2014).

Parts of this chapter have been adapted from Joel R. Beeke, *The Quest for Full Assurance: The Legacy of Calvin and His Successors* (Edinburgh: Banner of Truth, 1999), 83–98; Beeke and Salazar, *Works of William Perkins,* 6:xiii–xliv; Joel R. Beeke and Andrew Ballitch, "What William Perkins Teaches Us Today," in *The Beauty and Glory of the Reformation* (Grand Rapids: Reformation Heritage Books, 2018), 125–52; Joel R. Beeke, "The Greatest Case of Conscience," in *William Perkins: Architect of Puritanism,* ed. Joel R. Beeke and Greg Salazar (Grand Rapids: Reformation Heritage Books, 2019), chap. 3.

2. John Eusden, *Puritans, Lawyers, and Politics* (New Haven: Yale University Press, 1958), 11; Paul Seaver, *The Puritan Lectureships: The Politics of Religious Dissent, 1560–1662* (Palo Alto, Calif.: Stanford University Press, 1970), 114; Christopher Hill, *God's Englishman: Oliver Cromwell and the English Revolution* (New York: Harper & Row, 1970), 38; Packer, *An Anglican to Remember,* 1.

3. *The Works of William Perkins,* 10 vols., gen. ed. Joel R. Beeke and Derek W. H. Thomas

Perkins's attempt to wed decretal and experimental theology makes his works rich with insight into the theology-driven piety characteristic of the Puritan era.[4] In his teaching, Perkins sought to bring the legacy of the Reformation theology of God's sovereignty in salvation into further development, higher definition, and fuller application. Perkins saw himself as an heir of the Reformation and his mission—far from breaking with it—was to further its progress in England and abroad. Contrary to the charge of some scholars that Perkins deviated from the theology of Calvin,[5] Richard Muller rightly asserts

(Grand Rapids: Reformation Heritage Books, 2014–2020)—hereafter *Works*. Cf. Louis Wright, "William Perkins: Elizabethan Apostle of 'Practical Divinitie,'" *Huntington Library Quarterly* 3 (1940):171; Mosse, *The Holy Pretense*, 48. For other editions of Perkins's writings, see *The Workes of That Famovs and Worthy Minister of Christ in the Vniuersitie of Cambridge, Mr. William Perkins*, 3 vols. (London: John Legatt, 1612–13); Ian Breward, intro. and ed., *The Work of William Perkins*, vol. 3 of the Courtenay Library of Reformation Classics (Abingdon, England: Sutton Courtenay Press, 1970)—hereafter, *Work of Perkins*; Thomas F. Merrill, ed., *William Perkins, 1558–1602, English Puritanist—His Pioneer Works on Casuistry: "A Discourse of Conscience" and "the Whole Treatise of the Cases of Conscience"* (Nieuwkoop: B. DeGraaf, 1966). Additional printings of Perkins's writings include *A Commentary on Galatians*, ed. Gerald T. Sheppard (New York: Pilgrim Press, 1989), *A Commentary on Hebrews 11*, ed. John H. Augustine (New York: Pilgrim Press, 1991), and *The Art of Prophesying*, ed. Sinclair Ferguson (Edinburgh: Banner of Truth Trust, 1996).

4. Experimental or experiential preaching addresses how a Christian experiences the truth of Christian doctrine in his life. The term *experimental* comes from *experimentum*, meaning trial, and is derived from the verb, *experior*, to know by experience, which in turn leads to "experiential," meaning knowledge gained by experiment. Calvin used experimental and experiential interchangeably, since both words indicate the need for measuring experienced knowledge against the touchstone of Scripture. Experimental preaching seeks to explain in terms of biblical truth how matters ought to go, how they do go, and what the goal of the Christian life is. It aims to apply divine truth to the whole range of the believer's personal experience as well as in his relationships with family, the church, and the world around him. Cf. Robert T. Kendall, *Calvin and English Calvinism to 1649* (New York: Oxford University Press, 1979), 8–9; Joel R. Beeke, "The Lasting Power of Reformed Experiential Preaching," in *Feed My Sheep: A Passionate Plea for Preaching*, ed. Don Kistler (Morgan, Penn.: Soli Deo Gloria, 2002), 94–128.

5. Perkins's critics—both positive and negative—agree that he provided a major link in Reformed thought between Beza and the Westminster Confession. Those who view that linkage as largely negative include Perry Miller (*Errand into the Wilderness* [Cambridge: Belknap Press, 1956]); Karl Barth (*Church Dogmatics* [Edinburgh: T & T Clark, 1961], III/4:8); Basil Hall ("Calvin against the Calvinists," in *John Calvin*, ed. G. E. Duffield [Appleford, England: Sutton Courtney Press, 1966], 19–37); Robert T. Kendall *(Calvin and English Calvinism;* "Living the Christian Life in the Teaching of William Perkins and His Followers," in *Living the Christian Life* [London: Westminster Conference, 1974]; "John Cotton—First English Calvinist?" *The Puritan Experiment in the New World* [London: Westminster Conference, 1976]; "The Puritan Modification of Calvin's Theology," in *John Calvin: His Influence in the Western World*, ed. W. Stanford Reid [Grand Rapids: Zondervan, 1982], 199–214).

Scholars who have reacted positively to Perkins include F. Ernest Stoeffler (*The Rise of Evangelical Pietism* [Leiden: Brill, 1965]); Ian Breward ("William Perkins and the Origins of Puritan

that "Perkins's thought is not a distortion of earlier Reformed Theology, but a positive outgrowth of the systematic beginnings of Protestant thought."[6]

In Perkins we observe the convergence of the Reformation's purified

---

Casuistry," *Faith and a Good Conscience* [London: Puritan and Reformed Studies Conference, 1962]; "The Significance of William Perkins," *Journal of Religious History* 4 [1966]:113–28; "William Perkins and the Origins of Puritan Casuistry," *The Evangelist Quarterly* 40 [1968]:16–22); Richard Muller ("Perkins' *A Golden Chaine*: Predestinarian System or Schematized *Ordo Salutis?*" *Sixteenth Century Journal* 9, no. 1 [1978]:69–81; "Covenant and Conscience in English Reformed Theology," *Westminster Theological Journal* 42 [1980]:308–34; *Christ and the Decrees: Christology and Predestination in Reformed Theology from Calvin to Perkins* [Grand Rapids: Baker, 1988]); Mark R. Shaw ("Drama in the Meeting House: The Concept of Conversion in the Theology of William Perkins," *Westminster Theological Journal* 45 (1983):41–72; "William Perkins and the New Pelagians: Another Look at the Cambridge Predestination Controversy of the 1590s," *Westminster Theological Journal* 58 [1996]:267–302); Joel R. Beeke, *The Quest for Full Assurance.*

6. "Perkins' *A Golden Chaine*," 69–71, 79–81. In addition to the works cited above and Muller, much has been published on Perkins. Dissertations and theses that contribute to an understanding of Perkins's theology include Ian Breward, "The Life and Theology of William Perkins" (PhD diss., University of Manchester, 1963); William H. Chalker, "Calvin and Some Seventeenth Century English Calvinists" (PhD diss., Duke University, 1961); Lionel Greve, "Freedom and Discipline in the Theology of John Calvin, William Perkins, and John Wesley: An Examination of the Origin and Nature of Pietism" (PhD diss., Hartford Seminary Foundation, 1976); Robert W. A. Letham, "Saving Faith and Assurance in Reformed Theology: Zwingli to the Synod of Dort," 2 vols. (PhD diss., University of Aberdeen, 1979); R. David Lightfoot, "William Perkins' View of Sanctification" (ThM thesis, Dallas Theological Seminary, 1984); Donald Keith McKim, *Ramism in William Perkins's Theology* (New York: Peter Lang, 1987); C. C. Markham, "William Perkins' Understanding of the Function of Conscience" (PhD diss., Vanderbilt University, 1967); Richard Alfred Muller, "Predestination and Christology in Sixteenth-Century Reformed Theology" (PhD diss., Duke University, 1976); Charles Robert Munson, "William Perkins: Theologian of Transition" (PhD diss., Case Western Reserve, 1971); Willem Jan op't Hof, *Engelse piëtistische geschriften in het Nederlands, 1598–1622* (Rotterdam: Lindenberg, 1987); Joseph A. Pipa Jr., "William Perkins and the Development of Puritan Preaching" (PhD diss., Westminster Theological Seminary, 1985); Victor L. Priebe, "The Covenant Theology of William Perkins" (PhD diss., Drew University, 1967); Mark R. Shaw, "The Marrow of Practical Divinity: A Study in the Theology of William Perkins" (PhD diss., Westminster Theological Seminary, 1981); Paul R. Schaefer Jr., "The Spiritual Brotherhood on the Habits of the Heart: Cambridge Protestants and the Doctrine of Sanctification from William Perkins to Thomas Shepard" (PhD diss., Keble College, Oxford University, 1994); Rosemary Sisson, "William Perkins" (master's thesis, University of Cambridge, 1952); C. J. Sommerville, "Conversion, Sacrament and Assurance in the Puritan Covenant of Grace to 1650" (master's thesis, University of Kansas, 1963); Young Jae Timothy Song, *Theology and Piety in the Reformed Federal Thought of William Perkins and John Preston* (Lewiston, New York: Edwin Mellin, 1998); Lynn Baird Tipson Jr., "The Development of a Puritan Understanding of Conversion" (PhD diss., Yale University, 1972); J. R. Tufft, "William Perkins, 1558–1602" (PhD diss., Edinburgh, 1952); Jan Jacobus van Baarsel, *William Perkins: eene bijdrage tot de Kennis der religieuse ontwikkeling in Engeland ten tijde, van Koningin Elisabeth* ('s-Gravenhage: H. P. De Swart & Zoon, 1912); William G. Wilcox, "New England Covenant Theology: Its Precursors and Early American Exponents" (PhD diss., Duke University, 1959); James Eugene Williams, Jr., "An Evaluation of William Perkins' Doctrine of Predestination in the Light of John Calvin's Writings" (ThM thesis, Dallas Theological Seminary, 1986); Andrew Alexander Woolsey, "Unity

soteriology with the needs occasioned by the spiritual struggles of professing believers. Perkins's interest was not limited to the theoretical dimensions of salvation but focused especially on the faith-enabled apprehension and experience of it. His practical concern was to help God's elect understand, appropriate, and enjoy the benefits of salvation, that they may come to know the fullness of the gospel's grace, rest in Christ alone, and glorify God as the sole Architect of their redemption. Hence the doctrine of this master theologian was eminently pastoral in that it was put into the service of the spiritual needs of God's people. Above all, Perkins assessed that they needed help in discerning whether they had a well-grounded assurance of faith based on a genuine experience of salvation.

Perkins taught that while salvation is not limited to a believer's experience it nonetheless intersects with that experience and must be discerned and traced out in it. Such will aid in demonstrating to the unconverted that they have not yet experienced salvation so they may avert a soul-damning presumption and seek it. It will also serve to edify and comfort the converted by helping them to have confidence in God's saving purposes toward them. Perkins taught that the salvation preordained before the foundation of the world manifests in the life experience of God's elect in time; therefore, that experience can be examined for the sake of yielding evidence of God's electing grace. As the believer discerns the Spirit's work of grace in time, he or she can thereby be assured of God's predestined and unchanging love in eternity.

Perkins's synthesis of decretal and experimental predestination is Christologically centered and a natural outgrowth of Calvinism. It is particularly faithful to the theology of Theodore Beza, which promotes a healthy combination of Reformed theology and Puritan piety.[7] Interweaving supralapsarian predestination with experimental soul examination, Perkins attempted the daring feat of setting forth a lively order of salvation (*ordo salutis*) that challenged all people, whether converted or not, to search for the fruits of predestination within their own souls on the basis of Christ's work. Perkins used Beza's method for comforting people who lacked assurance, but he also provided a more schematic, experiential *ordo salutis* with which to examine faith and doubt. He organized insights from Puritan preachers like Richard Greenham, who explained conversion "as a progression of inner states."[8] Perkins's

---

and Continuity in Covenantal Thought: A Study in the Reformed Tradition to the Westminster Assembly" (PhD diss., University of Glasgow, 1988).

7. Breward, *Work of Perkins*, xi.

8. Charles Cohen, *God's Caress: The Psychology of Puritan Religious Experience* (New York: Oxford, 1986), 11. Cf. Ian Breward, "William Perkins and the Origins of Reformed Casuistry," *Evangelical Quarterly* 40 (1968): 3–20; Richard Greenham, *The Works of the Reverend and Faithfull Servant of Jesus Christ M. Richard Greenham* (repr., New York: De Capo Press, 1973).

legacy was a highly refined experiential predestinarianism, which fleshed out the practical theology of Beza and Zanchius and was subsequently validated by the Westminster Assembly.

In this chapter, I will provide a summary of Perkins's theology of the experience of salvation, particularly with a view to his doctrine of assurance and its relationship to the work of grace in God's elect. I will conclude with an examination of his short treatise that succinctly presents his greatest case of conscience entitled, "How a man may know whether he be the child of God, or no,"[9] since it illustrates precisely how Perkins portrayed the transformative effects of saving grace as markers of a genuine experience of salvation.

Election, Covenant, and Assurance of Faith
By the late sixteenth century, the question of personal assurance of faith, or "How one could be sure of his election," became prominent for at least two important reasons. First, second and third generation Protestants were compelled to clarify the Reformers' doctrine of assurance in part because of the tendency of many growing up in the church to take for granted God's saving grace. The early Puritans reacted to dead orthodoxy, which minimized the seriousness of sin and regarded mere assent to the truths of Scripture as sufficient for salvation. It thus became essential to distinguish between assurance of personal grace and certainty based on mere assent to Bible truth. In this context, Puritans like William Perkins labored to lead their flocks into a well-grounded assurance of their election and salvation.

Second, the construction of a doctrine of assurance became important within the Puritan movement because the Puritans took sin and self-examination seriously. The more people become occupied with sin and its gravity in God's sight, the more likely they are to despair over both sin and themselves. Such despair makes fertile soil for cases of conscience that revolve around assurance of election and salvation.

Ever the conscientious pastor, Perkins predictably sought to provide the means whereby a sincere seeker could be persuaded of his own favorable state before a merciful God. He wrote several books in the late 1580s and 1590s that explained how one may know he is saved: *A Golden Chain: Or, The Description of Theology: Containing the Order of the Causes of Salvation and Damnation;*[10] *A Treatise Tending unto a Declaration, Whether a Man Is in the Estate of Damnation or in the Estate of Grace;*[11] *A Case of Conscience, the Greatest That Ever Was:*

---

9. *Case of Conscience,* 8:595–613.
10. *Golden Chain,* 6:1–265.
11. *Treatise Tending unto a Declaration,* 8:441–594.

How a Man May Know Whether He Be the Child of God or No;[12] *A Discourse of Conscience: Where Is Set Down the Nature, Properties, and Differences Thereof: as Also the Way to Get and Keep a Good Conscience;*[13] and *A Grain of Mustard-Seed: Or, the Least Measure of Grace That Is or Can Be Effectual to Salvation.*[14]

Through his prolific writings, Perkins taught people how to search their consciences for even the least evidence of election based on Christ's saving work. Perkins viewed such efforts as part of the pastor's fundamental task to keep "balance in the sanctuary" between divine sovereignty and human responsibility.[15] Sinners had to be shown how God's immovable will moved the will of man and how to look for evidences of election and inclusion in God's covenant. They also had to be taught how to make their election sure by living as the elect of God.

Perkins taught that one primary means God uses to work out His election is the covenant of grace. The golden chain of salvation as recorded in Romans 8:29–30 (predestation, effectual calling, justification, sanctification, and glorification) was linked to the elect through the instrument of preaching God's gracious covenant. Consequently, while Perkins preached about God's sovereign grace toward His elect from eternity and God's covenant acts of salvation by which election is realized, he was particularly concerned in his practical theology with how this redemptive process breaks through into the experience of the elect. He wanted to explain how the elect respond to God's overtures and acts, that is, how the covenant of grace impacts the will of the elect so as to move them from initial faith to full assurance, which enables them to say, "I am sure that I am a child of God, elected by the Father, redeemed by the blood of the Son, and indwelt by the Holy Spirit."

Perkins offered the covenant as a basis for assurance, maintaining that "God becomes our God not by any merit of ours, but by means of the gracious covenant propounded in the Gospel, promising pardon and remission of sin in and by Christ." This prompts the question, "What must we do to say truly and in assurance that God is our God?" Here are the basics of Perkins's answer:

> We must for our parts make a covenant with Him, unto which is required a consent on either party. First, on God's part, that He will be our God.... Secondly, on our part is required consent...when we make an outward profession of faith, hear the word, receive the sacraments.... [Also] there is required in our consent a further degree, which stands in an inward

---

12. *Case of Conscience*, 8:595–613.
13. *Discourse of Conscience*, 8:1–94.
14. *Grain of Mustard Seed*, 8:639–58.
15. Irvonwy Morgan, *Puritan Spirituality* (London: Epworth Press, 1973), chap. 2.

consent of the heart whereby a man takes God for his God. Which is then begun when, first, a man acknowledges and bewails his sins...endeavors to be reconciled to God...purposes never to sin again. When this covenant is thus concluded by consent of both parties, a man may safely and truly say that God is his God. Now seeing we know these things, our duty is to labor to be settled and assured.... First, in this assurance is the foundation of all true comfort. All the promises of God are hereupon grounded.... And not only is it the foundation of all comfort in this life, but of our happiness after death itself.... For by virtue of this covenant alone shall we rise again after death to life, glory, and immortality.[16]

According to Perkins, then, man has a great deal of responsibility to fulfill in his covenant relation with God. Yet Perkins acknowledges that assurance can never be gleaned from a conditional covenant alone, for human conditionality can never answer all the questions conjoined with human depravity, divine sovereignty, and election. For Perkins, the covenant contains both a conditional and an absolute relationship. Assurance flows out of the covenant's absolute nature which is grounded in God's gracious being and promises, not out of the covenant's conditional nature which is connected with man's performance. Perkins writes, "God has spoken to us. He has made promise of blessing to us. He has made covenant with us. And He has sworn unto us. What can we more require of Him? What better ground of true comfort [is there]?" And earlier, he writes, "The promises of the gospel are not made to the work, but to the worker, and to the worker not for his work, but for Christ's sake, according to His work."[17]

Thus, though Perkins encourages people to strive after assurance, ultimately he thrusts us back on the one-sided grace of God for our assurance, declaring that the covenant itself is a divine gift rooted in the merits of Christ. Assurance, in the final analysis, rests on God's faithfulness to His covenant promises, making even the fulfillment of the condition of faith on man's part possible only by God's gracious gift.

The Christ-Centeredness of Faith

For Perkins, faith is a supernatural gift given by God to the sinner to take hold of Christ with all the promises of salvation.[18] The object of faith is not the sinner or his experiences or faith itself; it is Jesus Christ alone. Faith sees Christ, first, as a sacrifice on the cross for the remission of sins, then learns to

---

16. *Exposition of Jude*, 4:105–6.
17. *Commentary on Galatians*, 2:191, 177.
18. *Exposition of the Creed*, 5:12.

experience Him as the strength to battle temptation, the comfort in a storm of affliction, and ultimately grows to see in Christ all things needful in this life and in the life to come. In sum, faith shows itself when "every several person does particularly apply to himself Christ with His merits by an inward persuasion of the heart which comes none other way but by the effectual certificate of the Holy Ghost concerning the mercy of God in Christ Jesus."[19]

Faith has no meaning apart from Jesus Christ. "Faith [is] a principal grace of God, whereby man is engrafted into Christ, and thereby becomes one with Christ and Christ one with him," Perkins says.[20] All of Perkins's references to faith as an "instrument" or "hand" must be understood in this context. Faith is a gift of God's sovereign pleasure that moves man to respond to Christ through the preaching of the Word.

Perkins's use of the term "instrument" or "hand" conveys the simultaneously passive and active role of faith in this redemptive activity. As Hideo Oki writes, "The connotation of 'instrument' suggests activity. This activity, however, is never simply 'positive'; on the contrary, it means that when it is most active, then it is moved and used by something other and higher than itself. Thus, in the midst of activity there is passivity, and in the midst of passivity it [is] most efficient in activity."[21]

This is precisely what Perkins means. Initially, faith is the passive "instrument" or "hand" granted by God to the sinner to receive Jesus Christ. Yet precisely at the moment when Christ is received, faith responds to the gift of grace. Thus the response is most active when it has completely yielded to and is centered in the Person it has received.

This concept of faith, within the context of covenant, is the genius of Perkins's theology. His intense concern for the godly life rises alongside his equally intense concern to maintain the Reformation principle of salvation by grace alone. For man is never granted salvation on account of his faith but by means of faith.

Faith and Assurance

At times, Perkins seems to equate faith and assurance. He writes, "True faith is both an infallible assurance, and a particular assurance of the remission of sins, and of life everlasting."[22] On other occasions, he tends to separate faith

---

19. *Golden Chain*, 6:176.
20. *Three Books on Cases of Conscience*, 8:153.
21. "Ethics in Seventeenth Century English Puritanism" (ThD diss., Union Theological Seminary, New York, 1960), 141.
22. *Reformed Catholic*, 7:28.

and assurance: "Whereas some are of the opinion that faith is an affiance or confidence, that seems to be otherwise; for it is a fruit of faith," he says.[23]

Such apparent contradictions have led some scholars to assert that either Perkins was not a first-rate theologian or that he simply wrote from his limited context.[24] When opposing Roman Catholicism, scholars say, Perkins confirmed the certainty of faith. But when he spoke against the strong assertions of the early Reformers on assurance, Perkins tended to divorce faith and assurance.[25] Such views cannot be maintained in light of Perkins's own thought. Perkins knew very well what he was saying; he intended to teach that assurance both is and is not part of the essence of faith, depending on what kind of assurance is being discussed.[26]

To understand Perkins on faith and assurance, we must understand the two ways he used the term *assurance*. The first kind of assurance, which is more objective in nature, enables a sinner to be assured that his sins are pardonable apart from the personal realization of such forgiveness. The second kind, which is more subjective in nature, is the full assurance that enables the sinner to believe that God, for Christ's sake, has personally forgiven all his sins.

Then, too, Perkins (as well as many later Puritans) tended to categorize the operation of faith "into a succession of recognizable stages" beyond what Calvin did.[27] For example, in *A Golden Chain*, Perkins presents us with "five degrees" in "the work of faith," all of which, he says, are "linked and united together":

- Knowing the gospel by the illumination of God's Spirit.

- Hoping for pardon, "whereby a sinner, albeit he yet feels not that his sins are certainly pardoned, yet he believes that they are pardonable."

- Hungering and thirsting after the grace offered in Christ Jesus, "as a man hungers and thirsts after meat and drink."

- Approaching the throne of grace, "that there, flying from the terror of the law, he may take hold of Christ and find favor with God." The first part of this is "a humble confession of our sins before God particularly, if they be known sins; and generally, if unknown." The second part is "craving pardon of some sins with unspeakable sighs and in perseverance."

---

23. *Exposition of the Creed*, 5:13.

24. Marshall Knappen, *Tudor Puritanism: A Chapter in the History of Idealism* (Chicago: University of Chicago Press, 1939), 219.

25. Letham, "Relationship between Faith and Assurance," 29–30.

26. For a detailed treatment of Perkins's thought here, see Matthew N. Payne, "William Perkins's Doctrines of Faith and Assurance through the Lens of Early Modern Faculty Psychology," *Westminster Theological Journal* 83 (2021): 317–36.

27. Edmund Morgan, *Visible Saints* (New York: University Press, 1963), 68–69.

• Applying, by the Spirit's persuasion, "to himself those promises which are made in the gospel."[28]

These degrees of faith are dependent upon the preaching of the Word of God as well as the inner witness of the Spirit, which leads to a personal assurance of having been "grasped" by God's grace to embrace Christ. In this context, Perkins developed a major contribution to the discussion of assurance by making a distinction between *weak faith* and *strong faith*. Weak faith is like a grain of mustard seed or smoking flax, "which can neither give out heat nor flame but only smoke." Weak faith has low levels of illuminating knowledge and of applying to the promises (the first and last steps of saving faith mentioned above), but shows itself by "a serious desire to believe and an endeavor to obtain God's favor." God does not despise even the least spark of faith, Perkins says, providing the weak believer diligently uses the means of grace to increase it. He must "stir up his faith by meditation of God's word, serious prayers, and other exercises belonging to faith."[29]

For Perkins, even weak faith is a "certain and true" persuasion, since there can be no doubt in faith, but strong faith is a "full persuasion of the heart whereby a Christian much more firmly taking hold on Christ Jesus makes full and resolute account that God loves him and that He will give to him by name Christ and all His graces pertaining to eternal life."[30] Strong faith, or "full assurance," claims God's promises as a personal possession, remembering that evangelical promises exclude only those who exclude themselves (Isa. 55:1; Matt. 11:28). It accomplishes this by meditating upon the promises concerning Christ's life and work and by depending on the Spirit to stir up and increase faith.[31] Then, Perkins says, "to believe in Christ is not confusedly to believe that he is a redeemer of mankind, but withal to believe that he is my Savior, and that I am elected, justified, sanctified, and shall be glorified by Him."[32]

Several thoughts converge in Perkins. First, in weak faith God's promises are seen but the believer does not yet have freedom to appropriate them by the cowitness of the Spirit in his conscience. Second, the distinction between weak and strong faith is helpful pastorally to keep weak believers from despair by encouraging them to believe that weak faith is still authentic faith. Third, each believer must seek for strong faith, but the typical believer will not receive it "at the first, but in some continuance of time, after he has for a long space kept a

---

28. *Golden Chain*, 6:176–77.
29. *Golden Chain*, 6:178–79.
30. *Golden Chain*, 6:179.
31. *Golden Chain*, 6:196–97.
32. *Discourse of Conscience*, 8:23.

good conscience before God and before men, and has had divers experiences of God's love and favor towards him in Christ."[33] Finally, in strong faith, full assurance grows from a mustard seed to a full tree, ascertained by a personal, Spirit-worked appropriation of the benefits of faith.[34]

Perkins's teaching on faith and assurance must be situated within the experiential framework of his teaching on conversion, particularly within his delineation of identifiable aspects of conversion that reflect the Spirit's progressive work of grace in bringing sinners to Christ and sanctifying them out of the virtue of that vital union with the Savior. A balanced look at how Perkins understands the experience of salvation involves an examination of these precise stages to understand how the process of conversion and assurance was woven into Perkins's thought and preaching.

The Steps of Conversion

While Perkins divided conversion into steps or degrees, his primary list of ten stages may be summarized under four headings: humiliation, faith, repentance, and new obedience. Here is a basic description of those steps.

Step #1: Humiliation
According to Perkins, the first step of conversion includes four states or "actions of grace" that flow out of experimental predestinarianism: attentive hearing of the Word; awareness of God's commanding and prohibiting law; conviction of sin; and despair of salvation. Perkins defined these stages as follows:

> [Action of grace #1:] The ministry of the Word, and with it...some outward or inward cross to break and subdue the stubbornness of our nature so that it may be pliable to the will of God.

> [Action of grace #2:] God brings the mind of man to a consideration of the law, and therein generally to see what is good and what is evil.

> [Action of grace #3:] He makes a man particularly to see and know his own peculiar and proper sins whereby he offends God.

---

33. *Treatise Tending unto a Declaration*, 8:477.

34. More generally, on the faith and assurance question in Perkins's context, see Michael P. Winship, "Weak Christians, Backsliders, and Carnal Gospelers: Assurance of Salvation and the Pastoral Origins of Puritan Practical Divinity in the 1580s," *Church History* 70, no. 3 (2001): 462–81.

[Action of grace #4:] He smites the heart with a legal fear, whereby when man sees his sins, He makes him to fear punishment and hell and to despair of salvation in regard to anything in himself.[35]

These four "works of preparation" precede the work of grace. Since these are not fruits of grace per se (though they *may* be), and since the reprobate may travel this far in the garb of temporary faith,[36] several interpreters have labeled Perkins as an undiluted preparationist. For Perkins, however, these actions were preparatory because one would not know if these steps were saving until they led to further steps of grace.[37] In Perkins's theology, the needy sinner must be driven onward to find rest exclusively in Christ.

Step #2: Faith in Christ

The second step of conversion, Perkins said, includes four stages of grace. These stages separate the elect from the reprobate:

[Action of grace #5:] [God] stir[s] up the mind to a serious consideration of the promise of salvation, propounded and published in the gospel.

[Action of grace, #6:] [God] kindle[s] in the heart some seeds or sparks of faith, that is, a will and desire to believe, and grace to strive against doubting and despair.

[Action of grace #7:] So soon as faith is put into the heart, there is presently a combat, for it fights with doubting, despair, and distrust. And in this combat, faith shows itself by fervent, constant, and earnest invocation for pardon; and...prevailing of this desire.

---

35. *Three Books on Cases of Conscience*, 8:141.

36. For how far the reprobate may proceed with temporary faith, see *Golden Chain*, 6:243ff.; *Treatise Tending unto a Declaration*, 8:441ff.; cf. Tipson, "The Development of a Puritan Understanding of Conversion," 252–57, and Kendall, *Calvin and English Calvinism to 1649*, 67–76.

37. Perkins says the first four steps are "works of preparation going before grace," whereas of the subsequent steps he says, "by these degrees does the Lord give the first grace." The view of the Dutch Reformed divines such as Witsius is nuanced somewhat differently than the British divines in the former's locating regeneration earlier in the process of conversion. For a summary of Perkins's view of preparatory grace, see Joel R. Beeke and Paul M. Smalley, *Prepared by Grace, for Grace: The Puritans on God's Ordinary Way of Leading Sinners to Christ* (Grand Rapids: Reformation Heritage Books, 2013), 41–44. Cf. Shaw, "The Marrow of Practical Divinity," 128 with Pettit, *Heart Prepared*, 44ff., and Herman Witsius, *The Oeconomy of the Covenants between God and Man, Comprehending a Complete Body of Divinity*, trans. William Crookshank (London: Edward Dilly, 1762), III, vi., 11; see also Beeke and Smalley, *Prepared by Grace*, 240.

[Action of grace #8:] God in mercy quiets and settles the conscience as touching the salvation of the soul and the promise of life, whereupon it rests and stays itself.[38]

The objective assurance of the sinner's "forgivableness" lies in actions #5–7, whereas the subjective assurance of being forgiven is in action #8, which, for Perkins, is a further step in grace. Nevertheless, in neither case is the object of faith in the sinner or in his experience of faith, but solely in Jesus Christ.

Steps #3–4: Repentance and New Obedience

By placing *repentance* subsequent to faith as action of grace #9, Perkins emphasized that evangelical repentance refines the soul and persuades the elect to live wholly to God and to hate sin more than death. True gospel sorrow must thus flow from the inward conviction of having "offended so merciful a God and loving Father" and must yield a wholehearted Godward change "of the mind and whole man in affection, life, and conversation."[39]

The sequel to this is action of grace #10: *new obedience.* The whole man then endeavors "to keep the whole law in his mind, will, affections, and all the faculties of soul and body."[40] Here Perkins linked divine election and Reformed piety. The elect will walk in godly piety as a fruit of divine decree and personal assurance, he said. They will perform good works, often parallel to their degree of assurance, always in the strength of Christ who must cleanse all their works from corruption. In this manner, the golden chain is partly consummated on earth in a daily walk in the *assurance of sense* by means of *inward tokens* and *outward fruits*[41] and will finally be realized in heaven to the glory of an electing God.

Repentance and obedience augment the believer's assurance, strengthened by the means of grace, such as prayer and the sacraments. True prayer and a right use of the sacraments repeatedly remind the believer that he is elect.

Prayer indicates piety. For Perkins, to pray is to put up our request to God with assurance, according to His Word, from a contrite heart in the name of Christ.[42] He thus wrote: "Prayer is to be made with faith, whereby a man must have certain assurance to be heard. For he that prays must steadfastly believe that God in Christ will grant his petition."[43]

---

38. *Three Books on Cases of Conscience*, 8:142.
39. *Three Books on Cases of Conscience*, 8:147.
40. *Three Books on Cases of Conscience*, 8:148.
41. *Exposition of the Creed*, 5:338.
42. *Exposition of the Lord's Prayer*, 5:423–25.
43. *Exposition of the Lord's Prayer*, 5:426.

Conscience plays a key role in praying with assurance. Perkins wrote, "For unless a man be in conscience in some measure persuaded that all his sins are pardoned and that he stands reconciled to God in Christ, he cannot believe any other promises revealed in the Word nor that any of his prayers shall be heard."[44]

Perkins taught that a sacrament is "a prop and stay for faith to lean upon. For it cannot entitle us into the inheritance of the sons of God, as the covenant does, but only by reason of faith going before it does seal that which before was bestowed upon us."[45] Through the sacraments, the Holy Spirit confirms faith, restores piety, and works a new willingness in the heart to practice cross bearing and self-denial for Christ's sake, Perkins said. Moreover, the elements in the sacraments can strengthen assurance in God's promises. Perkins's syllogism for that is: "He who uses the elements aright shall receive the promises. But I do [use], or I have used, the elements aright. Therefore, I shall receive the promises."[46]

Faith, repentance, and obedience all have an intimate relationship with assurance, which is rooted in the finished work of Christ and ascertained through the Spirit's efficacious operations in harmony with the Father's eternal election. Understanding the big picture of Perkins's theology of the experience of salvation, however, involves situating the believer's assurance within his teaching concerning the proper grounds of assurance.

Grounds of Assurance

Perkins proposes three grounds of assurance: the *promises of the gospel*, which are ratified by God's covenant; the *testimony of the Holy Spirit* witnessing with our spirit that we are the children of God; and the *fruits of sanctification*. These three interconnected grounds, all of which depend on the applying ministry of the Holy Spirit, are so important that Perkins called them "the hinge upon which the gate of heaven turns."[47] The believer ought always to strive to grow in assurance by seeking as large a degree of assurance as possible from all three of these grounds or means.

The promises of God are always the primary ground of assurance. When embraced by faith, the promises of God bear the fruits of sanctification and often are combined with the witnessing testimony of the Spirit. The believer may have difficulty at times realizing one or more of these grounds in his own experience. That is particularly true of the testimony of the Spirit. Yet that ought not to distress the believer, Perkins says, because even when the Spirit's

---

44. *Exposition of the Lord's Prayer*, 5:426.
45. *Golden Chain*, 6:158.
46. *Discourse of Conscience*, 8:78.
47. *Galatians*, 2:260.

testimony is not felt deeply enough to persuade the believer of his election, the effects of the Spirit will be demonstrated in sanctification.

Perkins spent the most time expounding assurance by means of sanctification in part because this kind of assurance generated the most pastoral questions. Perkins asserted that the works of obedience are a "document of faith," not a principal ground or basis for it. Nevertheless, these works are important for assuring the believer of his election and salvation in Christ, for they provide assurance of the essential effects of justification. The believer can draw comfort from their heat even if no flame is visible.[48] These works are also benefits of Christ, and so they direct the believer's gaze to Christ. In no way do they justify the believer before God, but as Perry Miller says, "The chief value of a Puritan's actions in his own eyes was symbolical; they were emblems of his election rather than ethically commendable deeds.... His principal interest in behavior was its source."[49]

Perkins thus moves down his golden chain from God's assurance of salvation in eternity to the elect's assurance in time. The chain of divine sovereignty, covenant-establishment, mediatorial satisfaction, faith in Christ, and the Spirit's corroborating witness result in assurance within the soul through a "practical syllogism" (*syllogismus practicus*). A practical syllogism, simply put, is a conclusion drawn from an action. It involves a major premise, a minor premise, and a conclusion. The basic form of the syllogism Perkins uses to explain salvation is as follows:

Major premise: Only those who repent and believe in Christ alone for salvation are children of God.

Minor premise: By the gracious work of the Spirit, I repent and believe in Christ alone for salvation.

Conclusion: Therefore I am a child of God.[50]

Though assurance by syllogism provides secondary grounds of assurance dependent on the primary grounds (the sovereign work of the Father, the redeeming work of the Son, and the applying work of the Spirit), such assurance is nonetheless real. J. I. Packer says: "In my opinion, Perkins was right, first to analyse conscience as operating by practical syllogisms, and second to

---

48. *Golden Chain*, 6:182, 262.

49. Perry Miller, *The New England Mind, The Seventeenth Century* (Boston: Beacon Press, 1961), 52.

50. Cf. Kendall, *Calvin and English Calvinism*, 71; Beeke, *Quest for Full Assurance*, 65–72, 131–41.

affirm that scriptural self-examination will ordinarily yield the Christian solid grounds for confidence as to his or her regeneration and standing with God."[51]

Perkins stresses that the human spirit's syllogistic response to God's saving work does not degrade Christ in any way. Rather, it magnifies the unbreakable strength of God's golden chain of salvation merited by the Son and applied by His Spirit. Though one might argue that Perkins links these secondary grounds of assurance to a personal profession of faith, these grounds are only valid as evidence of the primary grounds. The smoke of sanctification must rise from the fire of grace; therefore, works, when evidenced as the fruits of grace, "certify election and salvation."[52] Perkins maintains, as did Calvin, that works do not save the elect but often succeed in assuring the elect. Works are the evidence of election, not the cause of it.[53] Scholars who assert that assurance is essential to faith in Christ and that sanctification cannot forward assurance in any way are guilty, as Andrew Woolsey says, of separating Christ and His benefits.[54]

In his writings, Perkins lists various marks or works of sanctification that the believer, in dependency on the Spirit, can use syllogistically. Here is one such list:

> (1) To feel our wants and in the bitterness of heart to bewail the offense of God in every sin. (2) To strive against the flesh—that is, to resist and to hate the ungodly motions thereof and with grief to think them burdensome and troublesome. (3) To desire earnestly and vehemently the grace of God and merit of Christ to obtain eternal life. (4) When it is obtained, to account it a most precious jewel (Phil. 3:8). (5) To love the minister of God's word, in that he is a minister; and a Christian, in that he is a Christian—and for that cause, if need require, to be ready to spend our blood with them (Matt. 10:42; 1 John 3:16). (6) To call upon God earnestly and with tears. (7) To desire and love Christ's coming and the day of judgment, that an end may be made of the days of sin. (8) To flee all occasions of sin and seriously to endeavor to come to newness of life. (9) To persevere in these things to the last gasp of life.[55]

---

51. Packer, *An Anglican to Remember*, 19.

52. Breward, "The Significance of William Perkins," 123.

53. Gordon J. Keddie, "'Unfallible Certenty of the Pardon of Sinne and Life Everlasting': The Doctrine of Assurance in the Theology of William Perkins," *The Evangelical Quarterly* 48 (1976): 30–44; Joel R. Beeke, *Assurance of Faith: Calvin, English Puritanism, and the Dutch Second Reformation* (New York: Peter Lang, 1991), 105–18.

54. Andrew A. Woolsey, *Unity and Continuity in Covenantal Thought* (Grand Rapids: Reformation Heritage Books, 2012), 481.

55. *Golden Chain*, 6:262–63.

If a believer has, even to a small degree, experienced some of these marks of grace, he can be assured that he is being sanctified by the Spirit of God. In turn, since the entire golden chain of salvation—election, vocation, faith, justification, sanctification, and eternal glorification, etc.—are "inseparable companions," the believer "may infallibly conclude in his own heart, that he has, and shall have interest in all the other in his due time."[56]

Mark Shaw summarizes Perkins: "The child of God can grab that link [of sanctification, or good works] in the golden chain and feel with certainty the tug of all the rest.... [Perkins's] general principle is clear: grab any part of the *ordo salutis* within reach and you have the whole chain. Anyone clutching the middle links (the covenant of grace, justification by faith, and sanctification by the Spirit) can be assured of possessing the end links (election and glorification)."[57]

It is impossible for the human will to foil the divine decree. Knowing that breeds certainty—not uncertainty—even in the weakest of saints. Assurance is assurance because election is the sinner's solid hope. As Dewey Wallace writes: "The piety of predestinarian grace as an experience was particularly focused on providing assurance and certainty, as anxieties dissolved in the experience of being seized, in spite of one's unworthiness, as one of the chosen of that awesome yet gracious number upon which one was totally dependent. It must be remembered that the powerful religious experience was always that of being chosen, not of being left out, and thus certainty and reassurance, not despair, were derived from the unique logic of this way-of-being-religious."[58]

Finally, Perkins taught that even full assurance might vanish in the midst of strong temptation. As long as believers are "in this world according to their own feeling, there is an access and recess of the Spirit,"[59] Perkins said. This lack of feeling could be due to a weak conscience, strong doubts, failure to grasp any part of the *ordo salutis*, or simply the sovereignty of the Spirit. The testimony of the Spirit, which could be temporarily lost at any moment, emphasizes the need for continual self-examination, repentance, and a godly walk.

How a Man May Know Whether He Be the Child of God, or No

Having given an overview of Perkins's theology of the experience of salvation and doctrine of assurance, I conclude by taking a closer look at his short treatise: *A Case of Conscience, The Greatest That Euer Was: How a Man May Know*

---

56. Merrill, ed., *William Perkins*, 111–12, spelling modernized.
57. Shaw, "The Marrow of Practical Divinity," 166.
58. Wallace, *Puritans and Predestination*, 195–96.
59. Wallace, *Puritans and Predestination*, 413.

Whether He Be the Child of God, or No. This treatise (not counting the attached article by Jerome Zanchius)[60] is six folio pages in length and primarily consists of a dialogue between the living church and the apostle John. The church, or the believer seeking assurance, asks questions, and John responds to the struggles of the soul with the exact words of his first epistle (Geneva Bible translation). To this Perkins adds marginal notes and minor clarifications in brackets.

In addition to this short treatise, Perkins wrote two major works on conscience. The first, *A Discourse of Conscience*, deals with the conscience from a theoretical perspective.[61] Perkins translates the biblical word for conscience as "co-knowledge" or "co-testimony." He shows that the word itself witnesses to the divine dimension of conscience, for who can "co-know" our deepest thoughts and feelings but God and ourselves? Hence Perkins says, "Conscience is of a divine nature, and is a thing placed of God in the midst between him and man, as an arbitrator to give sentence and to pronounce either with man or against man unto God."[62] Perkins concludes that the conscience has two main duties: to give testimony and to pass judgment.[63]

Perkins's largest work on conscience, *The Whole Treatise of the Cases of Conscience*, went through thirteen English and six Continental editions to become the paradigm for numerous Puritan manuals of practical divinity.[64] In this work, Perkins deals with a wide range of specific cases of conscience, covering man's relationship to himself, to God, and to others.[65] In the first section of this book, Perkins discusses what a person must do to be saved, how believers can be assured in their conscience of their salvation, and how they can be restored when they have fallen. Throughout this section, Perkins reverts back to questions that relate to assurance, making it clear that he regards assurance as the greatest case of conscience.

---

60. Zanchius emphasized three testimonies to the believer's salvation: the Spirit of God, which points the believer to Christ and His benefits; the preaching of the gospel, which commands our consciences to believe; and the effects of grace, such as a holy life and a clear conscience which "seal" assurance. By attaching material from Zanchius, Perkins shows that he will not stray beyond the boundaries already established by continental Reformed theology. *Case of Conscience*, 8:615–37.

61. Merrill, ed., *William Perkins*, 1–78.

62. Merrill, ed., *William Perkins*, 6, spelling modernized.

63. Merrill, ed., *William Perkins*, 7.

64. Breward, "William Perkins and the Origins of Puritan Casuistry," 3–20. Cf. James F. Keenan, "Was William Perkins' *Whole Treatise of Cases of Consciences* Casuistry? Hermeneutics and British Practical Divinity," in *Contexts of Conscience in Early Modern Europe, 1500–1700*, ed. Harald Braun and Edward Vallance (New York: Palgrave MacMillan, 2004), 29. Keenan concludes that Perkins's work is best classified as a spiritual directory rather than as casuistry, and argues that its uniqueness was not in its genre so much as in its broad scope (30).

65. Merrill, ed., *William Perkins*, 79–240.

By explicitly affirming assurance of faith as the greatest case of conscience in the title of his shorter work based on First John, Perkins is not falling into a kind of subjectivism which ultimately leads to unhealthy pietism, as some have affirmed. Rather, he has a more helpful goal in mind. Perkins stresses that if a person is assured of God's favor to him in Christ, he is able to live victoriously in whatever state he finds himself. Perkins was a practical theologian; he defines theology as "the science of living blessedly for ever." All his teaching on Christian living is based on a good conscience that rests with assurance of God's salvation in Christ Jesus.[66]

In each of these works, Perkins sees a good conscience as the major purpose of John's first epistle. In *A Discourse of Conscience*, Perkins devotes only one paragraph to prove this point.[67] In *The Whole Treatise of the Cases of Conscience*, Perkins summarizes the teaching of 1 John under three propositions:

- *Communion with God brings undoubted assurance* (1 John 1:3–7). If we have fellowship with God, Perkins asserts, we need not worry about God's eternal decree. In Christ we find certain salvation. We may know we are in Him by the forgiveness of our sins through the blood of Christ, the work of the sanctifying Spirit within us, holiness and uprightness of heart and life, and perseverance in the knowledge of and obedience to the gospel.

- *Every adopted son of God will undoubtedly be saved* (1 John 3). God's adopted sons will truly believe in the Son of God, will strive to obey Him as Lord, and will love other Christians as their brothers and sisters, thereby giving assuring evidence of their salvation.

- *Knowing the love of God provides assurance of salvation* (1 John 4:9). That love, in turn, will be manifest by our loving God and loving our brethren.[68]

Perkins offers more detail on 1 John in his short treatise *A Case of Conscience*. When John states that he is writing so that the joy of his readers might be full (1:4), Perkins adds, "i.e., might have sound consolation in your consciences."[69] Perkins repeatedly returns to the theme of conscience. He speaks of our consciences not accusing us for sin (commenting on 1 John 2:28; 3:19–21), of the

---

66. Breward, "William Perkins and the Origins of Puritan Casuistry," 14.
67. Merrill, ed., *William Perkins*, 53–54.
68. Merrill, ed., *William Perkins*, 114–16.
69. *Case of Conscience*, 8:599.

"checkings and torments of conscience" (on 1 John 4:18), and of a conscience "inwardly purified" (on 1 John 5:6).[70]

Other bracketed comments by Perkins are like a checklist of the marks of grace by which believers may be assured in their conscience that they are adopted of God. Here are a few of those marks:

- *Desiring to obey God's commandments.* On keeping God's commandments in 1 John 2:3, Perkins notes that "to keep is not to fulfill, but to have a care and desire to do it, for God of His mercy in his servants accepts the will for the deed."[71] Perkins is anxious not to set the bar of conversion too high, for the conscientious believer will be the first to admit that he does not keep God's commandments as he should, though he cannot deny his desire to do so. God's acceptance of the inward desire for the deed is most comforting for the trembling believer. At the same time it reaches the inward motions of the heart.

- *Possessing sincerity of heart.* In addressing 1 John 2:5, which speaks of the love of God being perfect, Perkins interprets *perfect* as "sincere and sound, perfection being opposed not to imperfection, but hypocrisy." When John speaks of loving in "deed and truth" (1 John 3:18), Perkins adds: "sincerely."[72] For Perkins, it is impossible to have a sound and healthy conscience without being sincere.

- *Delighting in God and His grace.* In commenting on 1 John 2:13, Perkins speaks three times of the delights of God's children. He addresses fathers "delighting to tell and hear of old and ancient matters," young men "delighting to shew your valor and strength," and children "who delight always to be under the Father's wing."[73] For Perkins, delighting in God is a key mark of grace, common to young children and old fathers in grace. Christianity that falls short of delighting in God is Pharisaism.

- *Fleeing the lusts of the world.* Commenting on 1 John 2:16, Perkins summarizes the lust of the flesh as "the corruption of nature, which chiefly breaks out in evil concupiscence," the lust of the eyes as the fruit of the lust of the flesh "stirred up by outward provocations…as it is manifest in adultery and covetousness," and the pride of life as "arrogance and ambition." Because believers live as adopted sons and daughters,

---

70. *Case of Conscience*, 8:610–11.
71. *Case of Conscience*, 8:601.
72. *Case of Conscience*, 8:601, 607.
73. *Case of Conscience*, 8:602.

they are reckoned as the "refuse and offscouring of the world" (on 1 John 3:1).[74]

- *Loving one another as believers.* This love is the fruit of God adopting us by His grace into His family. The church responds to 1 John 3:15 by saying, "You have shown us fully that love is a work of adoption." That adoption is possible because of God's love for us. Perkins comments on 1 John 4:12, "That love wherewith he loves, is thoroughly made manifest towards us by our love, as the light of the moon shining on us, argues the light of the sun shining upon the moon, from which, as from the fountain, the moon takes its light."[75]

- *Purifying of one's self.* On 1 John 3:3, Perkins makes clear that believers purify themselves, but he adds that they do so as a fruit of adoption and by the grace of God. In an accompanying marginal note, Perkins says that "a desire and an endeavor to use good means to cleanse ourselves of our corruptions and private sins is a mark of adoption."[76]

Perkins reinforces these and additional marks of grace by other marginal notes, such as:

1. Sincerity of life and religion [is] a note [mark] of communion with God (1 John 1:7).
2. Humble confession of sin to God is a note of remission of sin (1 John 1:9–10).
3. An endeavor to keep the commandments [is] a sign of faith (1 John 2:3).
4. Love of our brother [is] a sign of regeneration (1 John 2:10).
5. God's Spirit dwelling in the heart [is] a sign of perseverance (1 John 2:20).
6. Perseverance in the knowledge and obedience of the gospel [is] a sign of communion with Christ (1 John 2:24).
7. To love a Christian because he is a Christian (or godly man) is a note of God's child (1 John 3:14).
8. Compassion stirring in the heart [is] a note of love (1 John 3:17).
9. Works of mercy [are] signs of love (1 John 3:18).
10. Sincere love [is] a note of sincere profession (1 John 3:19).

---

74. *Case of Conscience,* 8:603, 605.
75. *Case of Conscience,* 8:607, 609.
76. *Case of Conscience,* 8:605.

11. Boldness in prayer [is] a sign of a pacified conscience (1 John 3:20).

12. The operation of God's Spirit in sanctifying us [is] a sign of communion with God (1 John 3:24).

13. A sincere confession of the gospel [is] a note of communion with Christ (1 John 4:15).

14. To be like God in holiness of life is a sign of His love to us particularly (1 John 4:17).

15. Our love of God [is] a sign that he loves us particularly (1 John 4:19).

16. An endeavor to obey the commandments [is] a sign of love of our brother (1 John 5:2).

17. A sign of our prayers granted us [is] if God does but hear them (1 John 5:15).

Several marginal notes describe the hypocrite:

1. Profession without practice [is] a note of a hypocrite (1 John 1:6).

2. To profess perfect sanctification in this life [is] a note of a hypocrite (1 John 1:8).

3. Faith without obedience [is] a note of a hypocrite (1 John 2:5–6).

4. Profession joined with hatred and malice [is] a note of a hypocrite (1 John 2:9).

5. Looseness of life, or the practice of sin, [is] a note of the child of the devil for the present time (1 John 3:10).[77]

Perkins is keenly aware of the need to set all marks of grace in a Trinitarian framework so that they do not result in a man-centered religion. In commenting on 1 John 4:7, Perkins writes that believers "by a special knowledge…are assured that God, the Father of Christ, is their Father; Christ, their Redeemer; the Holy Spirit their sanctifier."[78] All assurance is Christological. It is based on Christ's merits (commenting on 1 John 2:12), received by faith in Him (on 1 John 5:4), and patterned after Him (on 1 John 3:3).[79] It depends on the anointing of the Holy Spirit. Perkins views the ointment John refers to in 1 John 2:20, 27 as the grace of God's Holy Spirit, which is the fulfillment of the anointings in the Old Testament and the anointing that we receive of Christ.[80] In sum, one may know whether he is a child or God by examining the marks of saving

---

77. *Case of Conscience*, 8:599–613.
78. *Case of Conscience*, 8:609.
79. *Case of Conscience*, 8:602, 611, 605.
80. *Case of Conscience*, 8:603–4.

grace in his life as they flow out of Christ and are ratified by the anointing of the Holy Spirit.

Conclusion

Perkins's doctrine of assurance of faith emphasized the covenant, secondary grounds of assurance, active pursuit of assurance, subjective experience, and degrees of faith more than the Reformers did.[81] Perkins also stressed the role of conscience in relationship to covenantal obedience, particularly in his practical syllogism.[82] In his theology, growth in grace as a sign of assurance was inseparable from a close examination of the conscience.

Perkins did not abandon the Reformers' teaching on faith and assurance, however. Rather, his emphases rose out of pastoral concerns. Though at times Perkins emphasized salvation more than the primacy of God and His grace, he did not shift the ground of assurance from Christ, nor did he abandon *sola gratia*. He differed from Calvin and the Reformers in emphasis, but not in substance.

Perkins was not a voluntarist in matters of salvation. He asserted that the conditions of the covenant must be fulfilled, but he also said that God enables the believer to fulfill them. "He who turns to God must first of all be turned of God, and after we are turned then we repent," he wrote.[83] Perkins maintained that the object of saving faith is Jesus Christ and the primary ground of assurance rests in the Christological promises of a triune God as they are apprehended by faith.[84]

Perkins's dialogue on the first epistle of John and his other writings reveal a doctrine of assurance that resonates with biblical, warm piety along with "high Calvinism" and scholastic methodology. Perkins earned the titles of both "scholastic, high Calvinist" and "father of pietism."[85] His theology affirms divine sovereignty in the predestination decree of the Father, the satisfaction made by Christ for the elect, and the sanctifying work of the Spirit. Yet, Perkins also offers a practical, evangelical emphasis on the individual believer working out his own salvation as a hearer of the Word, follower of Christ, and warrior of the conscience. Divine sovereignty, individual piety, Spirit-worked assurance, and the gospel offer of salvation are always in view.

---

81. *Treatise Tending unto a Declaration*, 8:465–67; *True Manner of Knowing Christ Crucified*, 9:5–22.

82. Markham, "Perkins' Understanding of the Function of Conscience," 26.

83. *Nature and Practice of Repentance*, 9:129.

84. *Exposition of the Creed*, 5:12; *Treatise Tending unto a Declaration*, 8:466–67.

85. Heinrich Heppe, *Geschichte des Pietismus und der Mystik in der reformierten Kirche namentlich in der Niederlande* (Leiden: Brill, 1879), 24–26.

Perkins's emphasis on sound doctrine and the sanctification and assurance of souls influenced Puritanism for many years.[86] As J. I. Packer writes, "Puritanism, with its complex of biblical, devotional, ecclesiastical, reformational, polemical and cultural concerns, came of age, we might say, with Perkins, and began to display characteristically a wholeness of spiritual vision and a maturity of Christian patience that had not been seen in it before."[87]

Perkins's theology did not make him cold and heartless when dealing with sinners and saints in need of a Savior. Rather, his warm, practical theology set the tone for Puritan literature on the experience of salvation, particularly on assurance of faith and a host of other doctrines embraced by believers by faith in union with Christ that would pour forth from the presses in the seventeenth century.

---

86. Richard Muller, "William Perkins and the Protestant Exegetical Tradition: Interpretation, Style, and Method," in *Commentary on Hebrews 11*, 72.

87. Packer, *An Anglican to Remember*, 4.

6

Eschatological Glory
Matthew Hartline

Puritan eschatology is a complex subject.[1] Most scholars in William Perkins's day held to a "modified Augustinian historicist approach" to eschatology,[2] meaning they believed the millennium referred to a *literal* one-thousand-year period between Christ's two advents.[3] Among these scholars two popular views emerged.

First, some dated the start of the millennium from AD 1 (the birth of Christ) or AD 70 (the fall of Jerusalem) and its end in either AD 1000 or AD 1070.[4] During this time, Satan was bound and unable to deceive the nations and, therefore, the gospel spread freely among the nations. At the close of the millennium, however, Satan was loosed from the pit. This corresponded to the rise of pope Sylvester II (AD 999) or pope Hildebrand/Gregory VII (AD 1073). The Roman church increased in influence, the gospel was corrupted, and the true church was persecuted.

---

1. Crawford Gribben notes, "Writers documenting the development of the puritan apocalyptic tradition have repeatedly set puritan ideologies in a vacuum, failing to recognize that eschatology was not something puritans studied so much as something in which they believed themselves to be involved, for the implications of their eschatology were not purely theoretical." Crawford Gribben, *The Puritan Millennium: Literature and Theology, 1550–1682* (Eugene: Wipf & Stock Publishers, 2008), 13–14. For another important work on Puritan eschatology, see Iain Murray, *The Puritan Hope: Revival and the Interpretation of Prophecy* (Carlisle: Banner of Truth, 1975).

2. Peter Toon, ed., *Puritans, the Millennium, and the Future of Israel: Puritan Eschatology 1600–1660* (London: James Clark & Co., 1970), 6. Augustine viewed the millennium as an indeterminate period of time (as opposed to a literal one thousand years) between Christ's two advents.

3. See Robert Hill, *The Contents of Scripture: Containing the Sum of Every Book and Chapter of the Old and New Testament* (London, 1596); George Gifford, *Sermons upon the Whole Book of the Revelation* (London, 1599); and Thomas Brightman, *The Revelation of S. John, Wherein the Sense Is Opened by the Scripture and the Event of Things Fore Told* (Leyden, 1616).

4. Proponents of this view include John Bale, Heinrich Bullinger, William Fulke, George Gifford, Arthur Dent, Thomas Pickering, and Hugh Broughton. Also see the 1599 Geneva Bible.

Second, some dated the beginning of the millennium from AD 300 and its end in AD 1300.[5] They believed Satan was bound at the time of Constantine (AD 306–337) and released with the installment of pope Boniface VIII (AD 1294–1303) in the west and the establishment of the Ottoman Empire (AD 1299) in the east. The "papist" and the "Turk" were the two great threats to the gospel.[6]

William Perkins falls within the second group.[7] Given the prevalence of this eschatological position in his polemics against the Roman church, it is interesting that he never produced a detailed explanation of his position. He simply assumes it. What does figure prominently in his eschatological musings is the believer's eternal state—the hope of glory.

In *A Treatise Tending unto a Declaration Whether a Man Is in the Estate of Damnation or in the Estate of Grace*, William Perkins provides seven persuasive reasons for embracing Christianity. The sixth is the promise of "eternal life." This, says Perkins, "is a thing desired of all men, yet none shall be made partakers of it but the true Christian, and the glorious estate of this life would move any to be a Christian."[8] This is the case because of the great blessings attached to the "glorious estate." (1) Christians will be freed from "all pains, sicknesses, infirmities, hunger, thirst, cold, weariness; from sin, as anger, forgetfulness, ignorance; from hell, death, damnation, Satan, and from everything that causes misery." (2) They will enter the "presence of God's majesty in heaven, there to 'behold his face,' that is, His glory." (3) They will experience "such an excellent communion with God, that He shall be unto them 'all in all.'" (4) They will be filled with "an unspeakable joy and gladness." (5) They will "love God with all their hearts, with all their souls, and strength," and this love will show itself "in that they are eternally occupied in worshiping God by singing of songs of praise and thanksgiving unto Him."[9] The present chapter is dedicated to Perkins's understanding of this "glorious estate."

As recorded in Revelation 2–3, Christ sends seven letters to the seven churches in Asia Minor. According to Perkins, while the letters speak directly to these first-century churches, they are a "prophetic history" and, therefore, they also speak to "the state of the church to the end."[10] Perkins believes the

---

5. Proponents of this view include John Foxe, Laurence Deios, John Napier, John Foord, Robert Hill, Patrick Forbes, and Thomas Brightman.

6. John Napier, *A Plain Discovery of the Whole Revelation of Saint John: Set Down in Two Treatises: The One Searching and Proving the True Interpretation thereof: The Other Applying the Same Paraphrastically and Historically to the Text* (Edinburgh, 1593), 233.

7. *A Digest or Harmony of the Books of the Old and New Testament*, 1:69.

8. *Treatise Tending unto a Declaration*, 8:505.

9. *Treatise Tending unto a Declaration*, 8:505–6.

10. *Exposition of Revelation 1–3*, 4:324.

book of Revelation serves the church between Christ's two advents. While penned during the reign of Domitian (AD 81–96),[11] the book "concerns the present and future state of the church."[12] It makes known "things to come" for "the great good and comfort of [God's] children to the end of the world."[13] Perkins explains all this in *A Godly and Learned Exposition or Commentary upon the First Three Chapters of Revelation*. In this work he divides each of the seven letters into three main sections: *Preface*, *Proposition*, and *Conclusion*. As he expounds the *Conclusion* of each letter, Perkins gives special attention to the *Recipient* and the *Reward*.

The Recipient

In the conclusion to each of the seven letters, Christ extends a promise to those who "overcome."[14] Who are these people? For Perkins, they are those who prevail against all the "spiritual enemies" of salvation: "sin, Satan, hell, and condemnation."[15] They are those who have been born again, possess true faith, and persevere in the faith to the end.[16] In other words, they are those who are one with Christ.

Perkins begins his discussion of this reality by speaking of Christ's divine nature: "In respect of His Godhead, He is coeternal with the Father and with the Holy Spirit, living of Himself that uncreated and eternal life, which is all one with the Godhead, being eternal, without beginning or ending."[17] Yet the eternal Son of God became man, fulfilled all righteousness, died upon the cross, rose again, and then "ascended up to heaven, where in full glory He enjoys immediate fellowship with the Godhead.... His manhood being wholly and immediately sustained by His Godhead."[18] As the God-man, Christ now gives eternal life to every member of His body. Perkins explains that Christ's "manhood has quickening virtue in it, yet not of itself or by itself, but as it is the manhood of the Son of God; for from the Godhead it receives this quickening

---

11. *Exposition of Revelation 1–3*, 4:361–62.

12. *Exposition of Revelation 1–3*, 4:318.

13. *Exposition of Revelation 1–3*, 4:308.

14. See Rev. 2:7, 11, 17, 26; 3:5, 12, 21.

15. *Exposition of Revelation 1–3*, 4:452.

16. *Exposition of Revelation 1–3*, 4:452. Perkins explains these three as follows: "So by regeneration he is freed from the bondage of hell, death, sin, and Satan.... For when a man is in Christ, by faith he is made partaker of Christ's victory upon the cross and by it receives power to subdue his own corruptions, the world, and the devil.... [One] must keep faith—that is, true religion and a good conscience—standing out in life and death against all adversarial Power whatsoever." *Exposition of Revelation 1–3*, 4:452.

17. *Exposition of Revelation 1–3*, 4:405.

18. *Exposition of Revelation 1–3*, 4:405.

power to give eternal life unto the church."[19] He illustrates this reality as follows: "For as the root of a tree lives not for itself but for the body and for all the branches, even so Christ Jesus has eternal life in Him—not for Himself alone, but that He may convey the same to all His members."[20]

Christ is life and He conveys life to His people by "virtue of that mystical union which is between Him and every member of His church."[21] This means that His people inherit eternal life—that is, "glory and bliss in body and soul in heaven forever and ever."[22] When Christ is given to His people, His manhood "is given both for the *substance* and in regard of all the *benefits* that are conveyed to man by it."[23] Perkins explains:

> When God gives Christ to any, He does with all give unto the same party the Spirit of Christ.... This Spirit creates in his heart the instrument of faith by which Christ given of the Father is received and apprehended, both His body and blood and the efficacy and the benefits thereof.... And the same Spirit that works this faith does knit the believer unto Christ, really, though mystically, making him one with Christ, so as Christ is the Head and the believer a member. And thus is this mystical conjunction wrought, from whence proceeds this eternal life.[24]

In sum, by virtue of His divinity, Christ's humanity is exalted and glorified, and by virtue of His union with His people, He becomes to them the wellspring of life. Moreover, all that Christ's humanity receives in glory becomes

---

19. *Exposition of Revelation 1–3*, 4:406.

20. *Exposition of Revelation 1–3*, 4:406. John Calvin, commenting on Romans 6:5, writes, "[The] apostle does not exhort, but rather teach us what benefit we derive from Christ...for between the grafting of trees, and this which is spiritual, a disparity will soon meet us: in the former the graft draws its aliment from the root, but retains its own nature in the fruit; but in the latter not only we derive the vigour and nourishment of life from Christ, but we also pass from our own to his nature." John Calvin, *Commentaries on the Epistle of Paul the Apostle to the Romans* (Grand Rapids: Baker Book House, 2009), 223.

21. *Exposition of Revelation 1–3*, 4:406.

22. *Exposition of Revelation 1–3*, 4:406–7.

23. *Exposition of Revelation 1–3*, 4:406 (italics mine).

24. *Exposition of Revelation 1–3*, 4:406. Concerning eternal life, Perkins distinguishes between "uncreated life" and "created life." Uncreated life is "the very Godhead itself whereby God lives absolutely in Himself, from Himself, and by Himself, giving life and being to all things that live and have being...[and] is not communicable to any creature." Created life is a quality in the creature that is "natural and spiritual." Natural life is the understanding that men in this world "live by meat and drink and all such means by God's providence." Spiritual is "that most happy and blessed estate in which all the elect shall reign with Christ, their Head, in the heavens after this life and after the day of judgment forever and ever.... And it consists in an immediate conjunction and communion or fellowship with God Himself." *Exposition of the Creed*, 5:406–7.

theirs.[25] Perkins's understanding of Christ's nature and exaltation, and of the believer's union with Christ, is foundational to his view of eschatological glory.

The Reward

While "the power of grace does change [the elect's] carnal nature,"[26] Perkins insists that there is a future perfection that awaits God's people. This is the "reward"[27] (or prize) that they will receive in eschatological glory, and it is the chief cause of their hope.[28] Commenting on Hebrews 11:40, Perkins writes, "Indeed, all true believers before Christ were justified and sanctified and in soul received to glory before us; yet perfected in soul and body both they must not be before us, but we must all be perfected together."[29] This perfection will be realized at Christ's second coming. For Perkins, the eschatological rewards promised to the seven churches delineate exactly what this blessing will entail.[30]

Entering Paradise

"To him that overcometh will I give to eat of the tree of life, which is in the midst of the paradise of God" (Rev. 2:7). In this promise to the church at Ephesus, Christ says that they may "eat of the tree of life." For Perkins, the act of eating signifies "immediate fellowship with Christ."[31] At present, Christ conveys "quickening spiritual life to all that believe in Him."[32] In eternity, His people will enjoy an "immediate partaking with Christ in all His blessings. So

---

25. John Calvin writes, "As this secret power to bestow life, of which he has spoken, might be referred to his Divine essence, he now comes down to the second step, and shows that this *life* is placed *in his flesh*, that it may be drawn out of it.... But an objection is brought, that the flesh of Christ cannot give life, because it was liable to death, and because even now it is not immortal in itself; and next, that it does not at all belong to the nature of flesh to quicken souls. I reply, though this power comes from another source than from the flesh, still this is no reason why the designation may not accurately apply to it; for as the eternal Word of God is the fountain of *life* (John 1:4), so his flesh, as a channel, conveys to us that *life* which dwells intrinsically, as we say, in his Divinity. And in this sense it is called life-giving, because it conveys to us that life which it borrows for us from another quarter." *Commentary on the Gospel According to John*, trans. William Pringle (Grand Rapids: Baker Book House, 2009), 262.

26. *Sermon on the Mount*, 1:200.

27. "For as a reward is given to a workman after his work is done, so everlasting life is given unto men after the travels and miseries of this life are ended." *Exposition of the Creed*, 5:411.

28. See Phil. 3:11–14.

29. *Commentary on Hebrews 11*, 3:396.

30. For Perkins's views on the signs before Christ's coming, the signs at Christ's coming, the resurrection, and the final judgment, see *Fruitful Dialogue*, 6:460–62. Also see *Exposition of the Creed*, 5:286–303, 398–406; *Golden Chain*, 6:214–15.

31. *Exposition of Revelation 1–3*, 4:453.

32. *Exposition of Revelation 1–3*, 4:453.

that when Christ is all in all unto us immediately, then we do eat of the tree of life and thereby shall live eternally."[33]

Christ also says in the promise that His people will enter "the paradise of God." According to Perkins, this is the third heaven.

> The Lord does manifest Himself in His glorious majesty, and which He has prepared for the glory of all His elect...which is therefore called paradise, because it is a place of endless joy and pleasure...a great and most excellent place.... There, God communicates Himself to all the elect and becomes all things unto them immediately, so that this must needs be a place of all joy and comfort.... But the joys and glory of this paradise of God are endless and unspeakable.[34]

At the consummation Christ's members will hear these words: "Well done, thou good and faithful servant: thou hast been faithful over a few things, I will make thee ruler over many things: enter thou into the joy of thy lord.... Come, ye blessed of my Father, inherit the kingdom prepared for you from the foundation of the world" (Matt. 25:21, 34).

Escaping the Second Death
"He that overcometh shall not be hurt of the second death" (Rev. 2:11).[35] For Perkins, the second death is "the condemnation of the soul and body forever and ever.... When soul and body are both severed forever from God's comfortable presence."[36] The glory of this reward is that, although the regenerate will experience physical death (the separation of body and soul), they will never experience eternal death (or damnation). They will never be "severed from God to go into that lake that burns with fire and brimstone. Which is a most gracious and happy promise."[37] Instead, they will enjoy the fullness of joy found in the triune God.

---

33. *Exposition of Revelation 1–3*, 4:454.
34. *Exposition of Revelation 1–3*, 4:454.
35. In Revelation 2:10, Christ promises "a crown of life." It is given to those who are martyred for the faith. Perkins says they receive this crown "not for his sufferings, but because he is a member of Christ and by suffering death has shown his faith in Christ, for whose merit alone he is so rewarded. And so must this and all other promises of like sort be understood." *Exposition of Revelation 1–3*, 4:470.
36. *Exposition of Revelation 1–3*, 4:472.
37. *Exposition of Revelation 1–3*, 472.

Eating Hidden Manna

"To him that overcometh will I give to eat of the hidden manna, and will give him a white stone, and in the stone a new name written, which no man knoweth saving he that receiveth it" (Rev. 2:17). These three gifts, says Perkins, signify "the election, vocation, justification, and glorification of God's people."[38]

Specifically, "the hidden manna" is Christ—"the true food of life eternal."[39] "Our life," says Perkins, "comes out of Christ's death."[40] All that has been given to Christ's exalted and glorified humanity, by virtue of His Godhead, become ours by virtue of our union with Him. Elsewhere, Perkins states, "The exaltation of His humanity is the putting off from Him His servile condition and all infirmities and the putting on of such habitual gifts, which, albeit they are created and finite, yet they have so great and so marvelous perfection as possible can befall any creature." He adds, "The gifts of His mind are wisdom, knowledge, joy, and other unspeakable virtues; of His body, immortality, strength, agility, brightness."[41] Christ then bestows these same gifts upon His people in glory. "We shall then be," asserts Perkins, "partakers of the divine, not essence (for then we should be deified), but nature, that is divine virtues and qualities."[42]

Perkins defines "perfect glory" as "that wonderful excellency of the elect whereby they shall be in a far better estate than any heart can wish."[43] The reasons are as follows. (1) They will behold the face of God—His glory and majesty. (2) They will be conformed to Christ—"just, holy, incorruptible, glorious, honorable, excellent, beautiful, strong, mighty, and nimble." (3) They will "inherit the kingdom of heaven; yea, the new heavens and the new earth shall be their inheritance."[44] (4) They will have "dominion and lordship over heaven and earth."[45]

Turning to Philippians 3:21 and 1 Corinthians 15:44, Perkins notes the similarity between the glorified body of Christ and the glorified bodies of the elect. (1) As Christ's body is *incorruptible*, "so shall our bodies be void of all corruption."[46] (2) As Christ's body is *immortal*, "so ours in the kingdom of heaven shall never die." (3) As Christ's body is *spiritual*, "so shall ours be made spiritual." This means that we will have no need for food, drink, sleep,

---

38. *Exposition of Revelation 1–3*, 4:500.
39. *Exposition of Revelation 1–3*, 4:501.
40. *Exposition of Revelation 1–3*, 4:501.
41. *Golden Chain*, 6:61.
42. *True Gain*, 9:76.
43. *Golden Chain*, 6:217.
44. *Golden Chain*, 6:217.
45. *True Gain*, 9:76.
46. *Exposition of the Creed*, 5:410.

medicine, etc., because our body will be preserved "by the immediate power of God's Spirit forever and ever." (4) As Christ's body is now a "shining body," so "the bodies of the elect shall be shining and bright, always remaining the same for substance." (5) As Christ's body has a "property of agility" such as "swiftness to pass from earth to the third heaven," so the bodies of the saints "shall be able as well to ascend upward as to go downward and to move without violence, and that very swiftly."[47]

The second gift, promised to those who overcome, is "a white stone." According to Perkins, it is a "token of absolution."[48] He explains, "First, the judge in giving a sentence used white stones and black stones. The giving of a white stone was a token of absolution; the giving of a black stone, a sign of condemnation. Here then the giving of a white stone may signify absolution from Christ of all a man's sins and trespasses."[49] Because of the finished work of Christ, the overcomers receive a token of the reality that all their sins are forgiven. They live in true and eternal blessedness, knowing that there is no guilt, punishment, or condemnation.

The third gift is "a new name," written on the stone.[50] To explain this, Perkins turns to 1 John 3:1, and declares that it is an honor and privilege "to be called sons of God." "Beloved, now are we the sons of God, and it doth not yet appear what we shall be: but we know that, when he shall appear, we shall be like him; for we shall see him as he is" (1 John. 3:2). God's people will enjoy "the perfect vision," whereby they will behold the fullness of God with the eye of the mind and "be filled therewith…even as a vessel cast into the sea may be perfectly full of water, though it receives not all the water in the sea."[51]

Ruling the Nations

"And he that overcometh, and keepeth my works unto the end, to him will I give power over the nations: And he shall rule them with a rod of iron; as the vessels of a potter shall they be broken to shivers: even as I received of my Father. And I will give him the morning star" (Rev. 2:26–28). Perkins identifies two gifts in this promise.

The first is "power over the nations." As Christ received power and authority to rule over the nations, so too those who are in Christ participate in "the fruit

---

47. *Exposition of the Creed*, 5:410.
48. *Exposition of Revelation 1–3*, 4:504.
49. *Exposition of Revelation 1–3*, 4:503–4.
50. *Exposition of Revelation 1–3*, 4:504. Perkins adds, "We must not think this an idle name or a bare title only; but withal God gives him a new condition whereof this name is a token and title." *Exposition of Revelation 1–3*, 4:504.
51. *Sermon on the Mount*, 207.

and benefit of this power in his salvation."[52] Perkins describes this power in two ways. (1) Christ makes all His servants "partakers of His glory in heaven." They sit with Him and "there approve of the just condemnation of all the wicked." (2) Christ enables all His servants "to overcome all the enemies of their salvation." This means that all who are united to Christ and partake of His exaltation, by virtue of His power, will receive power "in themselves over their sins, over death, hell, the world, and all the enemies of their salvation."[53]

The second gift is "the morning star." This, for Perkins, is the full reception of Christ.[54] It consists of two principle "benefits." (1) Perfect illumination whereby "ignorance shall be whole taken away after this life, when man shall know God fully, so far forth as a creature can know the Creator. (2) Perfect glory whereby "we shall be made to shine as stars. Yea, we shall become saints in light."[55] Those who are in Christ will receive perfect knowledge and perfect holiness, so far forth as any creature may know and reflect the Creator.[56]

Receiving White Raiment

"He that overcometh, the same shall be clothed in white raiment; and I will not blot out his name out of the book of life, but I will confess his name before my Father, and before his angels" (Rev. 3:5). Just as the saints are arrayed with the glory of Christ, they will walk with Christ in white garments. This is the promise of living with Christ in glory. These garments, according to Perkins, "have always been used to signify joy, happiness, life, and glory."[57] Sin is that which separates man from God. The removal of sin, therefore, is the restoration of fellowship with God. This removal is secured by Christ and enjoyed in Christ. Perkins states:

> For when God will save any man, He gives Christ unto that man truly and really, so as he may say, "Christ is mine." And with Christ God gives His Spirit which works in his heart true saving faith, whereby he does receive

---

52. *Exposition of Revelation 1–3*, 4:539.
53. *Exposition of Revelation 1–3*, 4:539.
54. According to Perkins, the "morning star" is Christ for three reasons. (1) Christ illumines people with the "light of understanding and his church with the knowledge of the will of his father." (2) Christ is the fulfillment of Numbers 24:17; He is the "star of Jacob." (3) As the physical morning star rises at the end of night, before the sun dawns, likewise, "Christ came not in the beginning or middle of the dark time under the law, but in the last age of the world." *Exposition of Revelation 1–3*, 4:541.
55. *Exposition of Revelation 1–3*, 4:541.
56. *Exposition of the Creed*, 5:409–10.
57. *Exposition of Revelation 1–3*, 4:558.

Christ. And so Christ and His righteousness belong unto that man really, and by virtue thereof he is worthy [of] life everlasting.[58]

In addition to "white raiment," God's people receive two additional blessings. First, their names are included in the Book of Life.[59] Second, their names are confessed before the Father. Elsewhere, Christ declares, "Whosoever therefore shall confess me before men, him will I confess also before my Father which is in heaven" (Matt. 10:32). Perkins explains that, on that day, Christ will separate His people from the wicked, set them on His right hand, and advance them to glory. There Christ will pronounce before the angelic host and His Father that they are His. "He will confess [them] to be His and receive [them] to His own glory."[60]

Becoming a Pillar

"Him that overcometh will I make a pillar in the temple of my God, and he shall go no more out: and I will write upon him the name of my God, and the name of the city of my God, which is new Jerusalem, which cometh down out of heaven from my God: and I will write upon him my new name" (Rev. 3:12). It is here, says Perkins, that "Christ does most notably express the state and condition of eternal life."[61] When we want to remember a loved one or honor a heroic figure, we erect a monument (or pillar) in his name. In this way we "immortalize" them. Perkins makes the point that Christ does not merely erect a pillar to honor His people; rather, He "makes" them "a pillar durable and everlasting, whose memory shall always continue."[62]

The location of these pillars is extremely significant—God's temple. For Perkins, this is a description of "the church triumphant."[63] In the Old Testament, the temple was the place were God's people gathered to worship Him. It was also the place where God manifested His glory in a special manner. Likewise, in eschatological glory, God's people will dwell with Him in the "most glorious and comfortable manner." This dwelling has no duration, for they

---

58. *Exposition of Revelation 1–3*, 4:558–59. Perkins adds elsewhere, "Now if Christ is ours, then His obedience is not only His but ours also. [It is] His because it is in Him. [It is] ours because with Him it is given us by God." *True Gain*, 9:61.

59. For Perkins, the Book of Life is "nothing else but God's predestination or eternal decree of election whereby He has chosen some unto salvation upon His good pleasure." *Exposition of Revelation 1–3*, 4:559.

60. *Exposition of Revelation 1–3*, 4:561.

61. *Exposition of Revelation 1–3*, 4:590.

62. *Exposition of Revelation 1–3*, 4:590.

63. *Exposition of Revelation 1–3*, 4:590.

"shall go no more out," meaning they "shall remain forever and ever, and no time shall ever come wherein [they] shall cease to be a pillar in the same."[64]

Engraved on these pillars are three names: (1) the name of God; (2) the name of the city of God; and (3) Christ's new name. Regarding the first, Perkins explains that Christ will "manifest that this man is indeed the son of God, and that God is all in all unto him." The second name discloses the location of these pillars—the highest heaven. The third name reveals that they will share in Christ's exaltation—dignity, power, and glory.[65] Perkins concludes:

> And thus we have eternal life set out unto us by the author of life Himself. The sum whereof is this: that he which overcomes shall be made a true member of the triumphant church and there continue forever and shall have three names written on him, the name of God, having this made evident that he is the child of God; the name of God's city, being made partaker of the privileges of God's kingdom of heaven; and the new name of Christ, *communicating* with Christ in His glory and majesty.[66]

Sitting upon Christ's Throne

"To him that overcometh will I grant to sit with me in my throne, even as I also overcame, and am set down with my Father in his throne" (Rev. 3:21). Contained in this final eschatological promise is the reaffirmation of Christ's "gracious promise of fellowship" to all who are one with Him.[67] "For the saints of God," writes Perkins, "shall have an actual fruition of God Himself and be as it were swallowed up with a sea of His love and wholly ravished therewith."[68] When Christ promises, I will "grant to sit with me in my throne" (Rev. 3:21), He is guaranteeing them "fellowship with [Him] in glory."[69] They will participate

---

64. *Exposition of Revelation 1–3*, 4:590.

65. *Exposition of Revelation 1–3*, 4:591–92.

66. *Exposition of Revelation 1–3*, 4:592 (italics mine). "By this," says Perkins, "it is plain that no man can have fellowship with God but by Christ. We must not look to have immediate fellowship with God of ourselves or by any other, but by Christ. God hears not, God helps not, God saves not, but by Christ. Nay, God is no God unto us out of Christ. For first He is a God unto Christ, and then in Him and by Him unto us." Perkins goes on to expound that Christ will make the believer a partaker of that glory and dignity wherewith Christ himself is glorified since His death and resurrection. "Mark this," proclaims Perkins, "all that after this life must have Christ's new name must in this life become new creatures.... Would we then partake with Christ in His glory? We must here be partakers of His grace." *Exposition of Revelation 1–3*, 4:593–95.

67. *Exposition of Revelation 1–3*, 4:622.

68. *Exposition of the Creed*, 5:409.

69. *Exposition of Revelation 1–3*, 4:626.

in Christ's glory, "so much as shall suffice for [their] happiness." Christ will "advance" them into "the participation of His glory."[70]

Conclusion

"And every man that hath this hope in him purifieth himself, even as he is pure" (1 John 3:3). Perkins's view of the final state is to be applied in the present. His application falls into two broad categories: (1) polemical, and (2) personal. Naturally, as a Protestant, much of his application deals with the errors of Rome and includes warnings against its teaching and doctrine. As a pastor/teacher, he wanted to see his fellow believers walking in holiness in accordance with the gospel to which they have been called (Eph. 4:1). Therefore, he emphasizes the relationship between future and present realities. Biblical promises are to be made real in the life of believers in this life. They ought to create in them a sense of urgency to love Christ with all their heart, soul, strength, and mind and to obey all that He has commanded.

---

70. *Exposition of Revelation 1–3*, 4:626.

7

A Peculiar Company of Men:
The Nature of the Church

David M. Barbee

In his examination of William Perkins's views on grace and free will, Richard Muller astutely observes that they are best understood when contextualized within the environment of the intra-ecclesial debates within the Church of England, as well as within the larger structure of Protestant anti-Roman Catholic polemics.[1] This is equally true when Perkins attempts to delineate his doctrine of the church.[2] In doing so, he finds himself navigating a tortuous minefield. On one front, he critiques Roman Catholicism as a false church while also defending other versions of continental Protestantism, despite doctrinal disagreements. On another front, he champions the Church of England against both Roman Catholics who dismiss it as schismatic and from Protestant separatists who view it as too papist. These concerns place some boundaries on Perkins's ecclesiological reflections and provide some direction for his constructive account of the church. He deftly steers a course between these opposing forces through careful analysis of the nature of the church, peeling back layers that obscure the hidden nature of the church buried under external appearances. Along the way, he displays the irrelevance of some of the inconsequential differences among Protestant traditions while pointing toward the core of the church's nature in preaching of the Word and correct use of the sacraments. It is not defined by structures or standard traits like apostolic succession, but by concern for holiness and the presence of apostolic doctrine. In seeing the church as ultimately invisible, but manifested in visible churches, the catholic church for Perkins finally consists of those who are elected by God into union with Christ, drawn by preaching into a visible church, and presently moving toward glorification through the process of sanctification.

---

1. Richard A. Muller, *Grace and Freedom: William Perkins and the Early Modern Reformed Understanding of Free Choice and Divine Grace* (Oxford: Oxford University Press, 2020), 1.

2. See Donald John MacLean, *"Ours Is a True Church of God": William Perkins and the Reformed Doctrine of the Church*. St. Antholin Lecture, 2018 (London: The Latimer Trust, 2019).

The True Church

One of the most vexing ecclesiological problems bequeathed to post-Reformation Protestants was the need to refute the validity of Roman Catholicism while also finding unity among fractious but valid Protestant national churches. "One of the most frequent charges of Romanists against the Protestants," Anthony Milton explains, "was that, lacking any central authority, they differed among themselves on many fundamental issues, as the divisions between Calvinists and Lutherans demonstrated. This lack of unity, Romanists claimed, meant that the Protestants could not constitute the true church, which was indivisible."[3] Milton adds that the traditional English Protestant response was to accentuate shared points of unity while downplaying areas of disagreement over minor matters. In Perkins's justification of the legitimacy of continental Protestant churches, one can already begin to get a sense for the boundaries between a true church and a false church, as well as simply a sufficient church whose doctrine he deemed inadequate, but not so much as to delegitimize a church.

Regarding the Lutherans, Perkins comments that they are considered to be a true church, though not ideal, because they share a common foe and have a broad agreement regarding "the Father, the Son, and the Holy Ghost; and of the office of the Mediator, of faith and good works, of the Word, the church, and the magistrate," even though they disagree over the nature of receiving Christ's body and blood in the elements of the Lord's Supper.[4] The differences between the traditions leads to some curious theological hair-splitting. He condemns Lutheran belief in consubstantiation as reviving the ancient church heresies of Eutyches and Nestorius, who are typically interpreted as denying the full humanity and divinity of Christ, thereby overturning most articles of faith. He concedes that this was largely a private opinion held by Johannes Brenz and his followers, but not the whole church.[5] The Lutheran view is also radically different than the Catholic view, in Perkins's estimation, because Catholic transubstantiation is flatly against an article of faith, namely that Jesus had human flesh, and it destroys sacramental semiotics, whereas the Lutheran view only violates a philosophical principle that a body cannot be ubiquitous.[6] Lutherans were orthodox enough for Perkins to stand as a true church. Interestingly, he did not extend the same courtesy to any of the other Reformation era sects outside of the magisterial reformation, like the Anabaptists, whom he dismisses

---

3. Anthony Milton, *Catholic and Reformed: The Roman and Protestant Churches in English Protestant Thought, 1600–1640* (Cambridge: Cambridge University Press, 1995), 231–32.

4. *Exposition of the Creed*, 5:382.

5. *Exposition of the Creed*, 5:383.

6. *Exposition of the Creed*, 5:383.

as "conspiracies of monstrous heretics" and lumps together with other ancient heresies that were "by the malice of Satan renewed and revived in this age."[7]

Within England, radical Protestants questioned the legitimacy of the Church of England for decades prior to the beginning of Perkins's literary career on the grounds that it retained too much of Roman Catholicism. The pamphlet war triggered by the publication of the 1571 *Admonition to Parliament*, in which these concerns are aired, is often hailed as a seminal moment in the formation of Puritanism.[8] Defining Puritanism has proven to be a bit of an historiographical quandary and it should come as little surprise that there is a bit of variance in interpreting Perkins in relationship to Puritanism. Briefly investigating this matter will serve to illuminate his doctrine of the church in relation to his posture toward the Church of England. The overwhelming majority of scholars have consistently identified Perkins as a Puritan, even if they disagree on what exactly a Puritan is. John Coffey and Paul Lim define Puritanism as "a distinctive and particularly intense variety of early modern Reformed Protestantism which originated within the unique context of the Church of England but spilled out beyond it, branching off into divergent dissenting streams, and overflowing into other lands and foreign churches." This intensity culminates in attempts to reform the Church of England all the while remaining within it; although their rigorous spiritual praxis distinguishes Puritans from the broader category of Reformed Protestantism within the Church of England. Finally, Puritanism was "a uniquely fissiparous variety of Reformed Protestantism" that in turn spawned separatists, who may or may not be considered to be part of Puritanism.[9] Peter Lake draws attention to some of the ambiguity in situating Perkins within the Puritan tradition,

> What was distinctive about Perkins was the intensity with which his insistence on a direct and personal sense of assurance suffused his account of every other aspect of social life. If Perkins's status as a puritan is to be validated it must be done in terms of that distinctive zeal. He was not an overt nonconformist or Presbyterian and his works studiously omit the sort of consideration of the visible Church which would have involved

---

7. *Exposition of the Creed*, 5:382.

8. The classic study is Donald Joseph McGinn, *The Admonition Controversy* (New Brunswick: Rutgers University Press, 1949). But see also the more recent retelling in Peter Lake, *Anglicans and Puritans? Presbyterianism and English Conformist Thought from Whitgift to Hooker* (London: Unwin Hyman, 1988), 13–70. The separatist account is narrated in Stephen Brachlow, *The Communion of Saints: Radical Puritan and Separatist Ecclesiology, 1570–1625* (Oxford: Oxford University Press, 1988).

9. John Coffey and Paul C. H. Lim, introduction to *The Cambridge Companion to Puritanism*, ed. John Coffey and Paul C. H. Lim (Cambridge: Cambridge University Press, 2008), 1–5.

his pronouncing directly on such issues. On one set of criteria (perhaps on two, those of outward conformity and predominance) Perkins was an "Anglican." On others, broadly those employed by Dr Greaves in his first chapter, he was a puritan.[10]

This assessment is important because, first, it speaks to a regnant understanding of Puritanism as the "hotter sort" relative to other English non-Puritan Protestants and, secondly, it begins to give a sense of Perkins's ecclesiology insofar as it grants the Church of England validity in contrast to separatists who shared a common sense of piety but rejected the Church.

As the passage from Lake suggests, there is a smaller dissenting historiographical tradition that understands Perkins as an avowed member of the Church of England, in fact, an Anglican. This is based largely on his defense of the Church of England and his repudiation of English separatists. In his commentary on Zephaniah 2, Perkins maintains that, "For us in England the case stands thus: our church doubtless is God's corn field, and we are the corn heap of God, and those Brownists and sectaries are blind and besotted, who cannot see that the Church of England is a godly heap of God's corn."[11] He identifies the teaching of the Church as orthodox, writing "For we hold, believe, and maintain and preach the true faith—that is, the ancient doctrine of salvation by Christ, taught and published by the prophets and apostles—as the book of the articles of faith agreed upon in open Parliament does fully show."[12] Perkins simply does not suffer separatists who disavow the Church. A defense of the Church is implicit as well in Perkins's attacks on Roman Catholicism. The letter to the reader at the beginning of *A Reformed Catholic* is instructive in that it clearly juxtaposes what Perkins considered to be a deficient church in Roman Catholicism over and against a genuinely orthodox religion within the Church.[13] W. B. Patterson is the primary advocate for interpreting Perkins as an Anglican. Patterson largely describes Puritanism as a movement that sought reform of the Church and since Perkins did not do so, he was not a Puritan by definition.[14] Rather, Patterson views Perkins as "a mainstream English Protestant, notable for his systematic theology, his stress on 'practical divinity,' his

---

10. Peter Lake, "Puritan Identities," *Journal of Ecclesiastical History* 35 (1984): 118–19. The reference to Dr. Greaves is to Richard Greaves, *Society and Religion in Elizabethan England* (Minneapolis: University of Minnesota Press, 1981).

11. *Exhortation to Repentance*, 9:118.

12. *Exposition of the Creed*, 5:383.

13. *Reformed Catholic*, 7:5.

14. W. B. Patterson, *William Perkins and the Making of a Protestant England* (Oxford: Oxford University Press, 2014), 46. See also R. A. Sisson, "William Perkins, Apologist for the Elizabethan Church of England," *Modern Language Review* 47 (1952): 495–502.

rationale for the importance of preaching, and his social and moral concerns."[15] This is combined with Perkins's seeming dismissal of the pharisaic tendencies within those labelled as Puritans to remove him from their ranks.[16]

An appeal to Perkins's apologetic strategies does not really speak much to the question of his status as a Puritan, however. An attack on the Roman church was rather typical of English Protestants in his day and, in fact, served as a kind of rallying cry that only the boldest would not sound. Those who neglected to do so, like Richard Hooker, were regarded with a fair amount of disdain and mistrust.[17] Perkins's affirmation of the Church of England likely has much more to do with a broadly Reformed consensus within the Church during his literary career.[18] This outlook also weds Puritanism with separatism generally along the lines of church polity that are not historically tenable. It too readily connects Puritanism with forms of church government other than episcopalianism, namely congregationalism or Presbyterianism, a topic Perkins studiously avoided.[19] Finally, such a perspective also overlooks the manner in which the kind of moral reform he preached was perhaps strategic, as a necessary first step toward deeper reform.[20] The irony here seems to be that the very qualities that Patterson identifies as fortifying the Church are the very same attributes that other historians see as hallmarks of Puritanism. To understand Perkins as anything other than a Puritan is fraught with more problems than there are in trying to define Puritanism.

---

15. Patterson, *William Perkins*, 218.

16. *Sermon on the Mount*, 1:205.

17. See a pair of essays by Peter Lake, "The Significance of the Elizabethan Identification of the Pope as Antichrist" *Journal of Ecclesiastical History* 31 (1980): 161–78; and "Anti-Popery: the Structure of a Prejudice," in *Conflict in Early Stuart England*, ed. Richard Cust and Ann Hughes (London: Longman, 1989), 72–106.

18. The Church of England is generally understood now to be Reformed in orientation during Perkins's lifetime, but it is his teaching on predestination that will cause debate in the 1590s, leading to the beginning of the dissolution of the consensus. See Dewey D. Wallace Jr., *Puritans and Predestination: Grace in English Protestant Theology, 1525–1695* (Chapel Hill: University of North Carolina Press, 1982), 29–78; and Mark Shaw, "William Perkins and the New Pelagians: Another Look at the Cambridge Predestination Controversy of the 1590s," *Westminster Theological Journal* 58 (1996): 67–301.

19. See Peter Lake, "Matthew Hutton—A Puritan Bishop?," *History* 64 (1979): 182–204. There is a rather curious statement in Peter Heylyn, *Aerius Redivivus: or, the History of the Presbyterians* (Oxford: John Crosley, 1670), 342, that Perkins was a "professed Presbyterian." This is an unfounded claim.

20. See Raymond A. Blacketer, "The Rhetoric of Reform: William Perkins on Preaching and the Purification of the Church," in *Scholasticism Reformed: Essays in Honour of Willem J. van Asselt*, ed. Maarten Wisse, Marcel Sarot, and Willemien Otten (Leiden: Brill, 2010), 215–36.

Errors in Doctrines or Manners

The foregoing has begun to sketch out Perkins's doctrine of the church by contextualizing his ideas to show how polemical debates frame the boundaries between a true church and a false church. He offers something of a justification for his divergent assessment of churches. It is really a rather simple matter of making clear distinctions in kinds and degrees of errors. "The defects and corruptions of churches must be distinguished; and they be either in doctrine or manners," Perkins rationalizes. "Again, corruptions in doctrine must further be distinguished: some of them are errors indeed, but besides the foundation; and some errors directly against the foundation—and these overturn all religion, whereas the former do not."[21] As noted above, he can confess disagreement with the Lutherans and admit to internal debate within the Church of England, but in both instances the perceived errors are not significant enough to outweigh common theological ground.

This presents a rather slippery slope. If there are gradations of defects and corruptions within true churches, one might reasonably ask at what point does a church cross the threshold and lapse into being a false church? Perkins offers explicit advice in discerning the difference between the two. In his commentary on Galatians, he astutely observes that Paul still referred to the recipients of his epistles as "churches of Galatia," even though they had deviated from apostolic teaching significantly enough to warrant a scathing rebuke from the apostle. Paul's disposition is exemplary for Perkins and he elaborates upon his view on ecclesial error by identifying three rules to help discern whether a church is still a church. First, he again points toward a difference between an error in doctrine or in manners. He advises separation from immoral members of the church and that one ought to find a more moral church if possible. If the error is in doctrine, one must figure out whether the error is a majority position or a small faction. If the latter, then the church is still valid. Secondly, as noted above, if the error is foundational, then this invalidates the church. Finally, one must determine the cause of the doctrinal error. Perkins presents two options. Either it is due to human frailty or to obstinacy. "If it err of frailty, though the error be in the foundation," he avers, "yet it is still a church, as appears by the example of the Galatians. Yet if a church shall err in the foundation openly and obstinately, it separates from Christ, and ceases to be a church, and we may separate from it and may give judgment that it is no church."[22]

---

21. *Exposition of the Creed*, 5:383.

22. *Commentary on Galatians*, 2:19. This advice should be compared with his other comments on this topic in *Exposition of the Creed*, 5:378–80.

This description presents a quandary. Paul charges the Galatian church with a foundational error so severe that they are teaching another gospel, as Perkins acknowledges, and according to his own rubric, this should disestablish the church. This has obvious ramifications for his assessment of Roman Catholicism. The issue appears to be mostly procedural. Perkins seems to imagine Paul prosecuting the Galatians for their errors, exposing their mistakes in the same way that a prosecutor would lay out evidence against a defendant. Since they have not yet been found guilty, they are still entitled to be called a church, something the Roman church could not claim after decades of Protestant critique.[23] Perkins aptly summarizes his stance in his commentary on the Sermon on the Mount noting that, "This point must be remembered, as serving to rectify our judgments touching the state of a church or people that have many grievous wants and faults among them, both for doctrine and manners. For though a people do what in them lies to cut off themselves from God, yet till God cut them off from Him, they cease not to be His people; and therefore we must not judge them to be no people of God, till we see that God has cut them off."[24] This foreshadows election as a constitutive part of his definition of the church.

The Elect of God

The lines of the true church in Perkins's thought have been sketched out in very broad terms so far. He helpfully fills in this rough sketch with greater detail at various points in his writings by offering clearer delineations of the nature of the church. One of his most thorough examinations of the doctrine of the church can be found in his commentary on the phrase "I believe in the church" in the Apostles' Creed. The polemical context of the late sixteenth century shapes his introduction to the topic. He begins with a familiar maxim from Augustine, "He cannot have God for his Father which has not the church for his mother."[25] This is a reappropriation of a Catholic criticism of Protestantism that also serves to dismiss the separatists as dispossessed children and acts as a prolegomenon for a discussion of a point of debate with Roman Catholicism. The question is whether the Creed should say "I believe in the holy catholic church" or "I believe the holy catholic church." What appears to be a largely semantic matter is quite significant in the era. The former supplants Christ as a proper object of faith. This then permits for a doctrine of implicit faith which

---

23. *Commentary on Galatians*, 2:20.

24. *Sermon on the Mount*, 1:342.

25. *Exposition of the Creed*, 5:323. The footnote in the text cites Augustine, but the epigram originates with Cyprian of Carthage.

permits one to simply affirm the belief of the church, even if the teachings are not understood. Perkins explains that "where the speech is not of the Godhead but of creatures and mysteries, the preposition (in) is not added that it should be, 'in the holy church,' but that we should believe there is a holy church, not as God, but as a company gathered to God."[26] This comes as across as a usurpation of Christ's role again when he ponders the nature of what it means to believe "in" something. It is belief "in" Christ that allows one "to pass into Him and to be incorporated into His members."[27] While Perkins acknowledges that there is testimony from the early church and examples from Scripture to corroborate the use of "in the holy catholic church," the doctrinal ramifications for that phrasing outweighs that interpretation and it cannot mean anything more than belief that the church exists.

Having cleared the ground, Perkins now turns to consider the doctrine of the church proper. He defines the church rather succinctly as "a peculiar company of men predestinated to life everlasting and made one in Christ."[28] What ensues is an exegesis of his own definition, highlighting three primary points. "A peculiar company" is inspired by his reading of 1 Peter 2:9, "Ye are a chosen generation, a royal priesthood, an holy nation, and a peculiar people." This is extended to include not simply the church here on earth, but also the church in heaven as well. The next important phrase is "predestinated to life everlasting." This speaks to the question of the church's origins. "The first and principal cause of the church," Perkins avers, "is the good pleasure of God, whereby he has before all worlds purposed to advance His elect to eternal salvation."[29] This allows him to advance a streamlined definition of the church as simply the elect. The final point is "made one with Christ." This is the crux at which the predestining act of God is manifested. Perkins testifies, "This union makes the church to be the church; and by it the members thereof, whether they be in heaven or in earth, are distinguished from all other companies whatsoever."[30] In support of this, he cites Ephesians 3:15, Galatians 4:26, and Hebrews 12:22–23. This sets the stage for a lengthy treatment of predestination, as the efficient cause of the church, and mystical union, as the form of the church, neither of which are germane at this point. Perkins will ultimately summarize this clause of the Creed by stating that "'to believe the church' is nothing else but to believe

---

26. *Exposition of the Creed*, 5:323.

27. *Exposition of the Creed*, 5:323. Perkins tackles the matter of implicit faith again in *Reformed Catholic*, 7:121–25.

28. *Exposition of the Creed*, 5:324. Perkins defines the church in different places in his writings. See also *Exposition of Jude*, 4:71.

29. *Exposition of the Creed*, 5:324.

30. *Exposition of the Creed*, 5:324.

that there is a company of the predestinated made one in Christ, and that withal we are in the number of them."[31]

Three Rules

Once he returns to consider the church after his treatments of predestination and mystical union, Perkins adumbrates three rules regarding the church. The first is a delineation of ecclesial authority in which he affirms that Christ alone is head of the church, insofar as the church is Christ's body. This is an obvious repudiation of the Roman Catholic teaching of Petrine primacy, as Perkins will state in this section, but it is a point that resonated with separatists as well.[32] Headship consists of two duties. First, Christ governs the church "whereby He can and does prescribe laws properly binding the conscience of all His members." This is facilitated by the second duty, which "is by grace to quicken and to put spiritual life into them so as they shall be able to say that they live not, but Christ in them."[33] The second rule is that there is no salvation outside the church, "therefore everyone which is to be saved must become a member and a citizen of the catholic and apostolic church."[34] He uses the traditional imagery of the church as an ark to illustrate that one must be a member of a particular church which is a part of the catholic church. It is evident that Perkins structured his ecclesiology to allow for variances in particular churches while remaining catholic as noted earlier. This is further corroborated by his final rule, that the church is only one.[35]

These three rules touch on some important matters of dispute in the sixteenth century, namely, how one can discern the one church ruled by Christ outside of which there is no salvation. Some of this had been addressed in Perkins's defense of the Church of England and other Protestant assemblies, but he addresses it much more directly and positively. One of the most contested questions was the novelty of Protestantism. Roman Catholicism claimed a line of succession going all the way back to the New Testament era. Protestants seemed to break that chronological unity. Perkins flatly rejected antiquity as a

---

31. *Exposition of the Creed*, 5:371.

32. See also Perkins's dismantling of the doctrine of Petrine supremacy in *Reformed Catholic*, 7:129–33. Article 37 of the 1571 Thirty-Nine Articles states that the queen "hath the chief power in this realm of England...unto whom the chief government of all estates of this realm, whether they be ecclesiastical or civil." The article continues on to clarify that this does not mean that the queen has ministerial authority, but "only that prerogative which we see to have been given to all godly princes in Holy Scriptures by God himself." See Gerald Bray, ed., *Documents of the English Reformation* (Cambridge: James Clarke, 2004), 307–8.

33. *Exposition of the Creed*, 5:372.

34. *Exposition of the Creed*, 5:372.

35. *Exposition of the Creed*, 5:372–73.

valid metric for a true church. In his commentary on Galatians, he states that antiquity and apostolic succession "are no marks of the church unless they be joined with prophetical and apostolical doctrine. The kingdom of darkness has also antiquity, succession, universality, and unity."[36] He attempts to reclaim the high ground based, in part, upon how one should understand the nature of the church. In *Reformed Catholic*, he answers this charge of novelty once again by arguing that the hidden church of God was preserved within Roman Catholicism, thereby providing continuity with Protestantism that stretches all the way back to the apostles, although it was only revealed following Luther.[37]

Perkins ends up modifying what it means to be "catholic" to refute papist claims. He relies upon two traditional authorities, Vincent of Lérins and Augustine, to uproot Roman Catholic developments by showing that only those things which Vincent, Augustine, and other early church authors considered to be ancient could be received as universal. The so-called Vincentian Canon is critical here and Perkins quotes it here to define "catholic" as that "which has been held in all *places*, at all *times*, and of all *professors*, for that is truly and properly called catholic, as the very force and derivation of the word itself declares, comprehending all things truly universal."[38] This allows Perkins to root true catholicity in the apostolic age, as he says one or two centuries prior to Augustine and Vincent. In turn, this definition of catholicity permits a kind of minimalist list of the marks of the church. Perkins identifies only three, "The preaching of the word of God out of the writings of the prophets and apostles with obedience (John 10:27; Eph. 2:20). True invocation of God the Father in the only name of Christ by the assistance of the Spirit (Acts 9:14; 1 Cor. 1:2). The right use of the sacraments, baptism and the Lord's Supper (Matt. 28:19)."[39] When he turns to treat the matter of what he calls "forged Catholicism," he will appropriate the patristic legacy to deconstruct Roman Catholic beliefs and practices where it has exceeded the simplicity of the apostolic teaching through adding on to the catholic tradition in a way that undermines these core marks of the church.[40]

---

36. *Commentary on Galatians*, 2:308.
37. *Reformed Catholic*, 7:150.
38. *Problem of the Forged Catholicism*, 7:171.
39. *Commentary on Galatians*, 2:309.
40. On Perkins as a reader of the church fathers, see Ann-Stephane Schäfer, *Auctoritas Patrum? The Reception of the Church Fathers in Puritanism* (Berlin: Peter Lang, 2012), 31–63; and David M. Barbee, "A Refomed Catholike: William Perkins's Use of the Church Fathers" (PhD diss., University of Pennsylvania, 2013).

The Invisible Church

Part of the issue at hand is confusion regarding the relationship between the hidden church and the invisible church. Perkins sets out to distinguish between the two. He riffs on the traditional description of the church as Jerusalem in a way that will begin to separate and identify the two aspects of the church by listing six different ways this is an appropriate typology,

1. God chose Jerusalem to occupy in the same way that God chose the elect in the church.

2. Jerusalem is a community joined together by love and order as the church ought to be.

3. God's presence was in the sanctuary in Jerusalem and now the church is where one ought to seek God's presence.

4. Jerusalem was the throne of David and the catholic church is the throne of Christ, figured by the kingdom of David.

5. The citizens of Jerusalem and the church both yield obedience to their king.

6. The citizens of Jerusalem were listed in a census, as the elect are listed in Book of Life.[41]

One can see once again Perkins's definition of the church as the elect, organized and unified together communally under the headship of Christ, with incumbent ethical obligations, and oriented toward eternal salvation.

More simply, Perkins separates the church triumphant in heaven and the church militant on earth. The church triumphant "is a company of the spirits of just men, triumphing over the flesh, the devil, and the world, praising God."[42] It is those godly individuals who have passed away and whose souls have ascended to heaven after having conquered spiritual enemies, namely, the flesh, the devil, and the world, and who now praise God in the heavenly realm. It is fitting to refer to the church triumphant as Jerusalem because in both places, God's people worshiped him and he was present in a unique way.[43] On one hand, this appears to be a rather neat and tidy definition that clearly delineates between the two aspects of the church. On the other, Perkins makes connections between the militant church and the triumphant church by placing the militant church in heaven too. He explains that there are two ways in which the earthly church can be said to be in heaven. First, the divine act of

---

41. *Commentary on Galatians*, 2:305.
42. *Exposition of the Creed*, 5:373.
43. *Exposition of Revelation 1–3*, 4:590.

election originates with a gracious God and through Christ the Mediator who now serves as the root of the holiness and life of the elect. Second, the church can now be said to in heaven through union with Christ via faith.[44]

The church militant is a different matter. Perkins is more successful in disentangling the two aspects of the church once he more clearly defines the nature of the militant church. He denotes this simply enough as "the company of the elect or faithful living under the cross, desiring to be removed and to be with Christ." This limits the church to only those members of the elect who live upon earth, excluding those who are in heaven.[45] Perkins identifies two primary marks that help one to recognize the church militant. The first is that the members of the church militant suffer but benefit spiritually through suffering. In part, this is due to the fact that the church "consists of such as are subject to the contempt and reproach of the world."[46] This partly explains why Perkins thinks Paul can refer to the church as desolate in Galatians 4:21.[47] Perkins acknowledges that some are granted peace and welfare as a reward for faith and obedience, but, by and large, "the ordinary state and condition of God's church and people in this world" is "to be in affliction and under the cross," so that the members might waken from spiritual slumber by reforming their character.[48] The church is frequently disturbed by false doctrine, wicked examples of leaders, and the cruelty of tyrants or persecutors.[49] This provides the context for the second mark—that the members of the church have "a desire to depart hence and to be with Christ."[50] That the true church can be obscured by false doctrine as well as persecution is an explicit refutation of the Roman Catholic claim that a mark of the true church is visibility.[51]

The second estate of the church, as Perkins labels it, "is when it flourishes and is visible, not that the faith and secret election of men can be seen (for no man can discern these things but by outward signs), but because it is apparent in respect of the outward assemblies gathered to the preaching of the word and the administration of the sacraments for the praise and glory of God and their mutual edification."[52] Particular churches who manifest such outward signs ought not be imagined to be entirely separated from other true churches,

---

44. *Commentary on Galatians*, 2:305.
45. *Exposition of the Creed*, 5:373.
46. *Sermon on the Mount*, 1:312.
47. *Commentary on Galatians*, 2:310.
48. *Commentary on Hebrews 11*, 3:369, 282.
49. *Commentary on Galatians*, 2:339.
50. *Exposition of the Creed*, 5:374.
51. *Sermon on the Mount*, 1:231.
52. *Exposition of the Creed*, 5:377.

even if the doctrine is different. Perkins explains with an analogy. The church is divided up into several branches and every congregation that professes the gospel is a particular church, but all are members of the one catholic church. "As the sea is only one," he comments, "yet it consists of many parts, which taking their names of the countries whereto they adjoin are called so many particular seas, as the English Sea, the Spanish Sea, French, Italian, Scottish Seas, etc."[53] It is this underlying unity that prevents Perkins from getting too agitated when a particular church expresses liberty in declaring a time of fasting or rejoicing or any traditions "concerning things and actions of comeliness and government only, not pertinent any way to divine worship, or the articles of faith."[54] Functionally, this returns to the definition of a true church outlined above as a means to discern through external signs whether a church is authentic or not.

Perkins admits that "in the darkness of popery, the ministry of the gospel was hid from the world, and yet it gave some light to the hidden church, the house of God, to show them their calling, and the means of salvation."[55] This leads him to the conclusion that particular churches are mixed congregation of elect and reprobate and, following from that, the true catholic church is ultimately invisible. On the first point, he describes various kinds of people who compose the body of a particular church as a means to explain how churches fall into apostasy:

> In the visible church on earth, there are four kinds of believers. The first are they which hear the word without zeal, and they are like the stony ground. The second are they which hear, know, and approve the word. The third are they which hear, know, and approve the word, and have a taste of the power thereof, and accordingly yield some outward obedience. The fourth are they which hear, know, approve, and keep the word, in that they believe it, and are turned into the obedience of it. The three first may fall quite away; the fourth cannot. And by this means it comes to pass that visible churches upon earth may fall away, because of them that profess the faith, three to one may utterly fall away.[56]

Perkins also deploys the familiar language of wheat and chaff while describing the church as a threshing floor in which both lie until sorted, while also declaring that though the ungodly are in the church, "they are not more parts of it indeed than the superfluous humors in the veins are parts of the body."[57] This

---

53. *Exposition of Revelation 1–3*, 4:324.
54. *Golden Chain*, 6:98–99; *Problem of the Forged Catholicism*, 7:233.
55. *Sermon on the Mount*, 1:232.
56. *Commentary on Galatians*, 2:279.
57. *Exposition of the Creed*, 5:377.

is a universal truth, Perkins deduces, and he points toward the presence of Cain in Adam's family, Ham in Noah's, and Judas amongst Jesus's disciples before concluding that "we may not so much as dream of a perfection of the church of God upon earth, so long as wicked men be mixed with true believers."[58]

The all but inescapable conclusion is that the church is ultimately invisible.[59] In his commentary on Galatians, Perkins explains, "For the company of them that dwell in heaven by their faith cannot be discerned by the eye. John saw the heavenly Jerusalem descending from heaven, yet not with bodily eye but 'in spirit' (Rev. 21:10). The things which make the catholic church to be the church, namely, election, vocation, justification, glorification, are invisible."[60] A few pages later, he makes a similar point, but reframes it in privative terms when he deduces that "the catholic church is not a visible estate or company of men under one visible head because in respect of her outward estate she may be for a time in desolation."[61]

Perkins's belief in the invisibility of the church is a function of two issues. First, the simple reality that a particular church can fall into apostasy, as he claims the Roman Catholic Church did, necessitates the occlusion of the elect. Second, the way he conceived of salvation working and the nature of the church causes distrust of outward circumstances. In his elaboration of the notes of the church in his commentary on Jude, he states that "this catholic church is invisible and cannot by the eye of flesh be discerned, for what eye (except of faith) can see or discern the depth of God's election or whom He has effectually called? Yea, and who can infallibly determine the things that are within a man? And therefore this is a matter of faith, not of sense, an article of our belief, not the object of our sight, seeing faith is an evidence of things not seen."[62] Later in the commentary, he will describe right use of the word and sacraments as an indicator of the presence of the invisible church within the visible.[63] It is this ambiguity and pastoral concern over those who agonized over whether they

---

58. *Commentary on Galatians*, 2:83. Perkins uses the example of Cain compared to Abel again in *Commentary on Hebrews 11*, 3:34–35. He makes a similar point using Isaac and Ishmael, showing that everyone who is in the church is not of the church, followed by standard allegorical interpretations of the parables of the net, of the sower, and of the tares in Matthew 13. Here, Isaac and Ishmael are characterized as types of those whom God elects and condemns through his decrees. See *Commentary on Hebrews 11*, 3:235–37.

59. *Exposition of the Creed*, 5:324, 365, 377.

60. *Commentary on Galatians*, 2:306.

61. *Commentary on Galatians*, 2:311.

62. *Exposition of Jude*, 4:25.

63. *Exposition of Jude*, 4:71.

were part of the invisible church or not that will give rise to what R. T. Kendall has called "experimental predestinarianism."[64]

Conclusion

Speaking generally of the influence of Ramist philosophy on the whole of Perkins's *Exposition of the Symbol or Creed of the Apostles*, Donald McKim comments that "Perkins' concern to see the Church of England 'purified' and its members brought to a more zealous commitment to God in both thought and action was certainly the major impetus for keeping the concerns of ethics and piety alive in the midst of his theological writings."[65] This can certainly be seen in Perkins's approach to the doctrine of the church. He steers through tensions on all sides to arrive at an understanding of the church that emphasizes its incorporeal nature, specifically the election of individuals through time and across the globe united with Christ and moving toward holiness. It also has the benefit of sidestepping many of the ecclesiological debates of his day related to differently held theological convictions and church structure. Each are granted some leniency, provided the visible church still clings to Christ as the head, retains apostolic teaching, and does not commit idolatry. This is a minimalist position that allows for the Church of England and other Protestant traditions to be acknowledged as legitimate churches, even while admitting that they might not be perfect. Some may view this as a purely convenient pragmatism, but this stems from a deeply theological understanding of the church as a community of pilgrims assembled together through effectual calling into a particular church.

---

64. See R. T. Kendall, *Calvin and English Calvinism to 1649* (Oxford: Oxford University Press, 1979), 51–76. Kendall's overarching thesis has largely been discredited. For a different appraisal, his account should be read in concert with Joel Beeke, *Assurance of Faith: Calvin, English Puritanism, and the Dutch Second Reformation* (Berlin: Peter Lang, 1994).

65. Donald McKim, *Ramism in William Perkins' Theology* (New York: Peter Lang, 1987), 94.

8

The Ministry and the Means of Grace

Andrew S. Ballitch

William Perkins and his Puritan contemporaries strove to make the Church of England thoroughly and irreversibly Protestant in the Reformed mold. The Elizabethan Settlement reformed the church in doctrine but failed to extend that reformation into the arenas of church structure and liturgy. Further, the Church of Rome was a real and present danger, with Jesuit missionaries infiltrating the country and two of England's primary enemies, France and Spain, were armed with religious animosity. How would the Puritan task be completed? Through a learned ministry and the ordinary means of grace.[1] Perkins participated in the training of ministers through his Cambridge University tenure, his example of pastoral ministry at Great St. Andrew's Church, and his publications on the subject.[2] And what is clear, when surveying Perkins's surviving material, is that genuine pastoral ministry and true means of grace are saturated with Scripture.

The Ministry

Perkins lays out his vision of pastoral ministry in his *The Calling of the Ministry*, which originated as two addresses to the Cambridge University community. The presentations were expositions of Job 33:23–24 and Isaiah 6:5–8 respectively. William Crashawe, in his dedicatory epistle, praises the author as a model pastor, one especially suited for a profitable reflection on the minister's call and task. He also positions the work contextually between the Church of Rome's overevaluation of the minister as priest and the post-Reformation Church of England's pendulum swing in the other direction. In Crashawe's words, "By avoiding one extremity [they] have fallen into the other by taking too much

---

1. Diarmaid MacCulloch, *The Later Reformation in England, 1547–1603*, 2nd ed. (New York: Palgrave, 2001), 87–88.

2. For the larger Puritan effort, see Susan Doran and Christopher Durstan, *Princes, Pastors and People: The Church and Religion in England, 1500–1700*, 2nd ed. (London: Routledge, 2002), 168–74.

dignity and authority from our ministry, and by laying too much poverty, con-tempt, and baseness upon it."[3] If the Puritan project of spiritual reformation was going to succeed, the ministry had to receive appropriate investment. And in Perkins's estimation, there could be no greater investment, for his was as elevated a view of the ministry as possible without falling into the trap of sacerdotalism. This becomes clear upon investigation of his twin treatises on the subject.

The first treatise, again, springs from Job 33:23–24,[4] the "sum and sub-stance" of which,

> is that God uses means in His great mercy to preserve sinners from fall-ing into sin. But if they do [fall into sin], then He in much greater mercy affords them means and helps to rise again…. But the instrument by whom that great work is to be wrought is here in plain terms laid down to be a minister of God, lawfully called and sent by God, and appointed by His church to that great duty.[5]

Perkins unpacks the verses by observing the minister's titles, rarity, office, bless-ing, and commission and authority. Our purpose is not to trace his exegesis, but rather to pull from it the principles pertaining to the ministry, however, we will use Perkins's five points as the scaffolding.

First, the true minister is given two titles, namely, "messenger" and "inter-preter." As messengers from God, they preach God's Word, never their own, and they must demonstrate the Spirit of God through "admirable plainness and admirable powerfulness."[6] As interpreters, they mediate between God and His people by opening and applying the Scriptures and interceding for the people. Ministers are the people's interpreter to God, when in public prayer they are "able to speak to God for them, to lay open their wants and nakedness, to con-fess their sins, to crave pardon and forgiveness, to give thanks in their names for mercies received, and (in a word) to offer up all their spiritual sacrifices unto God for them."[7] To accomplish this, the minister must be educated and educated in divinity. But beyond what "by outward means be taught from man to man…. A true ministry must be inwardly taught by the spiritual scholar,

---

3. *Calling of the Ministry*, 10:199.

4. Perkins's translation: "If there be with him a messenger, an interpreter, one of a thousand to declare unto man his righteousness: Then will he have mercy on him, and will say, Deliver him, that he go not down into the pit, for I have received a reconciliation." *Calling of the Ministry*, 10:203.

5. *Calling of the Ministry*, 10:203–4.

6. *Calling of the Ministry*, 10:206.

7. *Calling of the Ministry*, 10:207.

the Holy Spirit."[8] Perkins is careful to protect against any whiff of extrabiblical revelation, while he insists on the necessity of the work of the Spirit upon the foundation of the Word.

Second, true ministers are exceedingly rare. There are several reasons why. For starters, they are treated with contempt by the world. The duties of the calling are difficult. Further, churches rarely compensate pastors properly. Third, the office of the minister is to declare righteous those who repent and believe the gospel, to preach law and justification, an unpopular prospect. This is the reason there is no higher calling, for "a good lawyer may be one of ten, a good physician one of twenty, a good man one of a hundred, but a good minister is one of a thousand. A good lawyer may declare the true state of your cause, a good physician may declare the true state of your body. No calling [and] no man can declare unto you your righteousness but a true minister."[9] The blessing the minister receives, fourthly, is upon his ministry, when God cooperates with the labors of the pastor as means to accomplish divine purposes. Finally, the ministers commission is such that "authority is given to the minister of God to redeem a penitent man from hell and damnation."[10] Returning to the illustration of various vocations, Perkins opines, "to some callings God says, 'Work you for man, build him houses, provide him sustenance.' To the physician, 'heal that man.' To the lawyer, 'do that man justice.' To the soldier, 'fight for him.' To the magistrate, 'defend him.' To the king, 'govern him, and see that everyone does his duty.' To none but the minister does He say, 'Deliver him that he goes not down into the pit.'"[11] This is the unique calling and privilege of the minister.

In the second treatise Perkins pulls from Isaiah 6:5–8, the prophet's commissioning.[12] He parses out the effect of Isaiah's vision of God, which was fear and astonishment, and then his consolation and renewal of his calling as a prophet among God's people. Isaiah was painfully aware of his sin and the sin of the people when he stood in the presence of God. This guilt was well placed as he claimed to be a man of unclean lips. The remedy was purification of course, in this instance, with a hot coal at the hand of an angel. The prophet's sin prob-

---

8. *Calling of the Ministry*, 10:208.

9. *Calling of the Ministry*, 10:221.

10. *Calling of the Ministry*, 10:226.

11. *Calling of the Ministry*, 10:226.

12. Perkins's translation: "Then I said, Woe is me, I am undone, for I am a man of polluted lips and dwell in the midst of a people of polluted lips: for my eyes have seen the King and Lord of hosts. Then flew one of the Seraphim unto me, with a hot coal in his hand, which he had taken from the altar with the tongs: And he touched my mouth, and said, Lo, this hath touched thy lips, and thine iniquity shall be taken away, and thy sin shall be purged. Also I heard the voice of the Lord saying, Whom shall I send? and who shall go for Us? Then said I, Here am I, send me. And He said, Go." *Calling of the Ministry*, 10:235.

lem accounted for, he is told to "go," to exit the presence of God and exercise his prophetic ministry. Again, the exegesis is not our concern, but rather what Perkins describes as the duties and the dignities of the ministry.

The duties of the ministry are manifold. First and foremost are conversion and humility. If pastors are ministers of reconciliation, preaching the necessity of regeneration, they must be reconciled to God themselves, having experienced the new birth. And humility is paramount. "All true ministers," Perkins declares, "must be first of all stricken into a great fear in consideration of the greatness of their function, yea into an amazement and astonishment in the admiration of God's glory and greatness, whose room they occupy and whose message they bring."[13] The high and excellent calling of the ministry tends toward pride, conceit, and narcissism, and therefore necessitates the cultivation of humility. The minister must have a tender conscience, experiencing conviction not only over gross or notorious sins, but the smallest of infractions. This is closely connected with the duty of holiness. Perkins thunders, "let us see the monstrous presumption of such ministers as dare venture rashly into the ministry, to tread upon the holy ground of God with unclean feat [and] to handle the holy things of God with unwashed hands."[14] He continues, "these men dare come into the sanctuary of God, yea dare take God's Word in their mouths [Ps. 50:16], and yet hate to be reformed, and do cast the glorious Word of God (which they preach to others with their mouths) behind their backs."[15] A lack of holiness hinders ministry effectiveness, so all ministers, "as they would see any fruit of their ministry, let them sanctify themselves, and cleanse their hearts by repentance, before they presume to stand up to rebuke the sins of others." Hypocritical ministers "may hap to confirm men who are already converted, but any such men shall hardly convert any souls from popery or profaneness." Further, "it is a vain conceit for men to imagine [that] there is any force in eloquence or human learning to overthrow that sin in others which rules and reign in themselves." And ministerial fruitfulness is not all that is at stake for the hypocritical ministers, for "because he would not, in this world, come into God's presence in sanctification and holiness, he shall therefore in fear and horror be hauled into the presence of God's glory at the last day, there to receive the

---

13. *Calling of the Ministry*, 10:237. Insightfully, Perkins identifies the unique temptation to pride for those ministers who are part of the university. He says, "now we have many occasions to be puffed up in self-conceits: we see ourselves grow in time, in degrees, in learning, in honor, in name and estimation, and God gives good portions of His gifts to many of us. What are all these but so many baits to allure our pride and vain opinions of our own worth?" *Calling of the Ministry*, 10:238. A sage observation!

14. *Calling of the Ministry*, 10:252.

15. *Calling of the Ministry*, 10:253.

just sentence of his condemnation."[16] Perkins was passionate about a regenerate, holy ministry. He summarizes this way:

> Let all men here learn the way to true courage and boldness before God; namely, to repent daily of their sins, and labor to grow in true holiness. Wealth or wit, learning or authority, cannot do this for you, but only a good conscience, which must be made good by grace and by repentance. Then, you shall rejoice in God's presence in this world, and delight to think of God, to speak of God, to pray unto Him, to meet Him in His Word and sacraments, and at the last day you shall stand with confidence before the throne of His glory.

The sweetest of motivations for the minister is delight in God Himself. The duties of the ministry consist of external responsibilities as well. There is preaching and pastoral care. Faithful pastors "must privately confer, visit, admonish, and rebuke, and principally they must preach, and that in such good manner, and in so diligent measure, as they may redeem and win souls."[17] We will look more in depth at preaching when explaining the means of grace, for not only is it the principal task of the minister, but it is also the primary means of grace in the process of discipleship. The minister must confess the sins of the people in public prayer, therefore, "he must not only have a flock, and know which is his flock, or have a general eye over it, but he must have a particular and distinct knowledge of the state of it, and the more particular the better."[18] A pastor must be in the trenches of life with his people, but at the same time he must be careful to remain unpolluted by the world. This is accomplished by ministers being "wary and choice of their company with whom they will most privately converse."[19] The pastor must take care about who his closest friends are. In short, the minister is obligated to pursue holiness, to know his people, and to preach the Word.

The dignities of the ministry, the special privileges, are primarily three: the external call, authority, and equipping. Perkins understands the external call of the church to be the call of God Himself. He clearly equates the two, claiming, "if any asks how he shall know when God calls him, I answer [that] God calls ordinarily by His church. Her voice is His. Therefore, whenever the church of God says unto you, 'you shall be sent, and you shall go for us,' even then does the Lord call us out to this holy function."[20] The church in this case is the

---

16. *Calling of the Ministry*, 10:254.
17. *Calling of the Ministry*, 10:227.
18. *Calling of the Ministry*, 10:245.
19. *Calling of the Ministry*, 10:248.
20. *Calling of the Ministry*, 10:272.

established church, for Perkins the Church of England, of course. This is balanced with the internal call. The individual conscience determines a willingness and desire, and the church judges the character and gifting. The individual is incapable of the latter, so the external call is nonnegotiable. But when it is present, "it is as effectual a calling as if you heard the voice of God from heaven."[21] We touched on this already, but a second privilege is a unique authority. This authority comes with the role of God's "deputy," "commissioner," and "ambassador," and consists in the ability to speak on behalf of God.[22] Finally, the calling of the ministry comes with the dignity of divine equipping for the task. Perkins beautifully reflects,

> If God bids them go, He will go with them Himself. If He sends them, He will not forsake them, but assist them, bless them, open their mouths, enlarge their hearts, harden their foreheads, and give power unto their words to convert His children and to confound and astonish the hearts of His enemies. If He sends them, He will defend and protect them, so that one hair on their heads shall not fall to the earth without His providence. If He sends them, He will provide for them, sufficiently reward them, honor them in the hearts of His own people, and magnify them in the faces of their enemies. And, lastly, if He sends them, He will pay them their wage, even an eternal weight of comfort here and of glory in heaven.

What precious, encouraging, and empowering promises.

The Word of God

As has been observed, the Word of God is central to pastoral ministry. It provides the pastor's marching orders, both for how he is to conduct himself personally in the private, familial, and societal spheres and how he is to go about his public responsibilities as a minister. Every one of his duties is infused with the Word. It is the content of his proclamation. It is the balm for troubled consciences and the hammer for the obstinate in counseling. It offers the only hope to the sick and dying. It provides the only perspective to one suffering loss. Pastoral ministry is Word-saturated through and through and for Perkins the Word of God is synonymous with Scripture. As such, what follows is a look at its nature and the task of biblical interpretation.

---

21. *Calling of the Ministry*, 10:279.
22. *Calling of the Ministry*, 10:278.

The Nature of Scripture

The excellency of Scripture flows from its inspiration. "Scripture is the Word of God," asserts Perkins, "written in a language fit for the church by men immediately called to be clerks (or secretaries) of the Holy Ghost."[23] The fact that Scripture is the inspired Word of God is accepted and truly believed only by the testimony of the Spirit. The lone proof of the nature of Scripture is "the inward testimony of the Holy Spirit speaking in the Scriptures, and not only telling a man within his heart but also effectually persuading him that these books of the Scripture are the Word of God."[24] That said, there are external witnesses or evidences as well, though they fall short of genuine proof without the Spirit's testimony. Perkins enumerates ten of these. First, there is the perpetual consent of the church throughout the ages, from Moses writing of the Pentateuch to the present day. Second, the corroboration of ancient pagan sources, verifying the facts referenced in Scripture. Third, the antiquity of the Word, namely, the narration of events such as creation for which there were obviously no eyewitnesses. Fourth, the fulfillment of specific prophecies. Fifth, the matter of Scripture being the revelation of the one true God. Sixth, the total absence of sincere contradictions. Seventh, the miraculous preservation of the Scriptures. Eighth, its operation "converts men, and though it is flatly contrary to the reason and affections of men, yet it wins them unto itself."[25] Ninth, its majesty in simplicity of language. Finally, the authors included their own shortcomings and corruptions. All of this compels the believer's faith that Scripture is indeed the very Word of God.

From the reality of inspiration, Perkins points to various features of Scripture. Scripture is pure, "whereby it remains entire in itself, void of deceit and error."[26] Scripture is sufficient, containing everything we need for salvation and godliness. It is eternal, such that it cannot pass away until all is accomplished. It is perspicuous in that "every article and doctrine concerning faith and manners, which is necessary unto salvation, is very plainly delivered in the Scriptures."[27] It is authoritative. Therefore, Perkins strongly claims, "the supreme and absolute determination and judgment of the controversies of the church ought to be given unto it."[28] Lastly, Scripture is a unity. The whole Old Testament points forward to the Messiah and the New Testament bears witness

---

23. *Art of Prophesying*, 10:292.

24. *Art of Prophesying*, 10:296.

25. *Art of Prophesying*, 10:299.

26. *Art of Prophesying*, 10:291. So much for inerrancy being a modern fundamentalist invention.

27. *Art of Prophesying*, 10:310.

28. *Art of Prophesying*, 10:292.

to Jesus as that Messiah. In this way, Christ Himself is the scope of Scripture. Given that Scripture is the Word of God and thus marked by these attributes, it behooves the Christian to understand rightly what God is communicating in His revelation. Perkins has a system for that.[29]

The Interpretation of Scripture

Perkins's biblical interpretation is "the opening of the words and sentences of the Scripture, that one entire and natural sense may appear." The Holy Spirit is the "principal interpreter" of Scripture. Given that He is the divine author, it makes sense that He would be the final authority on His intended meaning. The interpreter arrives at the Spirit's interpretation by using Scripture to interpret Scripture. In fact, "the supreme and absolute means of interpretation is the Scripture itself." The method by which this is accomplished is threefold: context, collation, and the analogy of faith. Perkins defines all three. He speaks of context in terms of "circumstances of place." Exegesis normally proceeds disproportionately, at this stage, when the interpreter interrogates the text with questions of "Who? To whom? Upon what occasion? At what time? In what place? For what end? What goes before? What follows?" Basically, questions one would ask when trying to understand any other text, but with the exception that context extends to the whole of the Bible, not merely the literary context of a single book. This brings us to collation. Collation is when "places are set like parallels one beside another, that the meaning of them may more evidently appear." Clearer passages shed light on the more obscure, delimiting interpretive options as they cannot by nature contradict and expanding them based on progressive revelation. The analogy of faith is "a certain abridgement (or sum of the Scriptures) collected out of [the] most manifest and familiar places." The parts of this summary are two. One concerns faith and is articulated in the Apostles' Creed. The other pertains to love, both for God and neighbor, spelled out in the Ten Commandments.

Perkins's threefold method of interpreting Scripture with Scripture and therefore arriving at the intention of the divine author works in unison when interpreting specific pericopes. Take for instance the institution of the Lord's Supper from the gospels where Jesus says, "This is my body"—a disputed phrase in the sixteenth century. The analogy of faith precludes the Lutheran view of consubstantiation because the fact that Christ's body is in heaven following the ascension is self-evidently true in the Reformed tradition, going all the way back

---

29. For the theological and historical context of Perkins's view of Scripture, see Richard A. Muller, *Post-Reformation Reformed Dogmatics: The Rise and Development of Reformed Orthodoxy, ca. 1520 to ca. 1725*, vol. 2, *Holy Scripture: The Cognitive Foundation of Theology*, 2nd ed. (Grand Rapids: Baker Academic, 2003).

to Zwingli. The context is Christ's institution of the ordinance, where he breaks bread and identifies it as a significant symbol. This means that the statement, "This is my body," is not literally true of the bread in wooden sense, but metaphorically true. Finally, in other places Jesus calls Himself the bread of life, the door, the good shepherd, etc., lending credence to the instance of symbolism in the upper room, as it is something Jesus did quite regularly. Not every passage may need all three tools of context, collation, and the analogy of faith, but they are available to the interpreter to guide toward the divine intent of the passage.[30]

The Means of Grace

Moving from the ministry to the means of grace, it is important to note two things at the outset. First, as a reminder, all means of grace are Word-centered, deriving their efficacy from the Word. Second, contrary to Puritan caricatures, growth in grace happens in the context of the local church. The visible church is the context where preaching takes place. The gathering of the faithful is where baptism and the Lord's Supper are practiced. It was within this framework of rituals and repetition that piety of a more personal nature flourished. Private and family worship in many ways served corporate worship on the Lord's Day, the apex of the Puritan week, the market day of the soul.[31] We will look at the Lord's Day and its ordinances, but, first, preaching demands our attention, as the primary means of grace and the one fixated upon by Perkins and his contemporaries. As Patrick Collinson noted, "accounts of the ministry in the later sixteenth and early seventeenth centuries were restricted to a remarkable extent to one function and one function only, that of preaching."[32] "The hearing of the Word preached is the means of the new birth," according to Perkins, and, of course, "unless a man be born anew by the Holy Ghost, he cannot enter into the kingdom of heaven."[33] For this reason, the pulpit demands our most significant treatment.

Preaching

Perkins wrote the book on preaching, at least for sixteenth-century England. His *The Art of Prophesying* (1592), a preaching manual, helped set the trajectory

---

30. For a full treatment of Perkins's hermeneutic, see Andrew S. Ballitch, *The Gloss and the Text: William Perkins on Interpreting Scripture with Scripture*, Studies in Historical and Systematic Theology (Bellingham, Wash.: Lexham Press, 2020).

31. Michael A. G. Haykin, "Word and Space, Time and Act: The Shaping of English Puritan Piety," *The Southern Baptist Journal of Theology* 14, no. 2 (Winter 2010): 442–43.

32. Patrick Collinson, *From Cranmer to Sancroft* (London: Hambledon Continuum, 2006), 48.

33. *Warning against Idolatry*, 7:497.

for Puritan preaching by influencing generations of pastors.[34] Perkins offers this definition: "Preaching the Word is prophesying in the name and room of Christ, whereby men are called to the state of grace, and conserved in it."[35] It is a most excellent gift that aims at a double end, namely, "(1) in that it serves to collect the church and to accomplish the number of the elect; [and] (2) in that it drives away the wolves from the folds of the Lord."[36] The only legitimate object of preaching is Scripture. Perkins argues, "the Word of God is the whole and only matter about which preaching is exercised. It is the field in which the preacher must contain himself."[37] This is precisely why Perkins was so concerned with correct interpretation, as we saw. If the preacher did not first grasp the meaning of the text of Scripture, then he had nothing to preach with any kind of authority, or worse, would engage in propagating heresy. But there is more to preaching than simply teaching the Bible, the preacher must communicate both doctrines and applications as well, what Perkins calls "right dividing of the Word."[38]

Part of dividing the Word appropriately is enumerating the doctrines contained in the text, which Perkins terms "resolution." Resolution is the process "whereby the place propounded is (as a weaver's web) resolved (or untwisted and unloosed) into sundry doctrines." This happens in one of two ways, either "notation" or "collection." Notation is simply recognizing the doctrines that are being directly communicated. This is common in the more didactic portions of Scripture, such as Paul's epistles. Collection, on the other hand, "is when the doctrine [is] not expressed [but] is soundly gathered."[39] Perkins illustrates this with a number of examples, showing how "collections ought to be right and sound, that is to say, derived from the genuine and proper meaning of the Scripture."[40] The fact that indirectly communicated doctrines may be legitimately derived does not give the preacher license to draw anything from anywhere. There are limits.

After the preacher decides what doctrines to focus on, next follows application, and this is where Perkins excels. He defines application as, "that whereby the doctrine rightly collected is diversely fitted according as place, time, and

---

34. W. B. Patterson, *William Perkins and the Making of a Protestant England* (Oxford: Oxford University Press, 2014), 114.
35. *Art of Prophesying*, 10:290.
36. *Art of Prophesying*, 10:285.
37. *Art of Prophesying*, 10:291.
38. *Art of Prophesying*, 10:329.
39. *Art of Prophesying*, 10:329.
40. *Art of Prophesying*, 10:331.

person do require."[41] This is why it is so important for the pastor to know his people well. Perkins conceives of seven conditions people may be in, which call for various applications of law and gospel. It is crucial to determine whether the text is a sentence of law or gospel, because the law declares to us our sin but offers no remedy. The remedy is Christ alone as He is offered to us in the gospel. Once this determination is made, the diverse conditions of the people come into play.

There are precisely seven conditions in Perkins's estimation. First, there are "unbelievers who are both ignorant and unteachable." They should be reasoned with and reproved, but unless they become teachable, they should be passed over. Second, "some are teachable, yet ignorant." These require both law and gospel, in the form of catechism. Third, "some have knowledge, but are not as yet humbled," needing the law to be applied before the gospel. Perkins says, "to the hard-hearted the law must be urged, and the curse of the law must be denounced with threatening, together with the difficulty of obtaining deliverance until they are purified in the heart.... But when the beginning of compunction does appear, they are presently to be comforted with the gospel." Fourth, "some are humbled," requiring the comforting and quieting balm of the gospel. Fifth, "some do believe," who require the gospel, the law as an instructor, and the curse of the law against remaining sins. Sixth, "some are fallen," demanding both law and gospel, for such persons must evaluate whether they are under law or under grace. Finally, there is "a mingled people." Because churches are a mix of people in various conditions, the preacher must strike a balance of law and gospel, especially over the course of a preaching ministry.[42]

These seven conditions of hearers are combined by Perkins with different kinds of application, driving the task of applying doctrine to be ever more specific. The kinds of application are derived from 2 Timothy 3:16–17, which Perkins translates, "the whole scripture is given by God's inspiration, and is profitable for doctrine, for redargution, for correction and for instruction in righteousness. That the man of God may be perfect, being perfectly instructed unto every good work."[43] From Paul's list of profitability, Perkins sees both mental and practical application.

Mental application has doctrine and redargution, or improving, in view. Doctrine is the positive proposal of truth to be believed, while redargution is the correction of the mind when in error. On the topic of mental application, Perkins offers two invaluable pieces of pastoral advice. First, "let those errors

---

41. *Art of Prophesying*, 10:334.
42. *Art of Prophesying*, 10:335–43.
43. *Art of Prophesying*, 10:344.

only be reproved which trouble the church in which we live. All others, which do either lie dead or are external, [are to be] let alone, unless some danger is ready to ensue from them." In other words, do not raise questions in people's minds or sow doubts that are not already there by correcting novelties. A second caution is, "if the error is out of the foundation of the faith, the confutation must not only be Christian-like (as it should ever be), but also a friendly, gentle, and brotherly dissension."[44] That is, correction should always be loving, but when the doctrine in question is not essential to the gospel, the preacher should especially tread lightly. But application is certainly not relegated to the mind, it is of course practical in nature as well.

Practical application is in the realm of instruction and correction in Perkins's evaluation. Instruction consists of how a person is to live out his or her faith in the spheres of family, society, and church. Scripture provides specific instruction for how believers are to conduct themselves in these overlapping domains. Then there is correction, which is admonition against ungodliness and unrighteousness in one's life needing reform. So the preacher is to instruct the people how they are to behave, both positively and negatively. Perkins concludes his section on application with a final appeal to preachers to know their context and people intimately. He writes, "any place of Scripture ought to be handled, yet so as that all the doctrines are not propounded to the people, but those only which may be fitly applied to our times and the present condition of the church. And they must not only be choice ones, but also few, lest the hearers are overcharged with their multitude."[45] The best preaching is pastoral preaching, because powerful application stems from a specific knowledge of particular people.

For being a preaching manual, *The Art of Prophesying* has relatively little to say to the delivery of a sermon. Yet what Perkins chooses to include in his direction is Puritan through and through. He teaches that in preaching, human wisdom is to be concealed and the Spirit is to be demonstrated.[46] Human learning should be downplayed both in the content and presentation of the sermon, namely, "because the preaching of the Word is the testimony of God and the profession of the knowledge of Christ and not of human skill, and again because the hearers ought not to ascribe their faith to the gifts of men but to the power of God's Word." At the same time, "if any man thinks that by this means barbarism should be brought into pulpits, he must understand that the minister

---

44. *Art of Prophesying*, 10:344.

45. *Art of Prophesying*, 10:347.

46. For more on plain style, see Leland Ryken, *Worldly Saints: The Puritans as They Really Were* (Grand Rapids: Zondervan, 1986), 104–7.

may, yea and must, privately use at his liberty the arts, philosophy, and variety of reading, while he is framing his sermon. But he ought in public to conceal all these from the people, and not to make the least ostentation."[47] Simply put, the minister should be educated and diligent in study, while at the same time refraining from the temptation to in any way show off his learning or abilities.

The preacher is not merely to hide human wisdom, but also demonstrate the Spirit of God. This is accomplished when "the minister of the Word does in time of preaching so behave himself that all, even ignorant persons and unbelievers, may judge that it is not so much he who speaks as the Spirit of God in him and by him."[48] With a series of Ramist bifurcations, Perkins unpacks what he means by demonstrating the Spirit, what it looks like in the ministry of the preacher.[49] He divides demonstration of the Spirit into speech and gesture. Speech is to be both spiritual and gracious. Spiritual speech is both simple and clear. Perkins has no time for preachers who reference the biblical languages or otherwise make their sermons inaccessible. He asserts, "neither the words of the arts nor Greek and Latin phrases and quirks must be intermingled in the sermon," because they disturb, hinder, and distract the minds of the hearers. Further, "the telling of tales and all profane and ridiculous speeches must be omitted."[50] Speech is also to be gracious, and grace is either the grace of the person or ministry. The grace of the person consists in holiness of heart and a blameless life, for "it is an execrable thing in the sight of God that godly speech should be conjoined with an ungodly life."[51] The grace of the ministry includes the ability to teach, the authority of being God's ambassador, and zeal, for in a very real sense, the preacher is executing God's decree of election when he proclaims the Word from the pulpit. Voice and the body make Perkins's category of gesture for demonstrating the Spirit. The preacher's voice must be audible for the people, and "in the doctrine he ought to be more moderate, in the exhortation more fervent and vehement." Regarding the gesture of the body, "it is fit that the trunk or stalk of the body, being erect and quiet, all the other parts (as the arms, hands, face, and eyes) have such motions as may express and (as it were) utter the godly affections of the heart." For example, "the lifting up of the eye and the hand signifies confidence...the casting down of the eyes signifies

---

47. *Art of Prophesying*, 10:349.

48. *Art of Prophesying*, 10:349.

49. For Perkins's adoption of Ramism, see Donald K. McKim, *Ramism in William Perkins' Theology* (Eugene, Ore.: Wipf & Stock, 2017).

50. *Art of Prophesying*, 10:350. It is worth noting that, while Perkins does use illustrations in his sermons, personal references are almost nonexistent in his preaching and writing.

51. *Art of Prophesying*, 10:351.

sorrow and heaviness."[52] Perkins has definite opinions about sermon delivery, but he is much more concerned about the content of preaching, which is betrayed by the relative attention he gives to preparation and delivery. Perkins concludes his preaching manual in this way:

> The order and sum of the sacred and only method of preaching: 1. To read the text distinctly out of the canonical Scriptures. 2. To give the sense and understanding of it, being read, by the Scripture itself. 3. To collect a few and profitable points of doctrine out of the natural sense. 4. To apply (if he has the gift) the doctrines rightly collected to the life and manners of men in a simple and plain speech. The sum of the sum: Preach one Christ by Christ to the praise of Christ.[53]

Baptism and the Lord's Supper

It comes as no surprise that most of what Perkins had to say about baptism and communion was consciously and decisively set in opposition to the teaching of Roman Catholicism. All Protestants recoiled at Rome's sacramental system of works-based salvation and the Reformation had just taken place less than two generations before. Lutherans and the Reformed, while agreeing on justification by faith alone, divided early on the issue of the sacraments. Further, there were internal debates about the spiritual presence of Christ in the Lord's Supper within the Reformed camp. All that to say that the stakes were extremely high. The Reformation was anything but complete in England in Perkins's mind and his understanding of the sacraments, specifically the Lord's Supper, was front and center of the debates raging at the time. In this context, Perkins's contributions are inevitably polemical, while retaining his impulse to make Scripture the determining factor.

Perkins unites the sacraments and the Word. In arguing that the sacraments do not automatically confer grace, he makes the point, "the Word preached and the sacraments differ in the manner of giving Christ and His benefits unto us because in the Word the Spirit of God teaches us by a voice conveyed to the mind by the bodily ears; but in the sacraments annexed to the Word by certain sensible and bodily signs viewed by the eye." Indeed, "sacraments are nothing but visible words and promises."[54] They are signs that represent Christ and His benefits, yes, but even more, they are "instruments whereby God offers and

---

52. *Art of Prophesying*, 10:354. For an extensive treatment of Puritan preaching, see Joel R. Beeke and Mark Jones, *A Puritan Theology: Doctrine for Life* (Grand Rapids: Reformation Heritage Books, 2012), 681–710.

53. *Art of Prophesying*, 10:356.

54. *Reformed Catholic*, 7:136.

gives" those benefits to His children. Now they are not physical instruments, which as such would betray a Roman Catholic view, but rather "voluntary instruments," in that "it is the will and appointment of God to use them as certain outward means of grace."[55] Because God has attached promises to the sacraments, they may be understood as "pledges," in that He has bound Himself to do what is symbolized. When they are received in faith, they therefore bolster faith and bring assurance of salvation. The sign affects the senses, which transmit the object of the symbol to the mind. The mind, guided by the Spirit, "reasons on this manner, out of the promise annexed to the sacrament: He that uses the elements aright shall receive grace thereby."[56] In this way, grace is received, and faith nourished.

The Lord's Day

Corporate worship, the gathering of the assembly of God, made the Lord's Day unique. Puritan Sabbatarianism was still young during Perkins's time, but it was, as one scholar puts it, an "increasingly frequent index of Puritan leanings."[57] Perkins, at the very least, refers to the Lord's Day as the Sabbath and understands it to be reserved primarily for spiritual exercises, like when he exhorts the Christian father, "to bring his family to the church or congregation on the Sabbath day, to look that they do there behave themselves religiously, and, after the public exercises [are] ended and the congregation is dismissed, to take account of that which they have heard, that they may profit in knowledge and obedience."[58] But his focus is on Lord's Day worship, which is the activity of the assembly, the church. To reiterate, the local church is fundamental to Perkins's conception of discipleship.[59] The Christian life consists of worship and if we want to truly worship God we must "join ourselves to the true church and people of God. For the church of God upon the earth is the kingdom of heaven, in which righteousness, peace of conscience, and joy in the Holy Ghost, with all blessings else are found.... And therefore, entrance must be made into heaven, in and by the church."[60]

Lord's Day worship includes preaching, fellowship, the sacraments, and public prayer, which Perkins takes directly from Acts 2:42. We have already

---

55. *Reformed Catholic*, 7:134.

56. *Reformed Catholic*, 7:135.

57. Theodore Dwight Bozeman, *The Precisionist Strain: Disciplinary Religion and Antinomian Backlash in Puritanism to 1638* (Chapel Hill: University of North Carolina Press, 2004), 113.

58. *Right Manner*, 10:190.

59. Paul R. Schaefer Jr., *The Spiritual Brotherhood: Cambridge Puritans and the Nature of Christian Piety*, Reformed Historical-Theological Studies (Grand Rapids: Reformation Heritage Books, 2011), 104.

60. *Warning against Idolatry*, 7:495–96.

looked at preaching and the sacraments in detail, but the implications of the Word spoken and seen are immense for congregants. Perkins could not have a higher view of preaching. By the power of the Spirit it was the means of salvation, and consequently church members have a role in hearing sermons. First and foremost, they "may not at their pleasure lie lolling at home, but they must join themselves to the congregation and serve God in the gospel of His Son." But further than merely showing up, they need to have a certain posture, one of fear and humility, and expectation, yielding themselves "in subjection to the Word [they] hear" and "fixing [their] hearts upon it."[61] Perkins understands fellowship as primarily the giving of alms. The Christian is to be generous in meeting the material needs of fellow brothers and sisters in Christ, and no one has so little that something cannot be offered. Public prayer, the fourth element of corporate worship, differs from private prayer in that despite only the minister verbalizing the prayer, the congregants are engaged and agreeing such that the collective "prayer of the congregation is of greater force than the prayer of private persons."[62] All of these elements that make up Lord's Day worship are enhanced by robust family and private worship.[63]

Perkins reserves some harsh words for families who do not engage in household worship. Families who do not worship God together, "are no better than companies and conspiracies of atheists."[64] Such families, "are fitly compared to a herd of swine, which are always feeding upon the mast with greediness, but never look up to the hand that beats it down nor the tree from whence it falls." While formal family worship is nonnegotiable, Perkins is not dogmatic about when or exactly how it takes place, but rather only suggests times such as morning, evening, and at meals, leaving the details up to the wisdom and discretion of the head of the household. However, there are some essential elements. First, there is "a conference upon the Word of God for the edification of all the members thereof to eternal life." Second, "invocation of the name of God with giving thanks for His benefits." This conference upon the Word is instruction on the commands of God, the ordinances of God, and the works of God. Instruction and prayer, led by the father or head of the house, make these families "little churches" and "a kind of paradise upon earth."[65] Family worship and public worship exist in a reciprocal relationship, where "teaching in the family is but a preparation to public teaching, that all persons may better profit

---

61. *Warning against Idolatry*, 7:500–501.

62. *Warning against Idolatry*, 7:509.

63. J. I. Packer, *A Quest for Godliness: The Puritan Vision of the Christian Life* (Wheaton, Ill.: Crossway, 1990), 240–41.

64. *Warning against Idolatry*, 7:510.

65. *Right Manner*, 10:121–22.

by public ministry."[66] It has a catechetical function, as they "grow in knowledge and reap the benefit of the public ministry."[67] On the other hand, "private teaching depends on public teaching, and must be ruled by it. For men may not teach at their pleasures what they will in their families, but such doctrine as they have learned and received from the public ministry."[68]

Private worship, which also undergirds Lord's Day corporate worship, is personal. The practice of personal worship includes two things. First, the private reading of the Scriptures. With reference to 2 Peter 1:19, Perkins says of the Scriptures, "We therefore must attend them while we are wandering in the night of this world, and we cannot attend unto them unless we read them." And lamenting the neglect of this duty in his own context while the reading of other things such as ballads proliferated, he writes, "when the stomach refuses meats, it is sick; and when there is no delight nor favor in God's Word, it argues the wickedness of the heart. For the Scripture is like a spice, which the more it is chafed and rubbed, the sweeter it is."[69] The second element is private prayer. Perkins illustrates the need for this secret prayer with the biblical examples of Isaac, Moses, Samuel, David, Paul, and Jesus Himself. Private prayer and Bible reading were to be regularly practiced, and especially on the Lord's Day.

Conclusion

To restate the thesis, genuine pastoral ministry and true means of grace are to be saturated with Scripture. Perkins was a man of the Bible. He brought the Scripture to bear on every area of faith and practice. The ministry and the means of grace were no exception. With urgency he sought to model pastoral ministry and train future pastors, all for the sake of establishing permanently the Reformed faith in England. His convictions about the nature of Scripture, its authority and sufficiency, necessitated a Scripture-focused strategy to such a task. If church members were to believe sound doctrine and live moral lives unto the glory of God, pastors needed to be able to exposit and apply the Word of God when churches gathered for Lord's Day worship. They needed godly men, qualified men, educated men, called by God to the awesome responsibility of ministry. And at the end of the day, the ministry and the means of grace were nothing if not motivated by, fueled with, and executed according to the Word.

---

66. *Warning against Idolatry*, 7:512.
67. *Right Manner*, 10:189.
68. *Warning against Idolatry*, 7:512.
69. *Warning against Idolatry*, 7:513.

9

The Ethics of Christian Conduct:
Law, Liberty, and Case Divinity

Roger L. Revell

William Perkins is clear that although no one is saved apart from justification in Christ, salvation cannot be reduced to divine pardon through grace and faith. Further to this, being saved also entails being sanctified, "delivered from the tyranny of sin" and "little by little renewed in holiness and righteousness."[1] In Perkins's mind, this experience is "vital evidence and a mark of true discipleship."[2] While this process of material renewal is unquestionably a work of the Holy Spirit, it is not a transformation in which believers are utterly passive.[3] To the contrary, their sanctification is a cooperative affair, one in which their decisions, actions, and habits are consequential even if not meritorious.[4] This basic perspective underpins Perkins's understanding of ethics.

In what follows, the three cornerstones of Perkins's ethics will be introduced and surveyed: his teaching about the role of divine law in Christian life, his doctrine of Christian liberty, and his case divinity. Taken collectively, these three facets of Perkins's legacy illuminate his perspective about how believers ought to behave.

Perkins on Divine Law and Christian Morality

For Perkins, the moral or godly life is one which endeavors "to do the will of God."[5] This, of course, begs a question: What is God's will for humanity? In answering this crucial question, Perkins points to Scripture, and especially

---

1. *Golden Chain*, 6:186. See also *Exposition of the Creed*, 4:30–37; *Treatise Tending unto a Declaration*, 8:483–88.

2. Geoffrey Thomas, "Pursuit of Godliness," in *William Perkins: Architect of Puritanism*, ed. Joel R. Beeke and Greg Salazar (Grand Rapids: Reformation Heritage, 2019), 40.

3. Perkins describes the Spirit as the "efficient cause" of sanctification, the one who enables Christians to pursue new obedience to God's will over the course of their life. *Golden Chain*, 6:187–90.

4. Repentance, for example, is an activity believers undertake in support of their sanctification. *Golden Chain*, 6:190.

5. *Exposition of Jude*, 4:36. See also *Commentary on Galatians*, 2:203, 209.

divine law. God's law, as first revealed through Moses and the prophets, and subsequently clarified and reiterated through Jesus and His apostles, supplies basic and authoritative definitions of right and wrong, good and evil.[6] As divine law bears upon Christian existence, it serves as a "rule and square" whereby they ought to "frame and fashion" all their actions.[7]

This outlook hearkens to John Calvin's teaching on the third and principal use of God's law, namely its role in helping the baptized to learn "the nature of the Lord's will to which they aspire, and to confirm them in the understanding of it."[8] More significantly, however, it is grounded in Jesus's teaching, as Perkins highlights in his exposition of the Sermon on the Mount. On this occasion Jesus does not impart "a new law" but rather clarifies "the true meaning of Moses and the prophets."[9] The upshot, as Perkins puts it, is that Matthew 5–7 stands as a robust affirmation of the enduring authority of divine law as the standard for a "godly, a holy, and blessed life."[10] In stressing this theme, he is careful to note that Jesus's affirmation of the law's ongoing authority for Christians pertains chiefly to its moral precepts, as opposed to those which are ceremonial or judicial.[11]

As a key point of access for the law's moral instruction, Perkins focuses on the Ten Commandments, regarding them as an "abridgment of the whole law."[12] In this move, he extends the Reformational determination to jettison the medieval Catholic custom of framing ethical exposition around the seven deadly sins.[13] He also takes it for granted that the Decalogue amounts to an explicit statement of the moral law "written in nature by creation."[14] In other

---

6. For Perkins, it is axiomatic that nothing can be good unless "it be appointed, ordained, and commanded of God." *Sermon on the Mount*, 1:234.

7. *Vocations*, 10:80.

8. Calvin, *Institutes*, 2:7:12.

9. *Sermon on the Mount*, 1:174.

10. *Sermon on the Mount*, 1:173. See also *Golden Chain*, 6:152; *Exposition of the Creed*, 5:285, 341–42; *Commentary on Galatians*, 2:196, 311, 320.

11. For a discussion of these distinctions, see *Sermon on the Mount*, 1:239–44. For an explanation of Christ's abrogation of Israel's ceremonial law, see *Commentary on Galatians*, 2:206; *Discourse of Conscience*, 8:18. Notwithstanding this abrogation, Perkins does sometimes draw ethical lessons out of the ceremonial law. For example, see *Commentary on Hebrews 11*, 3:37. For a discussion of the way in which Israel's judicial law is partially abrogated, see *Commentary on Galatians*, 2:206–8. For Perkins's ideas about how aspects of the judicial law should inform Christian ethics, based on his distinction between "common" and "particular" equity, see *Discourse of Conscience*, 8:16–17.

12. *Golden Chain*, 6:66.

13. Edmund Leites, introduction to *Conscience and Casuistry in Early Modern Europe*, ed. Edmund Leites (Cambridge: Cambridge University Press, 1988), 9.

14. *Exposition of Jude*, 4:54. See also *Exposition of the Creed*, 5:67.

words, Scripture's ethical ordinances are not arbitrary or capricious but in fact reveal God's creational intentions for humanity. They can thus be said to annotate the characteristics and behavior of a life which is properly and most authentically human, as this is defined by the one who brought humanity into existence. It is for this reason that Perkins regards lawful living as a restorative and ultimately happy affair, though such happiness does not equate to carnal or sensuous pleasure.[15]

In approaching the Ten Commandments, Perkins states that a bit of interpretive training is necessary. To this end, he proffers a series of rules meant to assist in properly drawing out their ethical import.[16] A first rule is that, in the negative, the affirmative must be understood and, in the affirmative, the negative. The moral injunctions of a given command are not, therefore, reducible to what it proscribes or prescribes but also locate in the inverse of such explicit edicts. Another key rule is that when a particular vice is forbidden so too are all other vices of that same kind. Thus, in forbidding murder God also forbids the hatred of one's brother, which is the seed of murder. Relatedly, even the "smallest sins are entitled with the same names that that sin is which is expressly forbidden in that commandment to which they appertain."[17] In this sense, looking at another person with a lustful eye is to be regarded as a form of adultery (as opposed to something less serious). In concluding this hermeneutical lesson, Perkins declares that all of God's commands remain in force unless God Himself countermands them.

At this point, to better understand how the Ten Commandments supply the content of Christian ethics, it is helpful to briefly rehearse Perkins's treatment of the sixth commandment.[18] He begins by commenting on the negative meaning of this command, namely its prohibition of both self-harm and harm to one's neighbor. With respect to the latter, he contends that the term 'murder' should be understood as a synecdoche, signifying not just the killing of one's neighbor but also "any kind of endamaging" of them.[19] Accordingly, the sixth commandment forbids fighting, beating, or maiming one's neighbors, as well as harboring any hatred, envy, or grudges against them. It also forbids harming the soul of one's neighbor; this can happen, as Perkins illustrates with

---

15. *Sermon the Mount*, 1:179. For more on this theme, see Sinclair Ferguson, "Life and Ministry," in *William Perkins: Architect of Puritanism*, ed. Joel R. Beeke and Greg Salazar (Grand Rapids: Reformation Heritage, 2019), 20–21.

16. *Golden Chain*, 6:66. See also *Commentary on Galatians*, 2:196.

17. *Golden Chain*, 6:66.

18. *Golden Chain*, 6:113–24. Perkins expounds the Decalogue as published in Exodus 20.

19. *Golden Chain*, 6:113.

appeal to Isaiah 56:10–11, when a minister fails "to preach the Word of God to their charge."[20]

As to its positive meaning, the sixth commandment enjoins preserving the lives of one's neighbors, pursuing their welfare in body and mind. Concretely, this means that believers should grieve with their neighbors in whatever miseries they face and avoid occasions whereby the "wants and infirmities" of their neighbors might be "stirred up and laid open."[21] They should also refrain from becoming angry with their neighbors over small offenses and instead strive to appease their neighbors' indignation when it is enkindled. This is all part of "following after peace" which the commandment exhorts.[22] The sixth commandment also requires a positive concern for the corpses and souls of others. We have a duty, writes Perkins, to ensure that our neighbors' dead bodies are properly committed to the grave; likewise, we have a responsibility to seek "all means to win [them] to the profession of Christian religion."[23]

This, then, is how the Ten Commandments supply the substance of Christian ethics. When read according to Perkins's protocol, they become deep wells of authoritative moral instruction. Through what they explicitly proscribe and prescribe, as well as through the inverse/inferential meaning of their edicts, they reveal how Christians should behave.

Yet what should a person do when two commandments of God stand at loggerheads? Perkins is sensitive to the possibility of such a predicament and proposes several principles for its resolution. First, he maintains that honoring God is more important than honoring worldly authorities. Thus, if one's parents (who are to be honored, according to the fifth commandment) urge one to do something which dishonors God (a violation of at least the first commandment), one should disregard the direction of one's parents. In this scenario, the command to honor God is weightier and should therefore be prioritized.[24] Second, Perkins teaches that if there is tension between obeying a moral injunction from the second table of the Decalogue and honoring a more ceremonial injunction from the first table, the latter is to give way to the former. Thus, if a Christian's neighbor's house is on fire on the Sabbath, she should readily cease in her cessation to help extinguish the fire.[25]

---

20. *Golden Chain*, 6:116.

21. *Golden Chain*, 6:119–20.

22. *Golden Chain*, 6:120.

23. *Golden Chain*, 6:121–22.

24. *Commentary on Hebrews 11*, 3:220–21. In making this point, Perkins draws additional support from Jesus's words in Luke 14:26. For another statement of these principles, see *Discourse of Conscience*, 8:14–15.

25. *Commentary on Hebrews 11*, 3:221.

Perkins's Doctrine of Christian Liberty

The second cornerstone of Perkins's ethical vision is his doctrine of Christian liberty. To be a Christian, he proclaims, is to possess a "spiritual and holy freedom, purchased by Christ."[26] Yet of what exactly does this freedom consist? Perkins answers this question in several ways.

For starters, Christian liberty denotes a complete release from needing to secure one's justification through obedience to the moral law. Moreover, it also encompasses freedom from what Perkins refers to as the "rigor of the law," namely the way in which the law "exacts perfect obedience and condemns all imperfection."[27] To the contrary, those who exist in Christ can be assured that their *imperfect obedience* will be accepted by God, so long as it is offered in faith and with a sincere heart. Bearing this in mind, Perkins's doctrine of Christian liberty makes it clear that when he affirms God's moral law as a "rule and square" for the conduct of believers, he in no way means to suggest that adherence to the law is in any way "satisfactory" with respect to one's justification.[28] Instead, Christian liberty means that striving to live in alignment with divine law is to be understood only as "a document of faith and a testimony of [one's] gratitude toward God."[29]

Additionally, Christian liberty denotes freedom of conscience with respect to adiaphora ("things indifferent"), that is, things "neither commanded by God nor forbidden."[30] In this domain believers enjoy discretion. This facet of Perkins's explanation of Christian liberty is especially germane to his ethical vision.

What sorts of matters are included in the category of things indifferent? Throughout his corpus, Perkins pinpoints many such things, including choices surrounding marriage or the single estate, the possession and use of riches, recreational activities, the consumption of meat and drink, fasting, and choices about apparel. Insofar as decisions pertaining to these sorts of matters are not dictated by divine law, they fall within the domain of believers' discretionary judgment.

In historical context, Perkins's defense of Christian liberty pertaining to things indifferent militates against what he and other Protestants saw as the heavy-handed Roman Catholic tendency to regulate or specify believers' conduct on many such matters. At a deeper level, this evinces his stalwart opposition to the Catholic claim that spiritual and ethical dictums issued by the church

---

26. *Discourse of Conscience*, 8:57. See also *Commentary on Galatians*, 2:318–24.
27. *Discourse of Conscience*, 8:57.
28. *Golden Chain*, 6:182.
29. *Golden Chain*, 6:182.
30. *Discourse of Conscience*, 8:59.

enjoyed a "co-active" authority alongside the moral precepts of Scripture, such that they should bind the conscience and command unquestioning obedience.[31]

Against this perspective, Perkins protests that Christ alone "is the only doctor and lawgiver of the church."[32] Practically, this gives rise to his insistence that the only proper "binder" of the conscience (that is, the only moral authority to which it ultimately owes unflinching deference) is "the Word of God written in the books of the Old and New Testaments."[33] As such, the church tramples on Christian freedom when it legislates the conduct of believers pertaining to things indifferent. It is in this spirit, for example, that Perkins opposes the rules of "Roman religion" pertaining to "set times of prayer," which bind believers "in conscience to observe them, upon pain of mortal sin."[34] Such superintendence over personal prayer is highly suspect insofar as Scripture "appoints no set time for this kind, but leaves it to liberty."[35]

This critique, it should be noted, does not mean that Perkins opposes any and all discretionary ecclesial regulation over the ceremonies or service patterns used in gathered worship. To the contrary, and in a manner which reveals his conformist sensibilities,[36] he maintains that the church is indeed permitted by God to issue "decrees concerning outward order and comeliness in the administration of the Word and sacraments," so long as such regulations comport with "the general rules of God's Word."[37] In this sense, his outlook is distinct from others such as William Bradshaw who, a few years after Perkins's death, argued that the ceremonies and rites of gathered worship were not in fact things indifferent but authoritatively set out in Scripture.[38]

At this juncture, a proximate question warrants brief attention: Does Perkins's opposition to the coactive authority of ecclesial injunctions carry any

---

31. *Discourse of Conscience*, 8:26. For more on this critique, see 26–38. See also *Problem of the Forged Catholicism*, 7:373.

32. *Reformed Catholic*, 7:73. See also *Exposition of the Creed*, 5:174; *Discourse of Conscience*, 8:30.

33. *Discourse of Conscience*, 8:13. Perkins elsewhere teaches that ministers play an important role in illuminating the moral teaching of Scripture and its application. *Exposition of the Creed*, 5:174.

34. *Three Books on Cases of Conscience*, 8:268.

35. *Three Books on Cases of Conscience*, 8:267.

36. See Article 20 of the Church of England's Thirty-Nine Articles of Religion.

37. *Discourse of Conscience*, 8:41–42.

38. William Bradshaw, *A Treatise of the Nature and Use of Things Indifferent* (W. Jones, secret press, 1605). For more on this debate, and Perkins's ideas about the application of the *adiaphora* principle to the "traditions and ceremonies" of the Church of England, see Peter Sedgwick, *The Origins of Anglican Moral Theology* (Boston: Brill, 2019): 205–7; Ethan Shagan, "Beyond Good and Evil: Thinking with Moderates in Early Modern England," in *Journal of Biblical Studies* 49 (2010): 505–6. Perkins's position is redolent of Calvin's in *Institutes*, 4:10:30.

implications for the duty of Christians to obey the ordinances of "magistracy" (that is, the law of the land)? Insofar as magisterial ordinances may venture beyond divine law in determining human conduct, can they to be disregarded by believers on account of Christian liberty?

In grappling with this important question, Perkins begins by robustly asserting that Christians are duty-bound to act in accordance with the law of the land. In support of this resolution, he reminds (with reference to the sweeping mandate of Romans 13:2–5) that magisterial jurisdiction is "an ordinance of God" and is thus something to which believers "owe subjection."[39] Additionally, he posits a distinction between "spiritual" and "civil" freedom, contending that Christian liberty pertains more to the former than the latter.[40] Consequently, believers do not enjoy "outward and bodily" freedom from the laws of their society. To suggest otherwise, as Perkins sharply quips, is to condone the unconscionable outlook of certain Anabaptist groups, who speciously appealed to "liberty by Christ" as an excuse for upending magistracy and behaving in a reckless and wanton manner.[41]

Notwithstanding this decided affirmation of magisterial authority, Perkins proceeds to affix several caveats to it. First, he highlights that such jurisdiction is not innate but derivative, founded upon God's authority-bestowing sovereignty. This means that the laws of the magistrate do not "have a constraining power to bind conscience as properly as God's laws do."[42] Accordingly, they only bind the consciences of believers to the extent that they echo laws which were "first made by God."[43] Among other implications, this means that adherence to the laws of the land by Christians may at times need only be a matter of "outward conversation" (which is to say *external* in nature, serving the orderliness of society), as opposed to a form of adherence grounded in inner conviction or allegiance. Second, Perkins admits at least one situation in which believers should not yield even external obedience to the magistrates laws, namely cases in which such ordinances are "flat contrary" to God's commands.[44] Along these lines, he writes that where the law of the land is made of "things that are evil and forbidden by God," Christians are "bound in conscience *not* to obey" it.[45] It is no doubt in an effort to preempt such an impasse that Perkins urges

---

39. *Discourse of Conscience*, 8:31, 39, 43. See also *Three Books on Cases of Conscience*, 8:138, 396.

40. *Discourse of Conscience*, 8:57.

41. *Discourse of Conscience*, 8:57.

42. *Discourse of Conscience*, 8:31, 35–38.

43. *Discourse of Conscience*, 8:39.

44. *Discourse of Conscience*, 8:15.

45. *Discourse of Conscience*, 8:39 (emphasis added).

England's magistrates to perform their duties in a manner harmonious with God's will.[46]

Having clarified how Christian liberty interacts with magisterial authority, it is now important to hone in on Perkins's ideas about how believers should exercise their discretion with respect to things indifferent. He has much to say about this topic. His remarks indicate that he in no way champions a modernist, libertarian conception of freedom, seeing Christians as licensed to negotiate their use of things indifferent according subjective preference or fancy. To the contrary, the people of God should strive to deploy their liberty respecting things indifferent in a "holy" or "spiritual" fashion.[47]

In contemplating what this necessitates, Perkins outlines a set of guiding principles meant to assist Christians in obeying and serving God according to His Word, which is "the end of [their] liberty."[48] To begin, he contends that things indifferent should be used as "signs and tables in which we may show forth the graces and virtues that God has wrought in the heart."[49] Thus, for example, believers should attire themselves in a manner which sets forth inner graces such as modesty, sobriety, and humility. The spiritual use of Christian liberty is also achieved through a willingness to suffer oneself "to be limited and restrained in the over-much or over-common use" of things indifferent.[50] In part, this sort of restraint equates to a refusal to behave in a manner which would cause hurt or offense to others, especially those in the household of God.[51] Third, Perkins writes that things indifferent should always be used to further believers in the course of godliness. As an illustration, he suggests that it is problematic to pamper one's body with meat and drink to such an extent that one is hindered from hearing God's Word, praying, and effectively undertaking one's ordinary work. Finally, he teaches that Christian liberty must be exercised within the compass of one's ability, degree, state, and condition in life. On this point, Perkins laments that during his own days "mean" people (that is, those of a lowly social stature) had taken to being "in meat, drink, apparel, [and] building" as if they were gentlemen and that gentlemen had taken to

---

46. *Grain of Mustard Seed*, 8:656.

47. *Discourse of Conscience*, 8:57. Perkins contrasts his notion of "holy freedom" with that of certain "Libertines" who erroneously "think that, by the death of Christ, they have liberty to live as they list." See also *Commentary on Galatians*, 2:348.

48. *Discourse of Conscience*, 8:61. See also *Commentary on Galatians*, 2:80–86, 347–50.

49. *Discourse of Conscience*, 8:60.

50. *Discourse of Conscience*, 8:60.

51. Correlative to this point, Perkins reflects on whether Christians should use their liberty before "such as are weak, and not yet persuaded of their liberty." The answer to this question, he argues, depends on *why* another believer may be unpersuaded of their liberty. *Discourse of Conscience*, 8:60.

using things indifferent in a manner more befitting of a knight (that is, someone of a comparatively higher social stature).[52]

These principles indicate that Christians should not conceive of their liberty unbounded, in libertarian terms. To the contrary, Perkins maintains that
even while Scripture affords believers a measure of genuine discretion with
respect to things indifferent, such discretion should nevertheless be exercised in a manner which is informed by the spiritual and moral teachings and
insights of the Bible. In short, the judgments believers are free to make by virtue of their God-given liberty should always strive to go with the grain of God's
revealed will. This theme exhibits the Augustinian hue of Perkins's conception
of liberty; in his mind, perfect freedom is found not in unlimited choice or
unencumbered autonomy but rather in conforming our decisions and actions
to God's will.[53] As he writes in his exposition of Jude, the "service of God is a
most happy and sweet liberty—any liberty else is straight bondage."[54]

Perkins's Case Divinity

The third cornerstone of Perkins's ethics is his case divinity or casuistry. This
pioneering and celebrated aspect of Perkins's legacy would be picked up and
extended by an array of successors over the course of the seventeenth century.[55]

Taken as a whole, this facet of his legacy is animated by two central concerns. On the one hand, as is evident in *A Case of Conscience: The Greatest
That Ever Was*,[56] as well as in the first book of *The Whole Treatise of the Cases
of Conscience*,[57] Perkins writes to provide comfort and assurance to those in
the church who were "troubled with fear that they [were] not God's children."[58]
In doing so, he extends the Reformational conviction that salvation assurance
"was absolutely essential to a healthy spiritual life."[59]

---

52. *Discourse of Conscience*, 8:60.

53. On the "Augustinian background" of Perkins's thought, see Richard Muller, introduction
to *Grace and Freedom: William Perkins and the Early Modern Understanding of Free Choice and
Divine Grace* (Oxford: Oxford University Press, 2020).

54. *Exposition of Jude*, 4:125. See also *Commentary on Galatians*, 2:314.

55. Perkins is regarded as the "father" of Reformed case divinity, standing as the "first great
master of [its] form in the context of Protestantism." Richard Muller, "Covenant and Conscience in
English Reformed Theology: Three Variations on a 17th Century Theme," *Westminster Theological
Journal* 42, no. 2 (1980): 309. For more on Reformed casuistry, see Joel R. Beeke and Mark Jones, *A
Puritan Theology: Doctrine for Life* (Grand Rapids: Reformation Heritage, 2012), 927–46.

56. *Case of Conscience*, 8:595–638.

57. *Three Books on Cases of Conscience*, 8:113–218.

58. *Case of Conscience*, 8:596. See also *Treatise Tending unto a Declaration*, 8:571–81.

59. Thomas Merrill, ed., *William Perkins (1558–1602): English Puritanist* (The Hague:
Nieuwkoop & B. de Graaf, 1966), xv.

On the other hand, Perkins's casuistical program is concerned to provide practical guidance for negotiating life's various spiritual and moral dilemmas. Along these lines, a large portion of his casuistical ruminations are devoted to elucidating the scope and extent of God's commands, as well as to discerning how Christian liberty afforded in the use of things indifferent might be holily exercised.

In committing himself to this endeavor, Perkins was impelled by an awareness of the hunger among England's Protestant populace for practical guidance on faithful and godly living. On account of this hunger, many of his countrymen had taken to consulting Catholic casuistical resources, of which there was no short supply.[60] One of Perkins's student, William Ames, would later compare this phenomenon to that moment in the Old Testament when the Israelites had resorted to going down to the Philistines to get their axes sharpened (1 Sam. 13:20).[61] Additionally, Perkins was motivated by a desire to develop a form of case divinity consistent with the core theological convictions of Protestantism. Along these lines, his program stands as an attempt to redress certain shortcomings in the "substance and circumstance" of its Catholic precursors.[62]

As Thomas Pickering, the editor of *Whole Treatise*, spells out in his dedication, one such shortcoming was the insufficient biblical basis of Catholic case writings, which were seen to stand on "weak and unstable grounds."[63] Another shortcoming was the fact that Catholic casuistry was by and large deployed in the context of the confessional, supplying priests with judgments to dispense to those under their care. From a Protestant vantage this was problematic insofar as it violated Christian liberty by perpetuating the ecclesiastical imposition of things indifferent upon the conscience rather than merely on the outward man, the latter case being within the purview of rightly instituted authority. Adding insult to this injury was the fact that casuistical judgments handed down by priests were frequently presented as a means to "appease the wrath of God"

---

60. *Three Books on Cases of Conscience*, 8:222. As reported by the volume's editor, Thomas Pickering. For firsthand accounts of early Protestant umbrage toward casuistical reflection, see *Luther's Works*, 2:314 and 26:405–6, as well as Calvin, *Institutes*, 4:10:1–2. For more, see Gordon Wakefield, *Puritan Devotion: Its Place in the Development of Christian Piety* (London: Epworth, 1957), 113; Thomas Wood, *English Casuistical Divinity During the Seventeenth Century* (London: SPCK, 1952), 38–40. On Catholic casuistical resources extant during this period, see Sedgwick, *Origins*, 187–88; James Keenan, "William Perkins and the Birth of English Casuistry," in *The Context of Casuistry*, eds. J. Keenan and T. Shannon (Washington, D.C.: Georgetown University Press, 1995), 107–11.

61. William Ames, To the Reader in *Conscience with the Power and Cases Thereof* (London: EG, 1643).

62. *Three Books on Cases of Conscience*, 8:98.

63. *Three Books on Cases of Conscience*, 8:101.

for whatever sins a confessant may have committed.[64] For Perkins and others of his ilk, this outlook denigrated Christ's atoning work. He thus set out to craft a form of casuistry decoupled "from Roman Catholic soteriology and ecclesiology."[65]

A Case Considered: The Right and Godly Use of Meat and Drink

So as to move toward a fuller grasp of Perkins's casuistry, let us now survey one of the moral cases which features in *Whole Treatise*. After this, attention will turn to clarifying the purpose of this third pillar of Perkins's ethics.

Whereas the first book of *Whole Treatise* considers an array of spiritual questions (for example, the nature of salvation, the achievement and preservation of assurance), and the second considers an array of theological queries (for example, the status of the Scriptures and the character of baptism), the third delves more straightforwardly into moral matters. Correlatively, it begins by invoking the notion of virtue and frames its subsequent ruminations around a fivefold series of virtues: prudence, clemency, temperance, liberality, and justice.[66] Within the chapter on temperance, Perkins considers the "use of meat and drink" by believers and develops the ensuing discussion around two questions.

The first query (whose answer is the foundation for the second) pertains to what the New Testament teaches about the use of meats and drinks and how this teaching applies in the present moment. Here, with appeal 1 Corinthians 8:13, Perkins submits that certain foods are "not to be used at some time," namely if their use would cause scandal to a brother.[67] He also avers that civil or political regulations surrounding food (for instance, forbidding the consumption of certain kinds of meats at certain times of the year) are to be honored, not as a matter of conscience but rather in support of the common good of the country. Finally, with a nod toward Acts 10:15, he stresses that believers enjoy "free use" of all meats, with respect to conscience.[68] In other words, no foods are to be regarded as innately unclean or defiling.

Following these preliminary remarks, Perkins makes a move typifying many of his cases: he treats ostensible scriptural tensions with respect to the issue at hand. On this occasion, he focuses on Acts 15:20, asking whether its prohibition of eating blood, as well as meat from strangled animals, remains in force. Perkins's conclusion is that it does not and is grounded in 1 Corinthians 6:12

---

64. *Three Books on Cases of Conscience*, 8:101.
65. Nigel Biggar, "A Case for Casuistry in the Church," *Modern Theology* 6, no. 1 (1989): 30.
66. *Three Books on Cases of Conscience*, 8:361–70.
67. *Three Books on Cases of Conscience*, 8:394.
68. *Three Books on Cases of Conscience*, 8:395.

and Titus 1:15, where Paul teaches that all things (including blood itself) can be lawfully consumed—so long as their consumption does not cause a scandal. As such, the dietary injunction of Acts 15:20 should be seen as having been put in place "in regard of offense, and for a time."[69]

With these conclusions in mind, Perkins turns to a second question: "How may we rightly use meats and drinks in such sort as our eating may be to God's glory and our own comfort?"[70] Here, he submits that the holy consumption of meats and drinks requires that certain things be done *before, during,* and *after* eating. Before eating, believers should bless that which they are about to ingest, an action which is part of seeking "grace that they may use the creatures holily to [God's] glory."[71] On this point, Perkins notes that as Christ did not dispense the fishes and loaves for consumption until after he had looked up to heaven and given thanks (Mark 6:41), so too should God's people acknowledge His provision each time they take sustenance.

With respect to the conduct of believers during eating, Perkins posits a distinction between what *may* be done and what *must* be done. In expounding the former, he suggests that Christian liberty allows for the use of meats and drinks not "sparingly alone, and for mere necessity, to the satisfying of our hunger and quenching of our thirst, but also freely and liberally, for Christian delight and pleasure."[72] In support of this view, he appeals to the festivity between Joseph and his brothers at their reunion (Gen. 43:34), David's words in Psalm 104:15 ("God giveth wine, to make glad the heart of man"), and the merriment of the wedding at Cana (John 2:10). Passages such as these suggest that, so long as the liberal consumption of meat and drink is undertaken with "hurtless and harmless joy, tending to the glory of God, and the good of our neighbor," it falls within the remit of Christian freedom.[73]

At the same time, to ensure that the liberal and delightful use of meat and drink do not assume a debauched tenor, Perkins elaborates on those things which *must* be done during their consumption. His advice here is fourfold. To begin, he argues that the eating and drinking of believers should not come at the expense of caring for their dependents. Second, he asserts that all consumption should be undertaken in a spirit of love and charity. Thus, if one's eating or drinking causes offense to another, it should be curtailed. Further, there should be no pampering of oneself with comestibles while the needy starve nearby. Third, the use of food and drink by believers should not be a profligate and

---

69. *Three Books on Cases of Conscience,* 8:396.
70. *Three Books on Cases of Conscience,* 8:397.
71. *Three Books on Cases of Conscience,* 8:397.
72. *Three Books on Cases of Conscience,* 8:399.
73. *Three Books on Cases of Conscience,* 8:399.

wanton affair. A person's intake, writes Perkins, "must not go beyond the condition, place, ability, and maintenance that God has given [him]."[74] In making this point, he takes care to note that the "holy moderation" to be practiced by Christians can vary "from person to person and place to place," such that there is no one-size-fits-all criterion.[75] Last, Perkins states that the eating and drinking of believers must be done with godliness. This entails receiving all that one eats and drinks as "from the hand of God Himself" and ingesting such gifts, not in the manner of swine (who devour their food without ever lifting "their eyes or hands unto [God]), but with continual recognition of the Lord, the one "of whom, and from whom" we are sustained.[76]

In reflecting on the postprandial conduct of believers, Perkins commends a moment of "holy remembrance," a conscious recognition that it is God who provides one's food.[77] He also urges a resolve to employ the strength of one's body in seeking God's glory by "walking according to all his laws and commandments."[78] And he even admonishes thriftiness with any leftovers, that they not be casually cast away but instead reserved for later use.

It is in this way, then, that Perkins envisions the holy exercise of Christian liberty with respect to the use of food and drinks. His handiwork is grounded in germane passages of Scripture and is careful to attend to ostensible tensions between such texts. Further, his meditations are attuned to pertinent intrapersonal factors (for example, how the size of one's body might impact one's consuming), as well as the circumstances of one's life (for example, a person's social position).[79] What results is a perspective which strives to honor individual discretion in the domain of eating and drinking while also promoting its godly exercise. To be sure, some might feel that Perkins's conclusions are excessively narrow and overly specified. However, when compared to the rigid dietary prescriptions imposed by the Roman Catholic Church of his day, they show themselves to be significantly less prescriptive and rigid.[80]

---

74. *Three Books on Cases of Conscience*, 8:401.

75. *Three Books on Cases of Conscience*, 8:401.

76. *Three Books on Cases of Conscience*, 8:402.

77. *Three Books on Cases of Conscience*, 8:403.

78. *Three Books on Cases of Conscience*, 8:403.

79. Perkins's casuistical disquisitions regularly account for a person's social station or condition. For another example, see his discussion on apparel in *Three Books on Cases of Conscience*, 8:408–9.

80. For some of Perkins's remonstrative remarks against Catholic dietary stipulations, see *Three Books on Cases of Conscience*, 8:396.

Clarifying the Purposes of Perkins's Case Divinity

It is now important to further comment on the purpose of Perkins's case divinity. To what end did he develop this facet of his moral theology?

In some instances, his case writings have been seen as an attempt to dictate the conduct of believers. Perhaps most famously this view is associated with Karl Barth, who reads Perkinsian casuistry as a *"Codex juris"* (or law code). According to Barth, Perkins's program is an attempt to specify the "correct individual decisions enjoined upon a Christian"[81] so as to resolve "every case in which the conscience might be in doubt."[82] Flowing from this interpretation, he censures Perkins (and Protestant casuistry in general) for attempting to "relieve [believers] of the…task of making [their] own orientations and decisions."[83]

Closer to our own moment, Peter Sedgwick has sustained this assessment, albeit in more nuanced terms.[84] His evaluation likewise leaves one with the impression that the primary mission of Perkins's case writings is to proffer authoritative resolutions on the use of things indifferent. Such resolutions would be consulted predominantly by ministers who, in turn, would hand down Perkins's judgments to those under their spiritual care. Within this arrangement, at least according to Sedgwick, there was little concern to engender understanding on the part of the ordinary believers, let alone to instruct them in the "arts of moral reasoning."[85]

Appraisals such as these suggest that Perkins's casuistry, even while it may have been soteriologically Protestantized, was essentially meant to function like its Catholic counterpart.[86] The primary objective, in other words, was to definitively specify the behavior of Christians, to dictate the godly use of their Christian liberty.

While certain aspects of this sort of evaluation are not entirely without basis,[87] it completely overlooks what is arguably the ultimate or chief end of Perkins's casuistical program. To wit, it obscures any meaningful recognition that his foremost aim is to equip all believers to exercise their liberty of judgment surrounding things indifferent in a godly manner. In this sense, it is not

---

81. Barth, *Church Dogmatics* (Peabody, Mass.: Hendrickson, 2010), III/4:8.

82. Barth, *Church Dogmatics*, III/4:6. For a parallel evaluation and critique, see Emil Brunner, *The Divine Imperative* (Philadelphia: Westminster Press, 1937), 134–37.

83. Barth, *Church Dogmatics*, III/4:8.

84. Sedgwick, *Origins*, 190–91, 193–94.

85. Sedgwick, *Origins*, 190.

86. For more on the way Catholic casuistry functioned, see Ian Breward, "William Perkins and the Origins of Reformed Casuistry," *Evangelical Quarterly* 41, no. 1 (1968): 15–17.

87. There is little doubt, for instance, that many of Perkins's case resolutions were received deferentially by his readers, marked as they are by a "great…measure of knowledge and understanding." *Whole Treatise on Conscience*, 8:102.

a *dictatorial* but rather a *didactic* concern which lies at the heart of Perkins's casuistical enterprise.

This corrective finds support in several observations, beginning with some of Thomas Pickering's remarks in his dedication to *Whole Treatise*. In commenting on the volume's aspirations, he notes that what is offered is not merely an array of sound case resolutions but also a series of rules for the "direction and resolution of the conscience."[88] In other words, what Perkins produced was not merely dependable advice but, more than this, instruction on how to reach godly determinations for oneself. Along these lines, as Pickering goes on to explain, Perkins's handiwork is "delivered…and disposed" to advance "understanding" in its users.[89] It means to "inform the judgment" (that is, the capacity for arriving at godly decisions) of all who might consult it, whether directly (in the case of pastors and literate laypersons) or indirectly, with assistance from a pastor (in the case of the unlettered laypersons).[90]

Commensurately, *Whole Treatise* is written (as it was from its inception) in English as opposed to Latin, composed "engagingly and directly" in the "language and idiom" of the men and women of Perkins's day.[91] Likewise, it exhibits a drive to translate "into simpler terms the technical language and subtleties that characterized Catholic cases."[92] Such features attest to a concern to bring "casuistry out of the realm of professional clerical adjudication [and] into the world of lay experience."[93]

Additionally, the didactic purpose of Perkinsian casuistry can be adduced from the tendency of its cases to remain "in the realm of general principles rather than detailed prescriptions."[94] Indeed, on a number of occasions Perkins's resolutions prove to be somewhat vague or indeterminate, coming up short in terms of offering "clear guidance."[95] Thus, for example, in deliberating on how the Sabbath is to be rightly observed, he writes that in "answering this

---

88. *Three Books on Cases of Conscience*, 8:102, 224.

89. *Three Books on Cases of Conscience*, 8:102.

90. *Three Books on Cases of Conscience*, 8:101–2.

91. W. B. Patterson, *William Perkins and the Making of a Protestant England* (Oxford: Oxford University Press, 2014), 113.

92. Meg Lota Brown, "The Politics of Conscience in Reformation England," *Renaissance and Reformation* 15, no. 2 (1991): 102.

93. Patterson, *William Perkins*, 113. See Henry McAdoo, *The Structure of Caroline Moral Theology* (New York: Longmans, Green, 1949). 80.

94. J. Stephen Yuille, "Preface to Volume 8," *Works*, xvii.

95. Elliot Rose, *Cases of Conscience: Alternatives Open to Recusants and Puritans under Elizabeth I and James I* (Cambridge: Cambridge University Press, 1975), 200. Cf. George Mosse, "William Perkins: Founder of Puritan Casuistry," *Salmagundi* 29 (1975): 99; and Kenneth Kirk, *Conscience and Its Problems* (London: Longmans, Green, 1948), 205.

question, I will not resolutely determine but only propound that which I think is most probable."[96] This restraint points to a pedagogical objective. Were Perkins to issue highly detailed, intricate resolutions, he would risk deterring his audience from cultivating their own deliberative capacities. Instead, they might be tempted to simply take his conclusions as their marching orders.

Finally, the central didactic aim of Perkins's cases comes into focus when they are set against the backdrop of his teaching about the conscience, which provides the "essential framework" for his casuistical program.[97] Perkins conceives the conscience as an organ of practical judgment which, among other duties, is meant to be a "companion and guide," showing us "what course we may take, and what we may not."[98] He also notes that, because of sin, the conscience malfunctions, failing to rightly lead humans in the way of godliness. Within the economy of salvation, however, the conscience can be healed. While its restoration originates in the punctiliar event of regeneration, it also encompasses a process of rehabilitation, something which believers must "labor to obtain."[99] More concretely, this rehabilitative process involves the cultivation of what Perkins sometimes refers to as "spiritual wisdom," that is, learning "the right use of God's Word in every particular action, that being by it directed we may discern what we may…do or leave undone."[100]

It is this very activity, of course, which is exhibited in Perkins's case writings. In this sense, they can be characterized as "paradigms of deliberation" meant to facilitate growth in spiritual wisdom.[101] Put another way, at the center of Perkins's program is a concern to model, commend, and teach the skill of biblically grounded, practical, moral reasoning—a hallmark of the renewed, properly functioning conscience.

The preceding observations frustrate the impression that Perkins's case writings are essentially an attempt to strip away the discretionary ethical judgment of believers by legislating Christian behavior respecting things indifferent. Against this view, they bring into focus the didactic orientation of his output, that which Ian Breward long ago pinpointed as its larger, "positive purpose."[102] As it stands, Perkins's casuistry is marked by a deep concern to

---

96. *Three Books on Cases of Conscience*, 8:344. This restraint also manifests in Perkins's remarks on the abrogation of oaths (322), consumption of meat (401), playing card games (420), and almsgiving (427), among other examples.

97. Yuille, "Preface to Volume 8," xiv.

98. *Discourse of Conscience*, 8:53. See also Muller, *Grace and Freedom*, 53.

99. *Discourse of Conscience*, 8:86.

100. *Discourse of Conscience*, 8:91. See also *Golden Chain*, 6:187.

101. Brown, "Politics of Conscience," 103. See also Wood, *English Casuistical Divinity*, 49.

102. Breward, "William Perkins," 16.

equip all Christians—beginning with but hardly limited to pastors—with a capacity for reasoning their way "to faithful and obedient moral decisions" in the exercise of their Christian liberty.[103] Along these lines, his case writings are better described as a training manual of sorts than as a compendium of definitive spiritual and moral injunctions. Unlike their Catholic counterparts, they do not mean to exclude their audience from the process of moral reasoning.[104] To the contrary, they are produced in the hope that all those in the church will become skilled casuists, men and women possessing sound consciences, increasingly able to determine for themselves the requirements of godliness as often as such discernment is divinely sanctioned.

Summation

In this chapter, we have surveyed the three cornerstones of Perkins's approach to ethics: his understanding of the role of divine law in the life of faith, his doctrine of Christian liberty, and his case divinity. Within this framework, the moral tenets of God's law—encapsulated in the Ten Commandments— provide believers with a foundational and authoritative understanding of how they ought to behave. As properly interpreted, the commandments illuminate the basic, nonnegotiable requirements of ethical righteousness.

At the same time, there is much in the realm of morality which divine law does not straightforwardly regulate. With respect to such "things indifferent" Perkins maintains that believers are afforded liberty of judgment or conscience; they are granted genuine discretion in determining what they do or do not do. While this discretion is not to be constrained by ecclesial laws which would claim a "coactive" authority to bind believers' consciences alongside God's revealed will, neither is it an excuse to blithely disregard the laws of the magistrate. Further, and perhaps most importantly, this discretion is not a license to behave in a wanton or hedonistic manner. To the contrary, it should be exercised in a holy fashion, informed by germane biblical insights and thereby wielded in a manner consistent with the will and wisdom of God.

The third cornerstone of Perkins's ethics, his case divinity, is a tool developed to promote the holy exercise of Christian liberty. In seeking to provide such support, Perkins's primary aim is not to dictate the conduct of believers through the various case resolutions he reaches, biblically sound and praiseworthy though they may be. More fundamentally, his casuistry is animated

---

103. Biggar, "Case for Casuistry," 30.

104. Brown, "Politics of Conscience," 109–10. See Leites, introduction 1–4. It is for this reason that Perkins's case divinity is better likened to a compass than to a map. Breward, "William Perkins," 16–17.

by a didactic concern. Its larger objective is to nurture in all believers an ever-increasing facility for discerning the requirements of godliness when they are not plainly and directly specified in God's law. To the extent that believers cultivate this capacity—and assuming they possess a solid grasp of God's moral law—they are, according to Perkins, well-positioned to conduct themselves ethically, which is simply to say, in a manner pleasing to God.

10

God's Imposition: The Nature of Vocation

Dee Grimes

According to Leland Ryken, medieval monasticism broke with New Testament Christianity by retaining "the terminology of calling" while "changing its meaning and application."[1] The term "vocation" was gradually restricted to a select few—namely, those who devoted themselves to a religious order.[2] As a result of this shift, several imbalances emerged.[3] For starters, the catechizing of all was replaced by the preparing of some for the monastic life. These few were "called" to the *vita contemplativa* (contemplative life), while ordinary believers gave themselves to an inferior pursuit—the active life (*vita activa*). It is at this point that the *sacred* vs. *secular* dichotomy became entrenched in people's thinking.[4]

This emphasis continued until the Reformation.[5] The Reformers insisted that "vocation" was not a reality restricted to religious orders, but an identity that belonged to all believers. Megan Devore notes, "A benchmark transformation occurred in the 16th century, when a novel envisioning of *vocatio* as 'one's specific occupation or profession' is often said to have arisen."[6] For the Reformers, all are called to glorify God by serving others in their vocation.

---

1. Leland Ryken, "'Some Kind of Life to Which We Are Called of God': The Puritan Doctrine of Vocation," *The Southern Baptist Journal of Theology* 22, no. 1 (2018): 46.

2. Paul Stevens sees a similar trend today: "The only people who speak of being 'called of God' are 'full-time' missionaries and pastors." R. Paul Stevens, *The Abolition of the Laity: Vocation, Work and Ministry in a Biblical Perspective* (Cumbria, UK: Paternoster Press, 1999), 72.

3. Perkins speaks to this in *Vocations*, 10:55.

4. See Paul Marshall, *A Kind of Life Imposed on Man: Vocation and Social Order from Tyndale to Locke* (Toronto: University of Toronto Press, 1996), 18–19; and Donald Bloesch, *Spirituality Old and New: Recovering Authentic Spiritual Life* (Downers Grove, Ill.: InterVarsity Press, 2007), 57–59.

5. For more on the Reformed view of vocation, see Marshall, *A Kind of Life*, 22–26; Stevens, *The Abolition of the Laity*, 73–79; and Gene Edward Veith Jr., ed., *God at Work: Your Christian Vocation in All of Life* (Wheaton: Crossway Books, 2002).

6. Megan Devore, "The Labors of Our Occupation: Can Augustine Offer Any Insight on Vocation?" *The Southern Baptist Journal of Theology* 22, no. 1 (2018): 23. See also Robert S. Michaelsen, "Changes in the Puritan Concept of Calling or Vocation," *The New England*

It was William Perkins who developed this concept in England. According to the historian, Ian Breward, Perkins's work "marked the first extended account in English of the theological and practical implications of one's calling."[7] Robert Michaelsen notes that Perkins's thinking on the subject was "an index of the importance of the concept of calling during the reign of Elizabeth."[8] He sought to strengthen the Church of England by affirming that sound doctrine should lead to godly practice, which should in turn be most evident in one's vocation. He explains:

> Man should use the place and office assigned unto him by God, in a holy manner, performing the duties annexed unto it in faith and obedience, and eschewing those vices that usually attend upon it with all care and circumspection. In this manner, God has disposed the whole estate of mankind, for the accomplishment of the foresaid end, the honor and glory of His name.[9]

Perkins believed that one's vocation and one's fulfillment of God's purpose are inextricably intertwined. He rejected the false dichotomy between sacred and secular and affirmed that one's vocation is the unique way in which love for God and neighbor is expressed. This conviction informed Perkins's understanding of "good works," which are not to be restricted to serving the poor, helping the sick, preaching the gospel, etc.; rather, the chief way in which one performs good works is in the faithful execution of one's vocation.[10]

Perkins gives this subject his full attention in *A Treatise of the Vocations, or Callings of Men, with the Sorts and Kinds of Them, and the Right Use Thereof*.[11] He begins by explaining that God issues two calls in the life of every believer. The first is a "general" call to salvation through faith in Christ. Flowing from the first, the second is a "particular" (or personal) call to be fulfilled in the

---

Quarterly 26, no. 3 (September 1953): 315–18; Jordan J. Ballor, "Doing Much Good in the World: The Reformed Tradition Emphasized Laboring in One's Calling for God and for Neighbor," ed. Jennifer Woodruff Tait, *Christian History: Callings Work and Vocation in the History of the Church*, no. 110 (2014): 28.

7. Ian Breward, "The Significance of William Perkins," *The Journal of Religious History* 4, no. 2 (December 1966): 125.

8. Michaelsen, "Puritan Concept of Calling," 318.

9. *Vocations*, 10:34.

10. This is an important observation, for one's interpretation of good works impacts one's understanding of vocation. Medieval Roman Catholicism maintained that works are a necessary perquisite for salvation. The Reformers affirmed that good works are a necessary result of salvation. For more on this, see Stevens, *The Abolition of the Laity*, 82; and Elizabeth Mehlman, "The Work and Faith of Theological Scholars: Converging Lessons from James 2 and Luther's Doctrine of Vocation," *The Southern Baptist Journal of Theology* 22, no. 1 (2018): 97–109.

11. *Vocations*, 10:31–107.

home, church, and commonwealth. Without the general call to salvation, the works of one's particular call are ineffectual because they "do not proceed from an upright heart, nor are they done in obedience to God's commandments, and for His glory."[12] Conversely, without the proper fulfillment of the particular call, a claim to have experienced the general call is mere hypocrisy. It means the individual is pursuing a "form of godliness without the power thereof."[13] It is for this reason that Perkins was motivated to write his treatise. In his own words, "Few men rightly know how to live, and go on in their callings so as they may please God."[14]

A Definition

Perkins defines the particular call (or vocation) as "a certain kind of life, imposed and ordained on man by God for the common good."[15] His definition contains three important elements. First, he describes the *nature* of vocation: it is "a certain kind of life." This means it is unique to every individual. For Perkins, the uniqueness of our vocations should cause us to consider "that we are placed in them by God, and therefore should practice the duties therein."[16] This act of "considering" involves searching our God-given affections (what we enjoy doing) and our God-given talents (what we do well). These reflect God's design and purpose for us. To ignore them, or to choose a vocation that is inconsistent with these, is to disregard the personal nature of one's vocation.

Second, Perkins identifies the *author* of vocation: it is "imposed and ordained on man by God." It has been observed that Perkins "believed that accenting the sovereignty of God and His decree gave God the most glory and the Christian the most comfort."[17] For this reason, he insists that one's vocation is perceived in the mind of God in eternity.[18] It is by God's design, then, that believers are able to do their part for maximum efficiency and effectiveness. Perkins states, "Behold here a notable resemblance of God's special providence over mankind, allotting to every man his motion and calling, and in that calling his particular office and function."[19]

---

12. *Vocations*, 10:78. These reasons distinguish the regenerate's works in their vocation from the same in the unregenerate. For more, see Charles H. George and Katherine George, "English Protestant Economic Theory: The World and Its Callings," in *The Protestant Mind of the English Reformation, 1570–1640* (Princeton: Princeton University Press, 1961), 127.

13. *Vocations*, 10:58.

14. *Vocations*, 10:43.

15. *Vocations*, 10:43.

16. *Vocations*, 10:57, 59.

17. Preface, *Works*, 6:xxix.

18. *Commentary on Galatians*, 2:52–53.

19. *Vocations*, 10:44.

Third, Perkins explains the *purpose* of vocation: it is for "the common good." This pertains to three main areas of life: family, church, and commonwealth. Simply put, devotion to one's vocation, while benefitting the individual, contributes to the well-being of society.[20] In Perkins's estimation, it is the sphere in which the greatest commandment is put into action (Mark 12:28–31). Through the God-honoring fulfillment of one's vocation, love for God and neighbor is made manifest. Closely related to this, Perkins believes that one's vocation is the principal means of sanctification. We honor God as we seek to obey Him amid temptations associated with our particular callings, such as the desire for wealth, power, and prestige, which incites envy, greed, and injustice. Learning to be faithful in the duties of our particular calling, according to Perkins, teaches "us much more to be constant in the general duties of Christianity."[21] It is the main arena in which we practice faith, repentance, and new obedience.

God's Design

Perkins's appreciation of the personal nature of vocation ("a certain kind of life") arises from his understanding of God's original design. Its first practical demonstration is found in the creation account.[22] Adam was called "to obey God and dress the garden."[23] In this way he was to mirror God's image in righteousness and holiness while executing wisdom and justice in the world.[24] The fall, of course, marred this original design. Now, under the covenant of grace, believers receive a double call.[25]

The first is to salvation. Perkins believes that God's grace in salvation (the general call) levels all people before God. He remarks, "God's church is a company of men ordained to salvation, taken from under the power of the devil." Thus, he adds, "No man is to stand upon his gentility or glory in his parentage for nobility and great blood, but only rejoice in this, that he is drawn out of the kingdom of darkness and from under the power of Satan and placed by Christ Jesus in the kingdom of grace."[26] By a work of God's saving grace, His image is

---

20. Conversely, Perkins argues it is an abuse to employ one's calling merely for oneself. *Vocations*, 10:45.

21. *Vocations*, 10:100.

22. *Golden Chain*, 6:26–31; *Exposition of the Creed*, 5:64–68.

23. *Golden Chain*, 6:31; *Exposition of Jude*, 4:89. See also George and George, "Callings," 132; and Stevens, *The Abolition of the Laity*, 78.

24. Perkins comments, "The Lord gives a particular commandment to him [Adam] and all his posterity, which binds all men to walk in some calling, either in the church or commonwealth (Gen. 3:19)." *Vocations*, 10:54.

25. *Sermon on the Mount*, 1:455; *Exposition of Jude*, 4:89; *Vocations*, 10:49–60.

26. *Exposition of Revelation 1–3*, 4:476. See also Christopher Hill, *Puritanism and Revolution: Studies in Interpretation of the English Revolution of the 17th Century* (London: Secker &

restored in the individual, resulting in newness of life.[27] Believers are thereby enabled to perform new obedience.

The second call is to a particular vocation. One responds to God's general call by first performing "specifically religious acts"[28] such as (1) praying, (2) serving for the good of the church, (3) serving others, and (4) walking worthy of Christ.[29] One also "responds in his work and in his whole life."[30] Perkins explains that "God manifests His fatherly care over us by the employment of men in His service according to their several vocations for our good."[31] The main end of our lives, therefore, is to serve God by serving others. This requires diverse callings, which contribute to the betterment of society. These distinctions (as ordained by God) are strategic, fashioned for the greatest efficiency and according to the nature of His creation—that is, the personal characteristics of each person. In other words, they are for our good.[32]

Some have argued that Perkins denies dignity to those who occupy "lesser" callings.[33] However, the evidence seems to prove otherwise. Perkins insists that every member of society contributes to the whole. "There are many wheels in a clock made by the art and handiwork of man," he writes, "and each one has its several motions, some turn this way, some that way, some go softly, some apace. And they are all ordered by the motion of the watch."[34] It is God who "orders" all things to accomplish His purposes. For instance, the farmer, teacher, and judge are owed deference simply because God appointed them to their vocations.[35] We are to honor all people in their diverse offices, whether they are our "superior, equal, or inferior," says Perkins.[36] As diverse members maintain the physical body, so diverse vocations are designed to maintain society. In this, a division of labor exists whereby unity and efficiency are established, not

---

Warburg, 1965), 237. Hill claims that the "Puritan revolution" was more akin to the English "bourgeois revolution," which prioritized the needs of the middle-class majority. For another view, see Paul S. Seaver, *Wallington's World: A Puritan Artisan in Seventeenth Century London* (Stanford: Stanford University Press, 1985), 133.

27. *Vocations*, 10:10–15.

28. Michaelsen, "Calling," 319.

29. *Vocations*, 10:49–53.

30. Michaelsen, "Calling," 319. Joel Beeke maintains that the Puritan concept of vocation fills "ordinary life with new spiritual motivations." Joel R. Beeke and Mark Jones, *A Puritan Theology: Doctrine for Life* (Grand Rapids: Reformation Heritage Books, 2012), 534.

31. *Vocations*, 10:58.

32. *Vocations*, 10:45.

33. Charles Constantin, "The Puritan Ethic and the Dignity of Labor: Hierarchy vs. Equality," *Journal of the History of Ideas* 40, no. 4 (1979): 546.

34. *Vocations*, 10:44.

35. *Commentary on Galatians*, 2:53.

36. *Treatise Whether a Man*, 8:437.

compromised. Perkins claims, "For if all men had the same gifts, and all were in the same degree and order, then all should have one and the same calling. But in as much as God gives diversity of gifts inwardly, and distinction of order outwardly, hence proceed diversity of personal callings."[37] God-given distinctions are for our good; they demonstrate unity in diversity and enable us to glorify God and serve others in the most efficient way.[38]

Rules to Be Obeyed

Perkins lists four main rules that are to govern our understanding of the particular calling. First, everyone has a vocation. Based upon the "measure of gifts" God has given us, we are to fulfill a role in the family, church, and commonwealth.[39] For Perkins, vocation extends well beyond the restricted world of monks and friars[40] to include all people in all places.[41]

Second, everyone is to consider their vocation "to be the best of all callings" for them.[42] To this end, we must (1) trust in God's plan, and (2) resist comparing ourselves to others (personally and materially) while striving for contentment in our personal calling.[43] Often times, differences in vocation (social order) incite a spirit of discontent. Perkins warns, "When we begin to mislike the wise disposition of God, and to think other men's callings better for us than our own, then follows confusion and disorder in every society."[44] He adds, "The greatest disorders that have fallen out in the church of God" are a result of discontent in one's calling. The same is true of the commonwealth.[45] We must strive, therefore, to believe that God's design in our vocation is the very best for us.

---

37. *Vocations*, 10:54.

38. Perkins affirms that it is the responsibility of "all Christian persons generally" to build up the church. *Vocations*, 10:51.

39. *Vocations*, 10:54–56. See also *Sermon on the Mount*, 1:238, 453, 455, 464; *Exposition of Jude*, 4:89–90; *Exposition of the Creed*, 5:67; *Golden Chain*, 6:137; *Grain of Mustard Seed*, 8:656. Perkins argues that "even the angels of God have their particular callings, in that they do His 'commandments in obeying the voice of his word' [Ps. 103:20]." *Vocations*, 10:55. For the Puritan, "The call to work is neither optional nor corporate, but imperative and personal." Chad Burchett, "Serious Joy: The Puritan Heritage of Leisure," *Puritan Reformed Journal* 10, no. 2 (July 2018): 224.

40. For Perkins, monks stood in the tradition of ascetic retirement from the world, whereby they served only themselves. *Reformed Catholic*, 7:76–77.

41. See Louis B. Wright, *Middle-Class Culture in Elizabethan England* (Ithaca, N.Y.: Cornell University Press, 1958), 170.

42. *Vocations*, 10:56, 100.

43. *Golden Chain*, 6:137–38.

44. *Vocations*, 10:56.

45. *Vocations*, 10:57. See also Constantin, "The Puritan Ethic," 547.

Third, everyone should unite their general calling and particular calling.[46] Perkins laments, "Few men rightly know how to live and go on in their callings so as they may please God."[47] It is due to "God's pleasure," Perkins asserts, that He chooses to use us as instruments to serve one another.[48] To be "unblameable both before God and man," we must therefore determine our vocation and "proceed to practice its duties."[49] This means, in particular, that we should obey the duties of the first and second tables—at church and work, with family and friends, and at home and abroad.[50] Without the general calling, the particular calling is "nothing else but a practice of injustice and profaneness."[51] It is, for Perkins, "a dangerous and lamentable course of life."[52]

Fourth, everyone is to ensure that their particular calling gives place to the general calling "when they cannot stand together."[53] Perkins describes a scenario in which a master (a zealous papist) asks his servant (a Protestant) to commit acts that are contrary to his religious beliefs. The directive is clear: the servant must honor and obey God over his earthly master. Therefore, despite possible repercussions, the believer must not compromise his faith. This rule is circumstantial. Perkins is not, in general, prioritizing the general call over the personal call. Some scholars interpret this rule as such. However, this interpretation refutes Perkins's third rule that the general and personal calls should always be united.

To close this section, Perkins divides callings into two categories. The first is composed of those which provide structure to society: "master, servant, husband, wife, parents, children, magistrates, subjects, minister."[54] The second is composed of those which supply the needs of the first: husbandmen,

---

46. *Vocations*, 10:57–59.

47. *Vocations*, 10:43.

48. *Vocations*, 10:58.

49. *Vocations*, 10:59.

50. *Vocations*, 10:57. See also *Sermon on the Mount*, 1:391; *Exposition of Jude*, 4:90; *Reformed Catholic*, 7:76–77; *Grain of Mustard Seed*, 8:656–57. Perkins connects this joining of the general call and particular call to the second commandment; i.e., a proper demonstration of "outward worship unto God." *Sermon on the Mount*, 1:665. His all-encompassing vision of vocation set the trajectory for the Puritan movement, as is evident in the numerous treatises (dealing with this subject) that emerged in the following century. By way of example, see George Swinnock, *Christian Man's Calling, or, A Treatise of Making Religion One's Business* (London: R.W. for Dorman Newman, 1668).

51. *Vocations*, 10:58.

52. *Vocations*, 10:59.

53. *Vocations*, 10:59–60. See also *Discourse of Conscience*, 8:14–15.

54. *Vocations*, 10:60.

merchants, doctors, soldiers, lawyers, tailors, carpenters, etc. They contribute to society's "good, happy, and quiet estate."[55]

Perkins is not suggesting that the first category is more important than the second. His point is that the first category of vocations forms society, whereas the second maintains it.[56] Both are essential. Charles Munson correctly states that, according to Perkins, the diversity of callings is the "very fabric" of a well-established society.[57]

Steps to Be Followed

For Perkins, the principal purpose of any vocation is that it is used "in a good and holy manner."[58] God does not favor any calling over another, or any work over another, for all are His. However, He does look "at the heart of the worker."[59] Perkins notes, "The action of a shepherd in keeping sheep, performed, as I have said, in its kind, is as good a work before God as is the action of a judge in giving sentence or a magistrate in ruling or a minister in preaching."[60] The "action" of each is deemed "good" when four steps are closely followed.

A Good Choice

To begin with, one makes a "good choice" of a vocation when it is "grounded upon the moral law." This means it must positively contribute to the family, church, and commonwealth. When this is the case, "it may be had, used, and enjoyed with good conscience."[61] In addition, one makes a "good choice" when the vocation best fits one's affections (what we enjoy doing) and talents (what we do well).[62] Perkins explains:

> Good choices are made when men try, judge, and examine themselves, to what things they are apt and fit, and to what things they are not. And every man must examine himself of two things: first, touching his affection; secondly, touching his gifts. For his affection, he must search what mind he

---

55. *Vocations*, 10:60.

56. *Exposition of Jude*, 4:89.

57. Charles R. Munson, "William Perkins: Theologian of Transition" (PhD diss., Case Western Reserve University, 1971), 103.

58. *Vocations*, 10:60. Remembering his master in heaven, the Puritan worker seeks to glorify God by the way he does the works of his calling. Peter J. Beale, "Sanctifying the Outer Life," in *Aspects of Sanctification: Being Papers Read at the 1981 Conference* (London: Westminster Conference, 1981), 72.

59. *Vocations*, 10:61. See also *Sermon on the Mount*, 1:238; *Three Books on Cases of Conscience*, 8:151.

60. *Vocations*, 10:61. See also *Sermon on the Mount*, 1:238; *Treatise Whether a Man*, 8:529.

61. *Vocations*, 10:61.

62. *Vocations*, 10:62–63.

has to any calling, and in what calling he desires most of all to glorify God. For his gifts, he must examine for and to what calling they are most fit.[63]

A process of trial and reflection is essential for discovering one's personal affinities and competencies. Perkins affirms, "The Holy Spirit signifies that all our goodness and all our dexterity to this or that office is merely from God because we are sanctified, dedicated, and set apart in the counsel of God from all eternity."[64] Richard Douglas expresses Perkins's symmetrical thought as follows: "Vocation is in one sense imposed, but in another it is chosen according to one's gifts."[65] Conversely, choosing a vocation without giving attention to one's suitability, in Perkins's estimation, results in disorder akin to a bone that is out of joint.[66]

Recognizing the difficulty of self-examination, Perkins counsels, "Because many men are partial in judging their inclination and gifts, the best way for them is to use the advice and help of others who are able to give direction herein and discern better than they."[67] God imposes a particular calling "mediately," that is, He uses people as instruments to identify and confirm it.[68] The counsel of devoted advisors aids the discovery of abilities and purifies motives.

By way of example, Perkins sees this in the relationship between parents and children.[69] It is never too early to notice God's design for a young life. Perkins explains that Athanasius, "that famous bishop," from a very early age was practicing the works of a minister by the seaside with his friends, "examining and baptizing them according the solemn order" he had witnessed in the congregation.[70] Perkins declares, "Parents cannot do greater wrong to their children, and the society of men, than to apply them to unfit callings; as when a child is fit for learning, to apply him to a trade, or other bodily service...

---

63. *Vocations*, 10:62. For Margo Todd's thesis that the Puritan theology of vocation draws from its contemporary humanist context to grant dignity to all people, see *Christian Humanism and the Puritan Social Order* (Cambridge: Cambridge University Press, 1987).

64. *Commentary on Galatians*, 2:52.

65. Richard M. Douglas, "Talent and Vocation in Humanist and Protestant Thought," in *Action and Conviction in Early Modern Europe; Essays in Memory of E. H. Harbison*, ed. Theodore K. Rabb and Jerrold E. Seigel (Princeton: Princeton University Press, 1969), 296.

66. *Vocations*, 10:61.

67. *Vocations*, 10:62.

68. *Vocations*, 10:45. See also *Commentary on Galatians*, 2:16; *How to Live Well*, 10:16; *Calling of the Ministry*, 10:27.

69. *Vocations*, 10:62–63; *Right Manner*, 10:176–78. Among the Athenians, parents took their children to markets and observed their delight in and skill with certain tools and occupations. Perkins remarks, "It will not be amiss for Christians to be followers of the heathen in this or any other commendable practice." *Vocations*, 10:62.

70. *Vocations*, 10:63.

this is like expecting toes to work like fingers."[71] He explains the value of both physical and mental gifts. As for mental capacity, adults and children alike are prone to either "active" or "passive" understanding. Recognizing the difference is useful in determining our callings.[72]

Following his first two points—namely, choosing a lawful and suitable calling—Perkins addresses how to choose a calling when a person is fit for more than one.[73] Paul advises the Corinthians to seek after the best spiritual gifts, that is, those gifts that best build up the body (1 Corinthians 14).[74] Based on this example, Perkins argues that we must seek for the best callings that most edify the church.[75] As a slave must seek freedom when offered it (1 Cor. 7:21),[76] so too we are free to pursue that area of service that is most beneficial to family, church, and commonwealth, and most glorifying to God.

Perkins's appraisal of what constitutes the "best" calling for an individual includes serious consideration of what best matches one's ability and what best contributes to society's good. After all, Perkins emphasizes, it is the diversity of ordinary callings that collectively meets the spiritual and physical needs of any society.[77] Therefore, according to Perkins, we make a good choice of a calling when it is consistent with God's Word, suited to our gifts, desires and abilities, and (in terms of the common good) is the most beneficial of all the options before us.

A Good Entry

Having made a good choice, one must make a good entry into a vocation. This necessitates two things, both of which serve to confirm that a good choice has been made. First, a person must "know in his conscience that God has placed him there."[78] This confidence is important because it provides comfort in adversity. "When our conscience cannot say thus much, the comfort is gone."[79] We arrive at this certainty when we possess the ability to do the work. God imparts gifts of "competence" (skill) and "convenience" (knowledge and dexterity).[80] A

---

71. *Vocations*, 10:63.

72. *Vocations*, 10:63.

73. *Vocations*, 10:63–64.

74. *Vocations*, 10:64. See Gordon D. Fee, *The First Epistle to the Corinthians*, ed. Ned B. Stonehouse, The New International Commentary on the New Testament, rev. ed. (Grand Rapids: William B. Eerdmans Publishing Company, 2014), 723.

75. *Vocations*, 10:100.

76. *Vocations*, 10:63.

77. *Vocations*, 10:58.

78. *Vocations*, 10:64.

79. *Vocations*, 10:64.

80. *Vocations*, 10:64.

"trial of gifts" confirms these things. If an individual is unable to perform the duties of a particular calling, then God has not called him to that work.[81]

Second, we must be confirmed by others in the calling. This necessarily involves those who are in positions of authority, such as "parents and masters in private families, the governors of the church for ecclesiastical callings, [and] the magistrate and men of authority for civil [callings] in the commonwealth."[82] Their recognition of one's suitability for a job ensures a good entry. Perkins notes that these two checks also aid in avoiding abuses, such as showing favoritism, buying and selling offices, and engaging in corruption. Perkins chides, "He who buys his office must say his money called him rather than God."[83]

At this point, Perkins addresses several potential problems that might arise when seeking to make a "good entry" into a calling.[84] For starters, what do we say to the person who has entered a calling for the wrong reason? Perkins answers, "He is not to forsake his place, but to repent of his bad entrance, and to do the duties of his calling with diligence and good conscience."[85] God will either bless his work or call him in time to a different vocation. Second, what do we say to those who are concerned about their "desire" for a certain vocation? Perkins responds by affirming that it is always acceptable to desire a particular calling for God's glory and man's good.[86] By contrast, "It is unlawful to desire work with a vain or greedy mind, for pleasure, or for lucre's sake."[87] Therefore, if the motive is honorable, desire is a good thing. Third, what do we say to those who have entered two callings or trades at the same time? Is this permissible?[88] Perkins makes allowance of this, as long as (1) neither calling contradicts what is permissible according to God's Word, (2) neither calling hinders the execution of the other, and (3) neither calling undermines the common good.[89] That said, in a densely populated community, it is "inconvenient,"

---

81. *Vocations*, 10:94. Veith makes a similar observation: "More often, acting outside of vocation is morally innocent, but it results in ineffectiveness, frustration, and wasted time." Veith, *God at Work*, 138.

82. *Vocations*, 10:65.

83. *Vocations*, 10:65.

84. *Vocations*, 10:66–70.

85. *Vocations*, 10:69.

86. *Vocations*, 10:70. Perkins appeals to 1 Timothy 3:1 as an example.

87. *Vocations*, 10:70. See also *Golden Chain*, 6:118.

88. The question does not concern holding a familial role and vocational role simultaneously. For Perkins, all familial roles are callings, as are all vocational roles such as merchants, government officials, pastors, tradesmen, farmers, physicians, publishers, and lawyers. Perkins refers to the Old Testament patriarchs—they were priests, prophets, civil judges, and family men. *Vocations*, 10:71–72.

89. *Vocations*, 10:71–72.

for one individual to occupy multiple livelihoods to the detriment of others.[90] Due to "presumption," people are tempted to overstep their abilities by "daring to enterprise things beyond their callings and above their power, which multiplies their anxieties."[91] Perkins warns, "He who does enlarge himself to bear the most offices, the fewer shall he discharge."[92]

In sum, a good entry into a vocation necessitates (1) testing one's ability, and (2) receiving an endorsement from others. These serve to confirm God's "imposition" of a particular calling. This is the way to make a good choice and a good entry into a vocation.

A Proper Continuance

Perkins devotes a significant portion of his treatise to explain what it means to persevere in a personal calling. There are multiple trials and temptations that threaten to undermine what it means to serve God and others in a vocation. This, coupled with Perkins's conviction that our particular calling is a means of sanctification, accounts for the attention he gives to this subject. Mark Shaw affirms that "sanctification is ultimately worked out in the rough and tumble of daily work."[93] In brief, to continue well, believers must know (1) the works of their vocation, and (2) the way it is to be done.

Perkins says that a good work possesses three essential properties. First, a work must be associated with our particular calling. He believes that the Holy Spirit "teaches us to search for the proper works of our callings and then afterwards do them."[94] However, some barely perform their own works but due to "vain curiosity" venture into the works of other men.[95] Perkins urges such people to follow Paul's advice to "live in peace by doing his own business (1 Thess. 4:11)."[96] Second, it must profit the worker and the commonwealth. By "profit," Perkins means the work should contribute to people's basic needs. Conversely, works that lead to vanity or indulgence are unprofitable.[97] Third, it must be necessary.[98] There are two kinds of works: principal and less principal.

---

90. *Vocations*, 10:72.

91. *Man's Imagination*, 9:222; *How to Live Well*, 10:3.

92. *Vocations*, 10:72.

93. Mark R. Shaw, "The Marrow of Practical Divinity: A Study in the Theology of William Perkins" (PhD diss., Westminster Theological Seminary, 1981),

94. *Vocations*, 10:73.

95. *Vocations*, 10:73.

96. *Vocations*, 10:73.

97. *Vocations*, 10:74.

98. *Vocations*, 10:74–77. See also *Treatise Whether a Man*, 8:369–70; Marshall, *A Kind of Life*, 42–43.

It is important to prioritize those works that are the essence of the calling over those that are less important.[99]

As for the manner of performing good works, Perkins emphasizes holiness and constancy (or perseverance). Regarding the former, he affirms that a double sanctification is required—first for the worker and second for the work.[100] The "blind divinity of the world" claims it is sufficient to live peaceably, work diligently, and not to harm anyone, but this simply is not true.[101] Without God's work of regeneration, and our constant cleaving to Him through the power of the Holy Spirit (sanctification), even our best works deserve condemnation.[102] "The good thing done by a natural man (unregenerate) is a sin in respect of the doer because it fails, both for his right beginning—which is a pure heart, good conscience, and faith unfeigned—as also for his end, which is the glory of God."[103] For the work of our calling to be blessed, the worker must be sanctified (or saved).

In addition, the work (or action) must be sanctified.[104] By this, Perkins means that it (and the motivation behind it) must be lawful. He cites Luke 18:10, where the publican and the Pharisee enact the same lawful work—prayer. But the former does it in humility, while the latter does it in pride.[105] Because the Pharisee's action was motivated by pride, his work was unsanctified.

There are two ways in which a work is sanctified: Scripture and prayer.[106] Perkins believes that daily time in God's Word makes a person more "skillful in the works of his calling."[107] When we are ruled by Scripture in vocation, vices (such as injustice) are exposed and discouraged, while virtuous practices (done in faith and love) are prompted and perpetuated.[108] As for prayer, Perkins proposes that believers should pray "for ability and good success."[109] They should also offer prayers of thanksgiving.[110] Asking for the Father's blessing should precede all works. In short, Scripture and prayer sanctify the works of every calling.

---

99. *Vocations*, 10:75.

100. *Vocations*, 10:77–80.

101. *Vocations*, 10:79. See also *Commentary on Hebrews 11*, 3:33–34.

102. *Vocations*, 10:78–79. See also *Treatise Whether a Man*, 8:398–99.

103. *Reformed Catholic*, 7:19.

104. *Vocations*, 10:79.

105. *Vocations*, 10:79. See also *Exhortation to Repentance*, 9:93. Due to the Pharisee's inability to find any sin of which to repent, Perkins identifies him as a "superficial searcher."

106. *Vocations*, 10:80. See also *Sermon on the Mount*, 1:237–38; *Golden Chain*, 6:96–97.

107. *Exposition of Revelation 1–3*, 4:322. See also *Reformed Catholic*, 7:66.

108. *Vocations*, 10:80–93.

109. *Vocations*, 10:93. See also *Sermon on the Mount*, 1:501.

110. *Vocations*, 10:93.

Inasmuch as works should be done in holiness, they should also be done with perseverance. A good choice of, and a good entry in, a vocation is irrelevant if endurance is lacking. As soldiers remain faithful to their post, so believers should persevere in their calling (1 Cor. 7:20).[111] Perkins acknowledges three obstacles: ambition, envy, and impatience. He warns that Satan will take advantage of each: "If a man be impatient of poverty, he [Satan] will seek to carry him to picking and stealing; if a man be prone to covetousness, he [Satan] will provoke him to fraud and oppression; if he be inclined to ambition, Satan will puff him up with pride and vainglory."[112] These impediments can be remedied with sufficient compensation, vacations, and necessary changes.[113] Thus, to persevere, namely, we must know the works of our callings and perform them diligently.

A Respectful Exit

When it is necessary to leave a particular calling, two things must be observed.[114] The first concerns the timing and manner of the exit. Whether a civil or ecclesiastical vocation, one must seek God's will. By contrast, the "wills of men for the attainment of greater wealth, pleasure, and preferment" cannot be the impetus for resigning from a calling.[115] As a mark of Christian witness, one should "resign in and with the testimony of a good conscience, which is when our conscience bears witness that we have in the works of our callings kept ourselves unblameable, and have endeavored in all things to do the will of God."[116]

Good Works

The fact that "we are bound" to be faithful in the works of our particular callings "must teach us much more to be constant in the general duties of Christianity."[117] For this reason, it is within the context of our particular callings rather than by any other "accidental or collateral courses" that we are sanctified, that is, "little and little renewed in holiness and righteousness."[118] With so much at stake, Perkins is careful to explain the nature of good works and the manner in which they should be done.[119]

---

111. *Vocations*, 10:94.
112. *Combat between Christ and the Devil*, 1:107.
113. *Vocations*, 10:96–100.
114. *Vocations*, 10:101–7.
115. *Vocations*, 10:101.
116. *Vocations*, 10:103.
117. *Vocations*, 10:100.
118. *Calling of the Ministry*, 10:243. See also *Commentary on Galatians*, 2:293.
119. *Three Books on Cases of Conscience*, 8:151. For more on remaining within the compass of one's calling, see *Combat between Christ and the Devil*, 1:9; *Exposition of Revelation 1–3*,

As Perkins writes, "A good work, is a work commanded of God, and done by a man regenerate in faith, for the glory of God in man's good."[120] The essence of good works, therefore, extends well beyond those of the general calling—namely, "prayer, thanksgiving, receiving the sacraments, hearing the Word, contributing to the good estate of the church, relieving the poor, and walking worthy of our calling."[121] Perkins insists, "All kinds of callings and their works" are the matter of good works.[122] These works pertain to "indifferent" duties which are performed by faith, for God's glory, and are sanctified by the Word and prayer.[123] By "indifferent," Perkins is comparing the personal works in the believer's particular calling to those corporate works of the general calling that are "directly" commanded by God. He does not mean that "indifferent" works are irrelevant, but that they may apply to one believer and not to another.

Moreover, the nature of these indifferent works exists within the compass of our particular callings, which "the Holy Spirit teaches us that we must search what are the proper works of our own callings, and then afterwards do them."[124] Therefore, "we must learn, that every action of a man's lawful calling, done in

---

4:382–83, 511, 540; *Exposition of the Creed*, 5:391; *Treatise Whether a Man*, 8:369. See also Shaw, "The Marrow of Practical Divinity," 244; and Breward, "The Life and Theology," 279.

120. *Sermon on the Mount*, 1:233. Regarding the papists "who hold them [good works] necessary, as causes of our salvation and justification," and some Protestants, "who hold them necessary, though not as principal causes (for they say, we are only justified and saved by Christ), yet as conservant causes of our salvation," Perkins remarks, "that good works are necessary, not as causes of salvation, or justification, but as inseparable consequents of saving faith in Christ, whereby we are justified and saved." *Sermon on the Mount*, 1:239. For more on good works, see *Sermon on the Mount*, 1:233–42, 392–405. For the scholarship on this, see Joel R. Beeke, *The Quest for Full Assurance: The Legacy of Calvin and His Successors* (Edinburgh: Banner of Truth Trust, 1999), 79–81, 92–95; R. T. Kendall, "Living the Christian Life in the Teaching of William Perkins and His Followers," in *Living the Christian Life: 1974 Westminster Conference Papers (Reprint)* (Huntingdon, Cambs.: The Westminster Conference, 1974); Richard A. Muller, *Grace and Freedom: William Perkins and the Early Modern Reformed Understanding of Free Choice and Divine Grace* (New York: Oxford University Press, 2020), 51, 118, 123–24, 132–35, 152; David M. Barbee, "A Reformed Catholike: William Perkins' Use of the Church Fathers" (Philadelphia, University of Pennsylvania, 2013): 232.

121. *Sermon on the Mount*, 1:236–37; *Vocations*, 10:49–53.

122. *Three Books on Cases of Conscience*, 8:151. Perkins argues against the "popish church, which teaches that only alms-deeds and building or maintaining of churches and religious houses are the matter of good works." He declares, "For not only alms-deeds, and large gifts to churches, and highways, are good works, but also the special duties of every man's lawful calling, done in faith, to the glory of God, and the good of men, be the calling ever so base, by the doing whereof, in faith and obedience, he may get sure testimony of his election." *Sermon on the Mount*, 1:242.

123. *Sermon on the Mount*, 1:237–38; *Vocations*, 10:60.

124. *Vocations*, 10:73. Perkins references 1 Thessalonians 4:11 and 1 Peter 4:15.

obedience to God, for the good of men, is a good work before God."[125] It is the right use of every calling that makes its works "good."[126]

The end of such works "is threefold."[127] First, concerning God—good works serve to sanctify us, and they evince our reverence, obedience, and thankfulness to Him. "True thankfulness stands in obedience, and our obedience is shown by doing good works."[128] Second, concerning ourselves—good works testify to "our faith," confirm our position in Christ and "title to all His benefits," and make us "answerable to our holy calling" whereby we become recipients of the "sweet promises" that Scripture makes to those who obey.[129] Third, concerning others—good works "win some to Christ, encourage believers in the obedience of the truth, and prevent offences, whereby many are drawn back."[130]

Good works follow "saving faith in Christ," and they are "the way of Christ." This means that those who are in Christ necessarily follow His ways.[131] Perkins says, "For where the fire of grace is, there it cannot but burn; and where the water of life is, it cannot but flow and send out the streams thereof, in good works."[132] And so, every believer must emulate the "virtues of Him that has called him (1 Peter 2:9)."[133] As Perkins states, "Faith in the heart is a light, and works are the shining of the light (Matt. 5:16)."[134] To that end, we "must practice the duties of the general calling in the particular, so as though they are two distinct in nature, yet they may be both one in use and practice."[135] God's pur-

---

125. *Sermon on the Mount*, 1:238.

126. *Vocations*, 10:60.

127. *Sermon on the Mount*, 1:240. See also J. Stephen Yuille, *Living Blessedly Forever: The Sermon on the Mount and the Puritan Piety of William Perkins*, Kindle ed. (Grand Rapids: Reformation Heritage Books, 2012), chap. 4.

128. *Sermon on the Mount*, 1:240.

129. *Sermon on the Mount*, 1:241. Perkins states, "For faith and good works are the fruits and effects of God's election." *Exposition of the Creed*, 5:332. He adds, "The care and endeavor to do good works" is a proof of election, but this proof is not for "God (for it was sure unto Him before the foundation of the world), but for ourselves and for our neighbors." *Case of Conscience*, 8:633.

130. *Sermon on the Mount*, 1:241. Perkins contends, "For a papist doing a good work, according to the rules of their religion, does it to satisfy God's justice, for the temporal punishment of his sins, and to merit heaven by it, and so errs quite from the right end of a good work, respecting therein, his own good, and nothing at all the good of others." *Sermon on the Mount*, 1:237.

131. *Sermon on the Mount*, 1:239. Perkins repeatedly cites 2 Peter 1:10, "Give diligence to make your calling and election sure." He insists that the believer's effort begins with God's grace.

132. *Sermon on the Mount*, 1:240.

133. *Sermon on the Mount*, 1:241.

134. *Commentary on Galatians*, 2:48. "One of the chiefest uses of good works, that by them, not as by causes, but as by effects of predestination and faith, both we, and also our neighbors, are certified of our election, and of our salvation too." *Case of Conscience*, 8:633.

135. *Three Books on Cases of Conscience*, 8:149.

pose in saving us is realized through the unity of these two callings. Perkins is so convinced of this that he affirms that our degrees of glory will depend upon the "diverse measures of gifts and graces" God has given us and our employment of them for His glory and the building up of the church.[136]

Conclusion

Perkins is adamant that everyone will give an account of the works of his calling before God. "Few are truly persuaded of this last and great account, because it is deferred. But we ought to be of better resolution, and prepare ourselves for it."[137] People will give an account for their actions as they relate to the general calling, but they will also give an account for their actions as they relate to their particular calling. Everyone will be answerable to God, for in His "infinite knowledge and providence" He has recorded all our thoughts, words, and deeds (Matt. 25:20–21).[138]

For this reason, Perkins exhorts his reader to prepare. Believers do so by making good use of what God has entrusted to them, namely, their vocation. As a shop owner keeps meticulous records of expenses and revenues, believers should draw up bills of receipts and expenses as they relate to their particular calling. The receipts reflect the things they have enjoyed (e.g., graces, blessings, and gifts—both material and spiritual).[139] The bill of expenses reflects their sins. In this accounting process "we find that our reckonings will be far short of that which God requires."[140] For this reason, we ought to "shake off that spiritual drowsiness which possesses our minds."[141] "While the day of grace remains," we should strive toward new obedience in our callings, thereby preparing to make a good account before our God.[142]

---

136. *Exposition of the Creed*, 5:412.
137. *Vocations*, 10:103. See also *Sermon on the Mount*, 1:449.
138. *Vocations*, 10:104.
139. *Vocations*, 10:105.
140. *Vocations*, 10:105–6.
141. *Vocations*, 10:106. Richard Lovelace explains, "The problem that confronts the Puritans as they look out on their decaying society and their lukewarm church is not simply to dislodge the faithful from the slough of mortal or venial sin, but radically to awaken those who are professing but not actual Christians, who are caught in the trap of carnal security." Richard C. Lovelace, "The Anatomy of Puritan Piety: English Puritan Devotional Literature, 1600–1640," in *Christian Spirituality*, ed. Louis K. Dupré and Don E. Saliers, 3rd ed. (New York: Crossroad Publishing, 1989), 303.
142. *Vocations*, 10:107.

11

The One Flesh Principle

J. Stephen Yuille

The English Reformation was a lengthy process, in which the country moved back and forth on multiple occasions between Catholicism and Protestantism. In a span of twenty years, the official religion shifted four times as monarchs came and went. But the reign of Elizabeth provided stability, thereby enabling the English Reformers to solidify the church's position. William Perkins played a pivotal role in this.

Despite the marked progress in advancing the Reformation, Perkins was troubled by the spiritual condition within the Church of England. He was convinced that many of his fellow countrymen suffered the ill-effects of the Roman Catholic dogma of implicit faith; that is to say, most assumed that they were good Christians simply because they confessed some basic points of religion. Perkins was particularly burdened by the prevalence of "civility" within the professing church. "If we look into the general state of our people," says he, "we shall see that religion is professed, but not obeyed: nay, obedience is counted as preciseness, and so reproached."[1] Prayer Book services, coupled with homilies and catechisms, introduced Reformation teaching to the people; however, most were content with minimal religious observance.

This lack of devotion was one of the main reasons why Perkins was not so concerned about the external forms of the Church of England. Instead of expending his energy on issues related to church polity, he was determined to address what he perceived to be widespread ignorance within the church. He was adamant that the church's most pressing need was not for ecclesiastical

---

1. *Sermon on the Mount*, 1:727. As R. C. Lovelace explains, "The problem that confronts the Puritans as they look out on their decaying society and their lukewarm church is not simply to dislodge the faithful from the slough of mortal or venial sin, but radically to awaken those who are professing but not actual Christians, who are caught in a trap of carnal security." "The Anatomy of Puritan Piety: English Puritan Devotional Literature, 1600–1640," in *Christian Spirituality*, vol. 3, World Spirituality, ed. Louis Dupré and Don E. Saliers (New York: Crossroad Publishing, 1989), 303.

innovation, but practical theological instruction. Perkins devoted his entire ministry to addressing this need. It shaped his preaching, lecturing, and writing. It informed his engagement in theological controversy. It fueled his commitment to training young men in the fundamentals of pastoral ministry.[2] And it caused him to champion the home as the chief means for cultivating and propagating his practical theology. Simply put, he recognized that the way to reform the church, transform the town, and alter the course of the country, was to spiritualize the home.[3]

Perkins articulates his convictions in *Christian Oeconomie; or, A Short Survey of the Right Manner of Erecting and Ordering a Family, according to the Scriptures.*[4] Having declared that "the only rule of ordering the family is the

---

2. For more on this, see J. Stephen Yuille, "'A Simple Method': William Perkins and the Shaping of the Protestant Pulpit," *Puritan Reformed Journal* 9, no. 1 (2017): 215–30.

3. *Right Manner*, 10:124. George Swinnock agrees: "The way to make godly parishes, and godly countries, and godly kingdoms is to make godly families." *The Works of George Swinnock* (1868; repr., Edinburgh: Banner of Truth, 1992), 1:330. By the end of the sixteenth century, there was a considerable body of literature about managing a household. By way of examples, see Richard Greenham, *A Godly Exhortation and Faithful Admonition to Virtuous Parents and Modern Matrons* (London, 1584); Henry Smith, *A Preparative to Marriage,* (London, 1591); and John Dod and Robert Cleaver, *A Godly Form of Household Government* (London, 1598). The historian, Christopher Hill, first wrote of the "spiritualization" of the Puritan household in 1964. Christopher Hill, *Society and Puritanism in Pre-Revolutionary England* (1964; repr., London: Panther Books, 1969), 429–66. As a Marxist, he was primarily interested in demonstrating how such a household served as the breeding ground for economic individualism and, therefore, the advent of capitalist values and practices. Whether employing Hill's exact phraseology or not, others have posited different theories as to the historical and sociological significance of the spiritual household. The German scholar of English literature, Levin Schucking, viewed it as the catalyst for the development of the close conjugal family, owing to its repudiation of celibacy and its celebration of intimacy. Levin Schucking, *The Puritan Family: A Social Study from Literary Sources* (London: Routledge & Kegan Paul, 1969). For a similar thesis, see Edmund Morgan, *The Puritan Family: Religion and Domestic Relations in Seventeenth-Century New England* (New York: Harper & Row, 1956). Predictably, the feminist historian, Lyndal Roper, decried the spiritual household as responsible for reinforcing repressive patriarchal structures and subjecting children to harmful indoctrination. Lyndal Roper, *The Holy Household: Women and Morals in Reformation Augsburg* (Oxford: Clarendon Press, 1991). More recently, the church historian, Alexandra Walsham, revisited the spiritual household, theorizing that it functioned at times as a support for the political and ecclesiastical establishment, and at other times as an impetus for clandestine resistance to authority. Alexandra Walsham, "Holy Families: The Spiritualization of the Early Modern Household Revisited," in *Religion and the Household* (Rochester: Boydell Press, 2014), 122–60.

4. For the full treatise, see *Right Manner*, 10:109–94. The title page indicates that Perkins first penned it in Latin, though it is noteworthy that he gave related lectures in English during the last few years of his life. The treatise was translated into English by Thomas Pickering. The original Latin MS is no longer extant, and it is unknown how Pickering came into possession of it.

written Word of God,"[5] he proceeds in eighteen chapters to expound what the Word says about marriage contracts, marital duties, the roles of husbands, wives, parents, children, and servants.[6] His desire is that "rightly ordered" families might become "little churches, yea even a kind of paradise upon earth."[7]

Central to Perkins's "spiritualization" of the household stands Genesis 2:24, "Therefore shall a man leave his father and his mother, and shall cleave unto his wife: and they shall be one flesh."[8] The man and woman "cleave" to one another, says Perkins, "as two boards are joined together with glue."[9] The nature of this conjunction is emotional, spiritual, and physical,[10] and its manner is "excellent" for it was God Himself who "joined" the first man and woman.[11] This *one flesh principle* is, for Perkins, the very essence of marriage—"the lawful conjunction…of one man and one woman into one flesh."[12]

---

5. *Right Manner*, 10:119. Perkins's definition of "oeconomie" is derived from Proverbs 24:3, "Through wisdom is an house builded; and by understanding it is established" "They went to Genesis for its institution, to Ephesians for its full meaning, to Leviticus for its hygiene, to Proverbs for its management, to several New Testament books for its ethic, and to Esther, Ruth and the Song of Songs for illustrations and exhibitions of the ideal." Packer, *A Quest for Godliness*, 263. Perkins pours over the written Word for any text that might shed light on God's will for the family. Perkins's treatise is saturated with Scripture references and inferences. Expectedly, he turns repeatedly to Genesis 1–2, Proverbs 31, 1 Corinthians 7, Ephesians 5–6, Colossians 3–4, 1 Timothy 3–4, and 1 Peter 3. He lives in the world of the patriarchs, the kings of Israel, and the New Testament saints, gleaning examples both to be shunned and emulated. In short, Perkins's right ordering of the family is the outworking of his biblical theology.

6. For an analysis of this treatise, see J. Stephen Yuille, "A Puritan, Spiritual Household: William Perkins and the 'Right Ordering' of a Family," *Puritan Reformed Journal* 8, no. 2 (2016): 158–79.

7. *Right Manner*, 10:122.

8. Perkins preached a series of sermons on Genesis 2:18–24. Eleven of them are preserved in the North Yorkshire County Record Office, Hutton of Marske family archive—Papers of Archbishop Matthew Hutton, MS ZAZ 75. These sermons are available in Matthew N. Payne and J. Stephen Yuille, *The Labors of a Godly and Learned Divine, William Perkins: Including Previously Unpublished Sermons* (Grand Rapids: Reformation Heritage Books, forthcoming 2022).

9. *Right Manner*, 10:123.

10. *Right Manner*, 10:156.

11. *Right Manner*, 10:123.

12. *Right Manner*, 10:123. Perkins cites Genesis 2:21, Matthew 19:6, and Ephesians 5:31. For significant Puritan works on marriage, see Richard Baxter, *A Christian Directory* (1673), in *The Practical Works of Richard Baxter* (London: George Virtue, 1846; repr., Morgan: Soli Deo Gloria, 2000), 1:394–449; William Gouge, *Of Domestical Duties: Eight Treatises* (London, 1622); and George Swinnock, *The Christian Man's Calling; or, A treatise of making religion ones business* (1661–1665), in *The Works of George Swinnock*, ed. James Nichol (London, 1868; repr., Edinburgh: Banner of Truth, 1992), vols. 1–3. For an overview of secondary sources related to Puritan views on marriage, see Joel R. Beeke and Paul Smalley, "Puritans on the Family: Recent Publications," *Puritan Reformed Journal* 10, no. 2 (2018): 227–44.

Of note, Perkins emphasizes that this "conjunction" is "an eternal law."[13] In his exposition of the debate between Christ and the Jews over the meaning of Moses's "bill of divorcement" (Matt. 19:3–12; Deut. 24:1–4), Perkins distinguishes between "civil" (or "politic") laws and "moral" (or "natural") laws.[14] The first are "for the good ordering of the commonwealth." At times, such laws "permit" an evil that cannot be avoided as a means of preventing "a greater evil."[15] Christ places Moses's "bill of divorcement" in this category and contrasts it with the moral law (or "the law of nature") concerning marriage as found in Genesis 2:24. In other words, the purpose of Moses's legislation was to control a problem that was out of hand. In making this concession, he did not intend to imply that God had abrogated His commandment concerning marriage. Moses simply introduced temporary legislation because of the prevailing conditions—the hardness of people's hearts (Matt. 19:3–12). As Perkins explains, God does not approve "of the giving a bill of divorce for every light cause," but tolerates "it for the preventing of greater mischief."[16] In Perkins's estimation, therefore, the "indivisible conjunction of one man and one woman only" is an eternal law, meaning it is always applicable to all people in all places.[17]

As such, it necessarily prohibits polygamy, for the "indivisible conjunction" can only exist between "two (and not three or four)."[18] It also prohibits homosexuality, for the "indivisible conjunction" requires "the distinction of the sex, which is either male or female."[19] Furthermore, it prohibits adultery, for the "indivisible conjunction" magnifies the marriage bed as "that solitary and secret society that is between man and wife alone."[20]

For Perkins, this eternal law (i.e., the one flesh principle) is important, not only for what it prohibits, but for what it promotes. In a word, it determines how the marriage relationship is to be viewed and valued. A concept of marriage, informed by the one flesh principle, prevents it from becoming a self-serving convenience or inconvenience, and elevates it as one of the most sacred callings the world has ever known. This conviction is front and center in Perkins's thinking, and it is on full display in what he has to say concerning marital "duties," "roles," and "ends."

---

13. *Right Manner*, 10:123.

14. For Perkins's view on divorce, see *Sermon on the Mount*, 1:316–23.

15. *Sermon on the Mount*, 1:316.

16. *Sermon on the Mount*, 1:317.

17. *Commentary on Galatians*, 2:298.

18. *Right Manner*, 10:123. For more on Perkins's view on polygamy (particularly his handling of Abraham's sin), see *Commentary on Galatians*, 2:298–300.

19. *Right Manner*, 10:130.

20. *Right Manner*, 10:166. For more on Perkins's view on adultery, see *Golden Chain*, 6:125–32.

Marital Duties

To begin with, the one flesh principle (i.e., "the lawful conjunction…of one man and one woman into one flesh") implies specific marital duties. Perkins identifies two. The first is "cohabitation." Because the husband and wife are one flesh, they enjoy the "quiet and comfortable dwelling together in one place."[21] This is an important duty, especially in the early stages of a marriage, as it gives the man and woman time to know "one another's conditions" and to cultivate "a settled affection one toward another."[22]

The second duty is "communion." Because the husband and wife are one flesh, they share "their persons and goods" for "their mutual help, necessity, and comfort."[23] A significant part of this communion is "the performance of special benevolence" in cherishing one another. "This cherishing," writes Perkins, "is the performing of any duties that tend to the preserving of the lives one of another. Wherefore they are freely to communicate their goods, their counsel, their labors, each to the other, for the good of themselves and theirs."[24] This special benevolence is also performed by rejoicing in one another. According to Perkins, the husband and wife delight in each other by a "mutual declaration of the signs and tokens of love and kindness."[25]

Essential to the "communion" between husband and wife is "the right and lawful use" of "the marriage bed."[26] Perkins grounds his positive view of the marriage bed on the creation narrative. As he surveys Genesis 1–2, he makes five observations.[27] (1) God "ordained" marriage "above and before all other states of life."[28] By this, Perkins means that marriage is God's intended design

---

21. *Right Manner*, 10:161. Perkins cites Deuteronomy 24:5, 1 Corinthians 7:10–13, and 1 Peter 3:7.

22. *Right Manner*, 10:161.

23. *Right Manner*, 10:166. Perkins cites Ephesians 5:28.

24. *Right Manner*, 10:170.

25. *Right Manner*, 10:170. Perkins cites Genesis 26:8, Proverbs 5:18–19, Canticles 1:1, and Isaiah 62:7. Without any explanatory word, he adds, "This rejoicing and delight is more permitted to the man than to the woman, and them both more in their young years than in their old age."

26. *Right Manner*, 10:166. Max Weber (among others) is responsible for promoting the stereotype of the Puritan marriage as somber and joyless. Max Weber, *The Protestant Ethic and the Spirit of Capitalism*, trans. Talcott Parsons, 2nd ed. (London: George Allen & Unwin, 1976), 118–19. For a more comprehensive (and accurate) analysis, see Joel R. Beeke and Paul Smalley, "Puritans on Marital Love," *Puritan Reformed Journal* 12, no. 1 (2020): 155–67.

27. *Right Manner*, 10:123–24.

28. "Marriage of itself," writes Perkins, "is a thing indifferent, and the kingdom of God stands no more in it than in meats and drinks." He also says that the "coming together of man and wife…is indifferent." *Right Manner*, 10:123, 167. For Perkins's convictions regarding "indifferent" things (*adiaphora*), and how they shape his view of marriage, see Seth Osbourne, "'Is Marriage Truly Open to All?': The Diverging Perspectives of Puritan Casuistry on the Christian's Freedom to Marry," *Puritan Reformed Journal* 8, no. 1 (2016): 84–109.

for men and women. Singleness, while laudable in the case of those who are called to it, only exists because of the fall.[29] (2) God triune instituted marriage "upon a most serious and solemn consultation among the three persons." The inference is that the triune God intended for this family (Adam and Eve) to be the context in which they would enjoy the kind of relationship enjoyed within the Trinity. That is why the expression, "they became one flesh," is so crucial. It highlights an experience of "diversity in unity" which is exclusive to the domain of marriage. (3) God joined Adam and Eve "together immediately," thereby indicating that "the manner of this conjunction" is "excellent." God's intention was (and is) that a husband and wife should delight in each other. This mutual delight is emotional, meaning they enjoy the support, comfort, and encouragement that a God-centered marriage provides. This mutual delight is also physical, meaning they enjoy the conjugal relationship—one of the most proper and essential acts of marriage. (4) God blessed the institution of marriage. God brought Eve to Adam. In effect, God gave them to each other. This necessarily implies that marriage is a divine gift. God created it, designed it, instituted it, and blessed it. (5) God appointed marriage "to be the fountain and seminary of all other sorts and kinds of life in the commonwealth and in the church."

What is interesting in these five observations is that the blessedness of marriage does not depend on its procreative purpose (although Perkins does acknowledge the importance of this elsewhere). Of primary importance, for Perkins, is that God instituted marriage, prior to the fall, as a manifestation of His goodness toward Adam and Eve. This necessarily means that the marriage bed ("the lawful conjunction…of one man and one woman into one flesh") is good.[30]

Given his positive view of the marriage bed, Perkins denounces those who view it as a sin.[31] He criticizes the Church of Rome for prohibiting "certain

---

29. *Right Manner*, 10:123. Perkins acknowledges that the "gift of continency" is in many respects better than marriage, "yet not simply, but by accident, in regard of sundry calamities which came into the world by sin." See 1 Corinthians 7:25–35.

30. For an overview of Puritan views of sexuality, see Daniel Doriani, "The Puritans, Sex, and Pleasure," *Westminster Theological Journal* 53 (1991): 125–43; and Roland Frye, "The Teachings of Classical Puritanism on Conjugal Love," *Studies in the Renaissance* 2 (1955): 149–55. For the common charge of Puritan prudery, see Lyle Koehler, *A Search for Power* (Urbana: University of Illinois Press, 1980), 10; and Lawrence Stone, *The Family, Sex and Marriage in England, 1500–1800* (New York: Harper & Row, 1977), 499, 523. For the opposite view, see Leland Ryken, *Worldly Saints: The Puritans as They Really Were* (Grand Rapids: Zondervan, 1986), 43–45.

31. The view that celibacy is a means to spirituality entered the church at an early date. Beginning in the second century, many allowed dualistic philosophies to influence their beliefs regarding sex (e.g., Gnosticism and Manichaeism). They held that lust taints all sexual activity and, therefore, affirmed that virginity is superior to marriage. From this premise, the church of the Middle Ages acknowledged two reasons for marriage: the procreation of children and

parties" from marrying because "they think this secret coming together of man and wife to be filthiness."[32] Perkins makes specific mention of Syricius (334–399), "that filthy pope of Rome, who determined that marriage was the uncleanness of the flesh, and to that purpose abused the words of the apostle (Rom. 8:8), affirming that they which are in the flesh, that is, in the state of matrimony, 'cannot please God.'"[33]

In his treatment of this subject, Perkins demonstrates no antipathy toward the physical body.[34] God's material gifts (including the marriage bed) are expressions of His kindness and are, therefore, intended for our enjoyment.[35] The fact that God created Adam and Eve, declared that they should not be alone, and brought them together (all prior to the fall), is sufficient evidence that the marriage bed is good. Perkins, therefore, has no problem with this "natural" delight. "We may use these gifts of God," says he, "not sparingly alone, and for mere necessity…but also freely and liberally, for Christian delight and pleasure. For this is that liberty, which God hath granted to all believers."[36] The way to holiness, therefore, is not found in abstaining from God's good gifts, but in enjoying them, echoing Paul's words: "Whether therefore ye eat, or drink, or whatsoever ye do, do all to the glory of God" (1 Cor. 10:31).[37]

---

the avoidance of fornication. These notions remained entrenched within the church until the Reformers departed from the accepted tradition by adding a third reason for marriage, namely, mutual society.

32. *Right Manner*, 10:166. For more on Perkins's critique of Rome as it relates to marriage, see *Problem of the Forged Catholicism*, 7:355–67.

33. *Right Manner*, 10:166. Swinnock makes the same observation in *Works*, 1:467.

34. Daniel Doriani argues that the Puritans never really freed themselves from their forefathers' dualistic tendencies. He writes, "The Puritans […] formulated so many warnings and restrictions that their protestations of the goodness and purity of sexuality lost their force." They maintain that marriage and sex are pure, that God requires couples to communicate their bodies to each other, and that sexual relations have beneficial products. However, he believes they fail to rid themselves of "the Greek and Roman Catholic idea that lust taints the procreative act so that it is shameful." "The Puritans, Sex, and Pleasure," 133.

35. There is nothing wrong with strong "desire" and "delight." As Edmund Leites remarks, "an outward fulfillment of the duties of marriage was not enough; the proper intentions and feelings toward your spouse must also exist." "The Duty to Desire: Love, Friendship, and Sexuality in Some Puritan Theories of Marriage," *Journal of Social History* 15, no. 3 (1982): 383. God's good gifts must be received with thanksgiving (1 Tim. 4:3–4). Because of sin, we can easily abuse food, drink, recreation, sleep, sex, etc. Thanksgiving prevents such abuse. We use God's gifts *sacredly*: we acknowledge that they come from God. We use them *soberly*: we do not make an idol of earthly delights. We use them *sensibly*: we do not make them more important than the soul.

36. *Three Books on Cases of Conscience*, 8:339.

37. The issue is not natural delights, but the abuse of natural delights, whereby we seek satisfaction in them apart from God. Speaking of the Puritans in general, Frye observes that "their fear was of an immoderate love, whose very violence precluded it from maintaining the stability necessary for the marriage relationship, and whose intensity of attachment was likely

For Perkins, the "coming together" of husband and wife is made "a holy and undefiled action" by means of God's Word and prayer (1 Tim. 4:3–5).[38] God's Word gives "warrant that [husband and wife] may lawfully do this action" and it prescribes "the right and holy manner of doing the same." This "holy manner" consists of two particulars. First, it must be done "in moderation." Perkins warns that "intemperance" (or "immoderate desire") is no different than fornication. Second, it must be done "in a holy abstinence," meaning the "coming together" of husband and wife is to be avoided when "a woman is in her flowers."[39] It is also to be avoided when "a solemn fast" has been instituted on account of some impending calamity.[40]

When a husband and wife commit their marriage bed to such a "holy usage," they can expect to enjoy its "fruits." Perkins identifies three.[41] The first is the possession of "a blessed seed." The second is "the preservation of the body in cleanness, that it may be a fit temple for the Holy Spirit to dwell in." The third is the representation of "a lively type of Christ and His church" whereby the "communion" of husband and wife serves as "a figure of the conjunction that is between Him and the faithful."[42] And it is this that infuses the marital relationship with inestimable worth and dignity.

Marital Roles

The one flesh principle (i.e., "the lawful conjunction…of one man and one woman into one flesh") also implies specific marital roles. Married persons are "either husband or wife," writes Perkins. Because they are "but one flesh," there is but one head—the husband.[43] As such, he has certain responsibilities to fulfill.[44] First and foremost, he is to love his wife, which includes "protecting her from danger" and "providing maintenance for her."[45] Second, he is to honor his

---

to burn itself out and die." "The Teachings of Classical Puritanism," 156. From his analysis of the primary literature, Leites concludes, "This sensuous love is not simply permitted, given the existence of a higher, holier, 'spiritual' relation between man and wife, nor is it allowed only to forward the other purposes of marriage. It is required as a constituent and intrinsic element of a good marriage. This sensual affection and delight must continue unabated, with the full intensity of youthful desire throughout the whole of married life." "The Duty to Desire," 388.

38. *Right Manner*, 10:167.

39. Perkins cites Leviticus 18:19 and Ezekiel 18:6.

40. Perkins cites 1 Corinthians 7:5.

41. *Right Manner*, 10:168.

42. Perkins cites Hosea 2:19 and Ephesians 5:23.

43. *Right Manner*, 10:170.

44. For more on a husband's duties, see Swinnock, *Works*, 1:489–500; and Gouge, *Domesticall Duties*, 349–426.

45. *Right Manner*, 10:170. Perkins cites Ephesians 5:33.

wife.[46] He does so by "making account of her as his companion."[47] God took Eve from Adam's side, "to the end that man should take her as his mate." He also honors her by patiently bearing her infirmities and receiving counsel and correction from her.[48]

For the performance of this role, Perkins believes four special "graces" are required.[49] The first is knowledge. This includes (in order of importance) knowledge of God, himself, his wife, and what it means to lead his wife. Perkins notes that this knowledge is so "necessary" that those who have not learned it, and are unmarried, are "unfit to marry." As for those who are married, they should "seek to learn" these things. The second grace is justice. In short, a husband must not commit any wrong toward his wife. The third grace is godliness. This means "he must sanctify his government with faith, which makes his government not only acceptable to his wife and others but makes [it] acceptable to God." The fourth grace is love. Perkins says the husband must lead in "meekness and gentleness." The reason for this is the one flesh principle: "it is his own flesh that he must govern, and therefore he must govern it in love."

The husband (the head) is to exercise leadership marked by the four special "graces" outlined above, while the wife is "to submit herself to her husband."[50] Moreover, she is "to be obedient unto her husband in all things."[51] Obviously, such a view is not without its detractors, but it is important to appreciate Perkins's full vision. Because of the one flesh principle, the husband and wife are "one by nature." This has three implications.[52] First, "they ought to agree together without any dissension or discord." Second, "they ought to have one

---

46. *Right Manner*, 10:170. Perkins cites 1 Peter 3:7.

47. *Right Manner*, 10:172. In this context, Perkins gives a practical example of the "one flesh" principle in action. He asks, "Whether the husband may correct his wife?" Having dismissed such a notion as contrary to Scripture, he affirms, "He may not chastise her either with stripes or strokes. The reason is plain: wives are their husbands' mates, and they two be one flesh. And no man will hate, much less beat his own flesh, but 'nourisheth and cherisheth it' (Eph. 5:29)." *Right Manner*, 10:172. See Swinnock, *Works*, 1:491; and Gouge, *Of Domesticall Duties*, 389–90.

48. *Right Manner*, 10:172. Perkins cites 1 Peter 3:7.

49. Sermon 10 (Gen. 2:24), 81–86 in Hutton MS. See n. 8.

50. *Right Manner*, 10:174–75. For Swinnock on a wife's duties, see *Works*, 1:504–11. Many argue that subjection necessarily implies a low view of women. There is no doubt that some Puritans view women as intrinsically inferior; however, this attitude is difficult to detect in Perkins, for whom subjection is no gauge of worth. He believes there are God-ordained roles in the marriage relationship. For the husband, this means he must love his wife as Christ loves the church. For the wife, this means she must submit to her husband as the church submits to Christ.

51. *Right Manner*, 10:175. Perkins cites 1 Peter 3:6. It is not difficult to see how quickly the principle of governance and obedience can become determinative in a marital relationship, especially if divorced from the "one flesh" principle. Likewise, it is relatively easy to infer (intended or not) intrinsic male superiority from some of Perkins's remarks.

52. Sermon 6 (Gen. 2:23–24), 60–66 in Hutton MS. See n. 8.

and the same affection toward the other." Third, they ought to "maintain" the "perfection" in "the union of two." It is for this reason that the husband must "cleave unto his wife"; that is, "love her so well that he shall prefer [her] above all others, because she is bone of his bone, and flesh of his flesh."

The exercise of headship in the home, therefore, is never an end itself but a means to an end. It exists so that life can flourish. Such authority functions within the one flesh principle, meaning it is based on self-giving, not self-serving. Such authority functions within the parameters of God's Word; thus, it is never arbitrary. Moreover, such authority functions within the context of mutuality—acting together, deciding together, working together, living together, etc. Its goal is to promote the relationship between husband and wife in which love is expressed in selflessness. In Perkins's estimation, when husbands and wives fulfill their roles within such a framework, the home becomes "a kind of paradise upon earth."[53]

Marital Ends

Closely related to marital roles are marital "ends." Perkins identifies four. The first is "the procreation of children," which ensures "the seed and posterity of man upon the earth." The second is "the protection of a holy seed," which ensures that "there may always be a holy company of men that may worship and serve God in the church from age to age." The third is the avoidance of "fornication." But this "end" has only existed since "the fall of mankind." In other words, the need to avoid fornication only exists because sin exists. The fourth is the fulfillment of personal callings. Marriage enables the "parties" to perform "the duties of their calling in a better and more comfortable manner."[54]

What is interesting is that Perkins's list is a slight (yet significant) modification of the Prayer Book (1559), which outlines "the causes for which matrimony was ordained" as (1) "the procreation of children, to be brought up in the fear and nurture of the Lord, and praise of God"; (2) "a remedy against sin and to avoid fornication, that such persons as have not the gift of continence might marry, and keep themselves undefiled members of Christ's body"; and (3) "the mutual society, help, and comfort, that the one ought to have of the other, both in prosperity and adversity."

Perkins essentially follows the wording of the Prayer Book, except he intentionally divides the first "end" into two, indicating that "the procreation of children" is both for the sake of humanity (i.e., "the seed and posterity of man upon the earth") and the church (i.e., "there may always be a holy company of

---

53. *Right Manner*, 10:122.
54. *Right Manner*, 10:124–25.

men that may worship and serve God in the church from age to age"). Here, Perkins isolates and amplifies this principal end in marriage, namely, the raising of children for the glory of God.

Children are, in Perkins's estimation, "the gift of God."[55] As one flesh, the husband and wife are charged with ensuring that their children "live" and "live well."[56] That is to say, they are responsible for their children's physical and spiritual well-being. Care for their physical well-being entails providing them with food and clothing, saving for their "future maintenance," and establishing them in "some honest calling and course of life" according to their "natural gifts of body and mind."[57] It also includes providing suitable "matches" for them to marry.[58] In this regard, says Perkins, "the parents ought to have a greater respect unto piety and wisdom than unto beauty or riches."[59]

As for their spiritual well-being, parents are "to sow the seeds of godliness and religion in the heart of the child, so soon as it comes to the use of reason and understanding; and as it grows in years, so care must be had that it grows in knowledge and grace."[60] This means that parents exercise authority over their children in raising them according to the tenets of God's Word. This is chiefly done by establishing "the private worship and service of God" in the home.[61] According to Perkins, family worship consists of two "parts." The first is "conferencing" upon God's Word for the "edification" of all the members of the family.[62] The second is calling upon "the name of God with giving of thanks."[63] These are to be done in the morning and evening and after meals. When this is

---

55. *Right Manner*, 10:167. Perkins cites Genesis 25:21, 1 Samuel 1:26–27, Psalms 113:9 and 127:3. In all this, Perkins strongly opposes a disembodied spirituality. The monastic ideal was that sinful nature must be subdued within the secluded environment of a monastery with a well-ordered regime for soul and body. In marked contrast, Perkins believes that godliness encompasses all of life; that is, everything is spiritual. Moreover, he believes there is a far better school for godliness than monastic isolationism—namely, the family, where we see our sinfulness and learn how to grow in Christlikeness.

56. *Right Manner*, 10:176. For Swinnock on parents, see *Works*, 1:395–416. For Gouge, see *Domesticall Duties*, 497–588.

57. *Right Manner*, 10:177.

58. *Right Manner*, 10:179.

59. *Right Manner*, 10:180.

60. *Right Manner*, 10:178. Perkins adds an interesting comment regarding the importance of so ordering children's religious learning that they "take it with delight." To this end, they should be allowed to "play and solace themselves in recreations fitting for their years."

61. *Right Manner*, 10:120.

62. *Right Manner*, 10:121.

63. *Right Manner*, 10:121.

faithfully followed, families become "little churches."[64] But when it is neglected, they are "no better than companies of profane and graceless atheists."[65]

Given the one flesh principle, Perkins looked to the "head" (the husband and father) as God's appointed instrument for effecting religious change in the home. It is his responsibility to ensure that the members of his household are devoted to the worship of God.[66] Perkins writes, "Governors of families must teach their children, and servants, and their whole household the doctrine of true religion, that they may know the true God, and walk in all his ways in doing righteousness and judgment.... But whereas they neglect their duty, falsely persuading themselves that it does not belong to them at all to instruct others, it is the cause of ignorance both in towns and families."[67]

Marital Cases

Perkins recognized that the one flesh principle entails the "conjunction" of two sinners and, therefore, the likelihood of marital problems.[68] Aware of this, he addressed a host of "cases"—perplexing situations, many of which he undoubtedly faced as a pastor. What happens if a young woman is unwilling to marry a man to whom she is engaged? What happens if a young man enters an engagement in a "furious and frantic" condition, and subsequently changes his mind? What happens if someone's prospective spouse becomes incapacitated? How

---

64. *Right Manner*, 10:122. For more on Perkins's views on "household service," see *Warning against Idolatry*, 7:509–12.

65. *Right Manner*, 10:122.

66. For examples of family devotional works, see Edward Dering, *Godly Private Prayers, for householders to meditate upon, and to say in their families*, 1578; John Parker, *A True Pattern of Piety, meet for all Christian householders to look upon, for the better education of their families*, 1592; Richard Jones, *A Brief and Necessary Catechism, for the benefit of all householders, their children and families*, 1583.

67. *Exposition of the Creed*, 5:105–6. The historian, Margo Todd, has challenged any notion of a Puritan spiritual household, arising from Protestant theology, arguing that the exaltation of marriage, the creation of the family church, the rise of religious education, the practice of disciplinary duties, and the recognition of spiritual equality emerged from "classical ideas transmitted to the Puritans by humanism." Margo Todd, "Humanists, Puritans and the Spiritualized Household," *Church History* 49, no. 4 (1980): 18. Kathleen Davies also disputes the suggestion that Puritanism represents "a very different and more elevated view of family life from that presented in pre-Reformation or early Protestant views of marriage." "The Sacred Condition of Equality—How Original Were Puritan Doctrines of Marriage?" *Social History* 2, no. 5 (1977): 563. For the opposite view, see Roland Frye, "The Teachings of Classical Puritanism on Conjugal Love," *Studies in the Renaissance* 2 (1955): 149–55.

68. Perkins's realism is a missing element from many of the funeral sermons and biographical accounts of his period, which tend to embellish domestic bliss while ignoring the messier aspects of family life. This is likely the result of apologetic intention. But Perkins provides a necessary reality check.

should a spouse handle a prolonged absence that is "prejudicial" to the marriage? When is it permissible to dissolve a marriage? What should one do in the case of abandonment? What should one in the case of abuse? What happens if a spouse requires something "intolerable" of the other? What happens if a spouse is unfaithful?[69]

In his handling of these cases, Perkins seeks to apply Scripture to broken people in broken relationships. Without going into the specifics, it is worth nothing that the one flesh principle looms large is in his application of biblical wisdom. It heightens the gravity of marital sins such as abuse, adultery, and desertion, while at the same time providing the only hope for change and reconciliation.

This emphasis is evident in Perkins's treatment of divorce. On the one hand, the one flesh principle means that divorce is forbidden. Marriage is an exclusive ("a man shall leave his father and his mother"), permanent ("shall cleave to his wife"), and God-instituted ("they shall become one flesh") covenant. On the other hand, the one flesh principle means that divorce is permissible in the case of "fornication."[70]

Conclusion

One of the principal strains upon marriage in our day is the Epicurean worldview, which ultimately posits no reality outside of the natural order. Faithfulness in marriage, therefore, is simply the result of personal and economic factors. Furthermore, marriage is merely a provisional convenience to be dissolved whenever one of the parties decides it is no longer in their interest. In sharp contrast, Perkins champions a lofty view of marriage rooted in the one flesh principle.

---

69. *Right Manner*, 10:148–54, 162–65.

70. Perkins acknowledges that there are those who disagree. For six objections and responses, see *Sermon on the Mount*, 1:322–23.

12

Reforging the Great Chain of Being:
Ramism Reconsidered

Simon Burton

Since Perry Miller's classic work, *The New England Mind*, the connection between Puritanism and Ramism has been the topic of considerable debate. For Miller, the alliance between Puritanism and Ramism manifested on both the philosophical and theological plane. In particular, he argued that Ramism— the system of logic developed by the sixteenth-century Huguenot philosopher Petrus Ramus—offered both English and American Puritans an exemplaristic[1] vision of the arts and sciences as grounded in the mind of God. It thus cohered closely with their desire to institute a scriptural reformation of all of knowledge. Indeed, Miller insightfully drew a direct link between Ramism and the Realism and Platonism of the thirteenth century.[2] While Miller's own work was swiftly eclipsed by that of his student Walter Ong, whose own assessment of Ramism was much more negative,[3] recent scholarship has begun to recover Miller's vision. In these terms Ramism must be understood as a Renaissance topical logic in which the systematic and methodical ordering of thought is intended to directly reflect reality.[4]

For Donald McKim precisely the same is true of William Perkins's Ramism. McKim's own work offers the most comprehensive study of Perkins's Ramism to date, charting its influence across his whole corpus and tracing its implications for his philosophy, theology, casuistry, art of memory, and

---

1. Exemplarism: the doctrine that divine ideas are the metaphysical basis of created realities and of their knowability to creatures.

2. Perry Miller, *The New England Mind: The Seventeenth Century* (Cambridge, Mass.: Harvard University Press, 1982), 64–153.

3. Walter J. Ong, SJ, *Ramus, Method, and the Decay of Dialogue: From the Art of Discourse to the Art of Reason* (Chicago: University of Chicago Press, 2004).

4. See especially Kent Emery, introduction to *Renaissance Dialectic and Renaissance Piety: Benet of Canfield's Rule of Perfection* (Binghamton, N.Y.: Medieval and Renaissance Texts and Studies, 1987), 26–44; and Grazia Tonelli Olivieri, "Ideale Lulliano e Dialettica Ramista: Le 'Dialecticae Institutiones' del 1543," *Annali della Scuola Normale Superiore di Pisa* 22:3 (1992): 885–929.

sermonizing.[5] McKim argues that one of the chief attractions of Ramism to Perkins was that it laid "bare the very mind of God Himself."[6] Like Miller, he therefore links Perkins squarely into the realist tradition, and sees him as anticipating the *Technometria* of William Ames.[7] Yet McKim's view of Perkins has not gone uncontested, and there has been a recent tendency to downgrade the importance of Ramism in his theological formation. Much of this follows on from Ong who viewed Ramism as a superficial movement devoid of intellectual content.[8]

In this chapter I seek to develop McKim's thesis and defend the centrality of Ramism for Perkins's philosophy and theology. Yet Perkins also must be seen as a distinctive Ramist who transposed Ramism into a more voluntaristic and covenantal key. In this way, he emerges not only as an important precursor of the encyclopedic turn of the seventeenth century but also of its decisive federal turn. Beginning from Perkins's Ramist logic and art of memory, this chapter demonstrates his profound debt to the French philosopher in elaborating a realist, natural, and exemplaristic logic. It then considers the intimate connection of this to the Augustinian and Franciscan tradition of Christian philosophy, newly reinvigorated by Ramus and his followers. Finally, it moves onto Perkins's systematic theology and his momentous reforging of the great chain of being.

The Shape of Perkins's Ramism

The shape of Perkins's Ramism emerges clearly from his celebrated controversy with Alexander Dickson. Traditionally this has been seen as a prime example of the clash of civilizations, with the medieval and Renaissance Neoplatonism of Dickson pitted against Perkins's Puritan Ramism. In such a reading this dispute over the art of memory becomes sublimated into an epochal conflict between a pre-Reformation culture of image and a Reformation culture of the Word. Thus, for Yate, the Ramist "image-less way of remembering through abstract dialectical order" became the supreme realization of the Protestant Reformation as

---

5. Donald K. McKim, *Ramism in William Perkins' Theology* (New York: Peter Lang, 1987).

6. McKim, *Ramism*, 130.

7. McKim, *Ramism*, 130–33.

8. Richard A. Muller, *Grace and Freedom: William Perkins and the Early Modern Reformed Understanding of Free Choice and Divine Grace* (Oxford: Oxford University Press, 2020), 14–15, 26, 36. Muller tends to view Perkins's Ramism as simply a way of organizing his theology. Paul Marshall, "William Perkins, A Ramist Theologian?" *Baptist Review of Theology* 7, no. 1–2 (1997): 49–68 denies outright that Perkins was a Ramist, arguing that he only organized his material in a Ramist fashion.

an "inner iconoclasm" or smashing of the idols of the mind.[9] However, recent scholarship has challenged such a view. For English Protestantism remained deeply embedded in the world of the senses and Puritans especially could draw on a rich store of biblical images for meditation and contemplation.[10] Moreover, as Barret Reiter has recently argued, Perkins's own epistemology shared many affinities with an Aristotelian-Thomistic understanding in which intelligible content is derived from sensible images through a process of progressive abstraction. Far from wishing to banish them, Perkins saw images as an inescapable and vital part of all true cognition.[11]

What Perkins opposed, therefore, was not images *per se*, but rather Dickson's use of images to frame an artificial system of memory. Dickson himself was a disciple of Giordano Bruno, the controversial friar whose visit to England in 1583 was the spark that ignited the Perkins-Dickson dispute. Bruno was a leading exponent of the Dominican art of memory which followed Classical precedent in using an ordered array of striking images, often placed systematically in different rooms in a house or palace, as a stimulus for remembering. Notably, Bruno also sought to fuse this established Dominican technique with the combinatorial art of Lullism, placing his images on moving wheels in order to generate infinite possible combinations intended to mirror the infinity of the human mind.[12] In 1584 Dickson published a mystical treatise, *De umbra rationis*, dedicated to the Earl of Leicester, in which he not only outlined the Brunian art of memory but also offered a scarcely veiled attack on Ramus. Perkins was incensed both by the attack on Ramism and by Dickson's attempt to woo Leicester and his nephew Sir Philip Sidney, key patrons of the Puritan party, over to Bruno's Neoplatonism. He responded immediately with the *Antidicsonus* and followed soon after with the *Libellus de Memoria*, a response to Dickson's defense of his system.[13]

From the opening words of the *Antidicsonus* Perkins set himself against "showy and irresponsible writers on memory," singling out for special mention Metrodorus of Scepsis, the Florentine friar Cosmas Rosselius, Bruno, and

---

9. Frances A. Yates, *The Art of Memory* (London: Pimlico, 2008), 270–71; McKim, *Ramism*, 57–58.

10. See Matthew Milner, *The Senses and the English Reformation* (London: Routledge, 2016).

11. Barret Reiter, "William Perkins, the Imagination in Calvinist Theology and 'Inner Iconoclasm' after Frances Yates," *Intellectual History Review* (2021): 1–23. For positive Puritan use of biblical images see also Susan Hardman Moore, "For the Mind's Eye Only: Puritans, Images and 'the Golden Mines of Scripture,'" *Scottish Journal of Theology* 59, no. 3 (2006): 281–96.

12. For Bruno's fusion of the Dominican and Lullist art of memory see Yates, *Art of Memory*, 197–227.

13. For the context of this see Yates, *Art of Memory*, 260–78 and McKim, *Ramism*, 51–58. While these treatises are anonymous, McKim offers a convincing defense of Perkins's authorship.

Dickson himself.[14] Elsewhere, he also attacked in no uncertain terms Peter of Ravenna, whose *Phoenix* was the most important fifteenth-century exposition of the Dominican art of memory.[15] For Perkins, these were the "dangerous cliffs" and "ravenous whirlpools" who threatened to shipwreck the art of memory, unless "it clung to the firm resolve of the Ramean men as to a column."[16] He thus sharply contrasted the "Scepsian" art of memory reliant on "places and suggestive images" and the true Ramist art of memory grounded on "dialectical arrangement."[17] Echoing Valla in his *Repastinatio Dialecticae* he held that Dickson had "tried to strip bare memory, the mistress and queen of very many virtues who resides in the citadel of the head, of all her most elegant raiment of logical disposition," replacing them with his own stinking undergarments.[18]

In all his attacks against Dickson it is notable that Perkins never denied the potential efficacy of the Dominican memory art.[19] In fact, in one place he even conceded that "artificial memory, which stands upon places and images, will very easily without labour teach how to commit sermons to memory."[20] Yet although Perkins held that memory images could indeed "aid the memory," he still held that they "utterly destroy intelligence."[21] His own objections to Dickson's artificial system were effectively threefold.

First, he held that it was cumbersome and inefficient, working well for short texts but quickly becoming unwieldy when applied to long texts or discourses. For the mind becomes "engulfed" in remembering so many images, then "truth inevitably breaks free and flies away."[22] What he had particularly in mind here was Dickson's attempt, inspired by the Lullist and combinatorial art, to frame a kind of alphabet of the mind, in which a complex system of images substituted for particular words, letters and numbers, meaning that whole sentences could thus be directly "written" on the mind.[23] Drawing directly on Ramus,

---

14. *Antidicson*, 6:477. Perkins references the reputed origin of the art of memory in Simonides and Metrodorus (6:425). See further Yates, *Art of Memory*, 42–62.

15. Perkins, *Libellus in quo dilucide explicatur*, in *Antidicsonus* (London, 1584), 45, and *Libellus de memoria* (London, 1584) 4r. See also in English translation *Antidicson*, 6:517–18 and *Handbook on Memory*, 525. For Peter of Ravenna, see Yates, 119–22.

16. *Antidicsonus*, "Epistola" (*Antidicson*, 6:477).

17. *Antidicsonus*, "Epistola" (*Antidicson*, 6:477).

18. *Antidicsonus*, 5 (*Antidicson*, 6:477–78); cf. Lorenzo Valla, *Lorenzo Valla: Dialectical Disputations*, ed. and trans. Brian P. Copenhaver and Lodi Nauta, 2 vols. (Cambridge, Mass.: Harvard University Press, 2012), Book II "Proem" (p. 7).

19. *Antidicsonus*, 29–30 (*Antidicson*, 6:504, 525); *Art of Prophesying*, 10:348.

20. *Art of Prophesying*, 10:348.

21. *Libellus in quo dilucide explicatur*, 48 (*Antidicson*, 6:521).

22. *Libellus in quo dilucide explicatur*, 41–43, 47–48 (*Antidicson*, 6:515–16, 521).

23. *Libellus in quo dilucide explicatur*, 37–43 (*Antidicson*, 6:509–16).

Perkins held that "orators completely disorder the memory of words by an endless number of images."[24]

Second, there can be no doubt, as Yates and McKim have argued, that Perkins saw Dickson's memory art as wicked and impure.[25] Fundamental to the Dominican memory art was not only the use of images but also their movement and animation so that they could be imprinted more deeply on the memory.[26] Perkins did not dispute the principle, but held that it was dangerous to deliberately arouse "perverse emotions in the mind" such as anger, hatred, fear, and lust. Singling out Peter of Ravenna particularly, he roundly attacked him for his celebrated advice to young men to use images of their girlfriends in order to stimulate desire and improve the memory.[27] For Perkins, such advice bore the "glaring stain of impiety" and he warned against it again in his *Art of Prophesying* saying "the animation of the image, which is the key of memory, is impious, because it requires absurd, insolent and prodigious cogitations, and those especially which set an edge upon and kindle the most corrupt affections of the flesh."[28] In similar vein, the Renaissance occultic and astrological associations of the Brunian art of memory were also objectionable to Perkins and he certainly rejected his animating of images with Zodiac wheels.[29] While Perkins extolled mathematics, viewing it as a "divine" art,[30] he rejected Dickson's use of pyramids, cubes and "shades" of light as "clumsy and bizarre."[31] Like Ramus he despised the cult of mystery in which Renaissance Neo-Pythagoreanism and the Brunian art of memory were often veiled.[32]

Third, and most significantly, Perkins attacks Dickson's memory art as fundamentally illogical. In particular, he held that Dickson had become so "blinded by error" that he failed to see that reason and memory are the same thing.[33] The result was that the Scot had constructed a memory system which violated almost every canon of reason. Drawing on Ramus, Perkins held that

24. *Libellus in quo dilucide explicatur*, 43 (*Antidicson*, 6:515–16).

25. Yates, *Art of Memory*, 260–78; McKim, *Ramism*, 57–58.

26. *Libellus in quo dilucide explicatur*, 38, 44–45 (*Antidicson*, 6:510, 517); cf. Yates, *Art of Memory*, 121–22.

27. *Libellus in quo dilucide explicatur*, 44–46 (*Antidicson*, 6:517–18); cf. Yates, *Art of Memory*, 267.

28. *Art of Prophesying*, 10:348.

29. *Golden Chain*, 6:55; cf. McKim, *Ramism*, 56–58.

30. *Handbook on Memory*, 6:554.

31. *Antidicsonus*, 13 (*Antidicson*, 6:486–87).

32. Petrus Ramus, *P. Rami Professoris Regii Prooemium Mathematicum* (Paris, 1567), 216, 266–301 championed Regiomontanus's more scientific approach to mathematics. See also Robert Goulding, *Defending Hypatia: Ramus, Savile, and the Renaissance Rediscovery of Mathematical History* (Dordrecht: Springer, 2010), 36, 57n.

33. *Antidicsonus*, 21 (*Antidicson*, 6:495).

Dickson had failed to see that "an exquisite art is refined with glorious definition, set apart by a complete and compact division of subjects, and filled with
constant and clear examples."[34] Dickson's use of images thus subverted the
Ramist and Aristotelian rule of definition,[35] inverted the correct division by
prioritizing sensible images over intelligible reasons,[36] and obscured the application of memory by making use of flawed examples.[37]

In order to demonstrate the complete failure of Dickson's memory art, Perkins also drew extensively on Ramus's celebrated three laws, seeking to weigh
the precepts of his art "as though upon the exact scale of a goldsmith."[38] Thus,
he violated the law of truth as his system contained many false principles and
was in fact "utterly devoid of truth."[39] Dickson also went against the law of
justice as he mixed the arts indiscriminately, not confining them to their own
"particular banks and channels."[40] It also contravened the law of wisdom which
ordered all things from the more universal to the more particular and argued
that "all things must be explained reciprocally," since Dickson's images were not
reciprocal with objects and words.[41] What this meant overall was that Dickson committed that supreme Ramist sin of violating not only invention and
judgment but also method itself, proving "inept at constructing these same
topics into a proper system."[42] In the final analysis, Dickson's art of memory
was unmethodical, and that is why Perkins rejected it.

In supreme contrast, Perkins's own art of memory was intended to be both
systematic and methodical in character. It had been Ramus's contention that
the art of memory was identical with logic itself, and Perkins shared this revo-
lutionary attitude entirely.[43] As he put it, "There exists no other teaching than
this logical disposition by which the ability to call things to mind—which up
to this point is still bitter and coarse—can be rendered more sweet and mild."[44]
True to his claim to belong to the "school of Cicero and Ramus," Perkins
affirmed from Cicero that dialectical disposition is a crucial aid to memory.
In fact, drawing on Ramus's *Brutinae Quaestiones* he went further holding that

---

34. *Antidicsonus*, 9 (*Antidicson*, 6:483).
35. *Antidicsonus*, 9–10 (*Antidicson*, 6:482–83, 509; *Handbook on Memory*, 6:546).
36. *Antidicsonus*, 26–27 (*Antidicson*, 6:500; *Handbook on Memory*, 6:547).
37. *Antidicsonus*, 28 (*Antidicson*, 6:502).
38. *Handbook on Memory*, 6:547; cf. Ramus, *P. Rami Scholae in Liberales Artes* (Basel, 1578), col. 333–37.
39. *Antidicsonus*, 26–27 (*Antidicson*, 6:500, 507; *Handbook on Memory*, 6:546).
40. *Handbook on Memory*, 6:546, 555–56.
41. *Antidicsonus*, 26–27 (*Antidicson*, 6:500–501; *Handbook on Memory*, 6:546).
42. *Handbook on Memory*, 6:548.
43. Yates, *Art of Memory*, 228–30, 265–79.
44. *Antidicsonus*, "Epistola" (*Antidicson*, 6:477–78).

logical disposition is the only, true art of memory.[45] Since memory and reason are inseparable, it follows that "logical ordering of words" is the "only method for equipping memory."[46] Indeed, it not only "helps the memory" but also "greatly sharpens the intelligence, and vigorously molds and fashions a person's natural genius."[47] In fact, echoing Ramus's own extravagant claims, he held that "spending just one hour can make anyone a sufficiently competent practitioner of the art of memory."[48]

For Perkins the logical order followed by the art of memory was naturally that of Ramus himself. Notably, he expressed this in terms of a threefold division of dialectic into invention, judgment and memory—thus cementing even further the intimate Ramist bond between logic and memory.[49] For Perkins, these three operations are innate and "inborn" to every act of cognition.[50] For this reason he held that "the artificial memory system should not be derived from the clever design and conjecture of any philosopher, nor from any school in particular, but from the natural practice of memory that shines forth in everyone."[51] What this meant was that by organizing everything according to neat chains of arguments, propositions, syllogisms, and system, Ramist dialectic could allow anyone to remember even an "infinite series of items," binding them all together such that each naturally follows its predecessor according to a tight, well-defined, logical order.[52]

Ramus's system of logic was thus supreme for Perkins since it already embodied method through its conformity to the three laws of truth, justice, and wisdom in its very construction.[53] Since logic is natural, it is also empirical in character and, like Ramus, he was emphatic that logic should be derived from ordinary experience.[54] In this sense, logic was a process of generalizing from everyday life in order to find the laws which govern all of thought. As Perkins elegantly expressed this, "Since these topics which apply to common experience are unique, they certainly will never be able to be reduced to the narrow compass of any skill, unless, by some rationale, they become universal."[55] Adapting Ramus's principles he held there to be a fourfold way

---

45. *Antidicsonus*, 30 (*Antidicson*, 6:504).
46. *Antidicsonus*, 20 (*Antidicson*, 6:494).
47. *Libellus in quo dilucide explicatur*, 48 (*Antidicson*, 6:521).
48. *Libellus in quo dilucide explicatur*, "*Lectori*" (*Antidicson*, 6:507).
49. *Antidicsonus*, 29–30 (*Antidicson*, 6:504).
50. *Antidicsonus*, 29–30 (*Antidicson*, 6:504; *Handbook on Memory*, 6:546).
51. *Handbook on Memory*, 6:544.
52. *Libellus de memoria*, c. 4 (*Handbook on Memory*, 6:533).
53. *Handbook on Memory*, 6:546–47.
54. *Handbook on Memory*, 6:543–44.
55. *Handbook on Memory*, 6:542.

of achieving this. Thus perception recognizes individual instances, observation marks them off, induction gathers together these specific instances, and practice strengthens them.[56] For a logician to ignore experience was for Perkins to be like those philosophers who theorized an uninhabitable, fiery zone of the earth, only to have their theories utterly exploded by the expansion of navigation and Columbus's discovery of the new world.[57] In this he shared to the full that new empirical and inductive approach to reality pioneered by his contemporary Francis Bacon, a thinker who was also nurtured on Ramist principles.[58]

For Perkins, it was also clear that a natural logic should be realist in character. As he elegantly put it, logical order should derive from "what nature herself abounds in and has produced."[59] Like Ramus, he therefore recognized a direct correspondence between the logical categories of the human mind and extramental reality. What this meant was that the systematic ordering of all reality into a connected hierarchy of genera and species was not something constructed or imposed by the mind, but something truly present in things themselves.[60] Ramism had the advantage of every other system of logic since it automatically and spontaneously configured itself to this innate order of genera and species, which it was even capable of graphically representing in its branching charts. In doing so, logic arranges everything with a "view to the perspicuity of the subject's own nature."[61]

Unfortunately, Perkins is not explicit on exactly how logical concepts relate to reality. He is certainly highly critical of Aristotle's definition of genus in his *Topics*, followed by his "ape" Dickson,[62] and surely preferred Ramus's alternative definition of a "whole essential to its parts."[63] Perkins held it to be "a principle in logic that the genus is actually in all the species and a rule in the optics that the general species of things are perceived before the particular."[64] This certainly has a Thomistic ring to it but elsewhere he also affirms with Scotus that

---

56. *Handbook on Memory*, 6:542–43. For this Ramist pattern see Friedrich Beurhaus, *De P. Rami Dialecticae Praecipius Capitibus Disputationes Scholasticae* (Dortmund, 1581), "Prooemium," 1–10.

57. *Handbook on Memory*, 6:543.

58. For Bacon's Ramist background see Paolo Rossi, *Francis Bacon: From Magic to Science*, trans. Sacha Rabinovitch (London: Routledge, 2009).

59. *Libellus in quo dilucide explicatur*, 48 (*Antidicson*, 6:521).

60. *Antidicsonus*, 25 (*Antidicson*, 6:499; *Handbook on Memory*, 546–47).

61. *Handbook on Memory*, 6:547.

62. *Handbook on Memory*, 6:543.

63. Ramus, *Scholae in Liberales Artes*, col. 371, 377–78.

64. *Art of Prophesying*, 10:331.

a genus is naturally prior to its species.[65] Perkins's discussion is taken directly from Ramus, stating that mathematical objects such as points and lines must be understood as not purely abstract but "really joined with and connected to individual objects in such a way that you can in no way force them apart."[66] This is in direct contradiction to Dickson's claims. But even more significantly, Perkins's discussion carries distinct echoes of Scotus's formal distinction.[67] If so then Perkins is best connected to the loose Realism and topical Scotism which characterized the Agricolan school.[68]

In contrast to Ramus and his fellow Puritan Ames, Perkins has a rather more muted exemplaristic view of reality. He does on occasion parallel created forms and their eternal exemplars in the divine mind.[69] He also clearly assumes an overarching Neoplatonic framework of illumination. Thus, when he launches a frontal attack on Dickson's "shadowy" method, pitting against it the "radiant brightness" of the laws of logic, he cites in support Plato who "said many things about light," noting by comparison that Aristotle only "made certain comments." His further citations of the Islamic philosopher Alhazen, the Franciscan Witelo, and the Renaissance philosopher Patricius suggest an appreciation for the optics and light metaphysics pioneered by the Franciscan school.[70]

By contrast, to Dickson's Brunian account of seeking the "shadow of the light of the divine mind,"[71] Perkins thus clearly adheres to an Augustinian view of the luminous clarity of intellectual light.[72] Expressing his exemplarism and illuminism, he thus holds that ideas must be "vivid and gleaming, so that the

---

65. Todd Bates, "Fine-Tuning Pini's Reading of Scotus's *Categories*," in *Medieval Commentaries on Aristotle's Categories*, ed. Lloyd A. Newton (Leiden: Brill, 2008), 271.

66. *Handbook on Memory*, 6:554–55.

67. For Scotus's formal distinction see Allan Wolter, "The Formal Distinction," in *John Duns Scotus, 1265–1965* (Washington, D.C.: Catholic University of America Press, 1965), 45–60.

68. See Lodi Nauta, "From Universals to Topics: The Realism of Rudolph Agricola, with an Edition of His Reply to a Critic," *Vivarium* 50 (2012): 190–224.

69. *Case of Conscience*, 8:620. Muller, *Grace and Freedom*, 65, suggests his interest in divine exemplars, although Richard A. Muller, "Calvinist Thomism Revisited: William Ames (1576–1633) and the Divine Ideas," in *From Rome to Zurich, Between Ignatius and Vermigli: Essays in Honor of John Patrick Donnelly*, ed. Gary Jenkins, W. J. Torrance Kirby, and Kathleen Comerford (Leiden: Brill, 2017), 107, points out that he apparently has no explicit discussion of such divine ideas. *Exposition of the Creed*, 5:75, follows Aquinas and other medieval theologians in holding that the natural law reflects the eternal law of God. For Ames's exemplarism, see William Ames, *Medulla S. S. Theologiae* (Amsterdam, 1659), 1:7:15–17.

70. *Handbook on Memory*, 6:549, 557. For more on the Franciscan metaphysics of light see Roger K. French and Andrew Cunningham, *Before Science: The Invention of the Friars' Natural Philosophy* (Abingdon: Routledge, 2016).

71. Yates, *Art of Memory*, 261.

72. *Handbook on Memory*, 6:549.

mind can be quickly affected and compelled by grasping these ideas."[73] Like
Ramus, he clearly sees the logic as revealing the "ideas of the...arts,"[74] such
that correct logical arrangement "sparkles with the truth."[75] For Perkins, the
goal of logic is thus to yield the intelligible structure of reality which he views
as shining with its own light. Indeed, turning the tables on the imagistic art
of memory, Perkins can claim that the "dialecticians' method" employs well-
delineated and luminous images far superior to Dickson's evanescent "fleeing
shadows and puffs of smoke."[76] Indeed, echoing Ramus's early works, Perkins took up his Neoplatonic understanding of dialectic as the lively image
of the mind, referring to definitions, distinctions and examples as the "living
and natural images" employed by method—to be contrasted with the impious
moving images employed by Bruno and Dickson.[77] The skilled logician is thus
like Apelles producing lifelike images of the world, and his memory a kind of
"picture and type of remembering everyday experiences."[78] It is thus Ramist
logic, and not Dickson's Brunian method, which is the true imaging of reality.[79]

Christian Encyclopedism and Mosaic Philosophy

Following Ramus and Johann Thomas Freige, his "most ardent German
disciple,"[80] Perkins understood dialectic as a universal method valid for all the
arts.[81] The same logical structure and methodology could therefore be seen as
underpinning all the arts as its "correct and generic theorem."[82] In his *Scholae*, well known to Perkins, Ramus had offered his own logical discussion of
all the arts, as a kind of prototypical Ramist encyclopedia.[83] Developing this
model, Freige's *Professio Regia* presented all the arts and sciences as a set of

73. *Antidicsonus*, 15 (*Antidicson*, 6:489).

74. *Antidicsonus*, 18 (*Antidicson*, 6:492).

75. *Libellus in quo dilucide explicatur*, 48 (*Antidicson*, 6:521).

76. *Handbook on Memory*, 6:557.

77. *Libellus in quo dilucide explicatur*, 44 (*Antidicson*, 6:517). Petrus Ramus, *Institutiones
Dialecticae* (Paris, 1543; facsimile edition Stuttgart: Friedrich Frommann Verlag, 1964), 7r–8v,
42v–43r. For the Lullist roots of this see Ramon de Sebonde, *Theologia Naturalis* (Venice, 1581), c.
152, 155 (130r, 132v).

78. *Antidicsonus*, 20–22 (*Antidicson*, 6:494–96); cf. Ramus, *Institutiones*, 7r–8v, 42v–43r.

79. *Antidicsonus*, 21–22 (*Antidicson*, 6:496).

80. Hotson, *Commonplace Learning*, 61.

81. For Perkins's approbation of Freigius see *Antidicsonus*, 22–23 (*Antidicson*, 6:496–97;
Handbook on Memory, 5:557). On 496–97 Perkins defended Freige directly from Dickson's
attacks.

82. *Handbook on Memory*, 6:543.

83. Howard Hotson, *Commonplace Learning: Ramism and Its German Ramifications, 1543–
1630* (Oxford: Oxford University Press, 2007), 114–26.

interconnected Ramist charts.[84] In just the same way, Perkins offered for illustration a Ramist chart showing all the "heads of ethics" and their principal divisions and sub-divisions. In this, the intelligible structure—or "idea"—of the art of ethics becomes revealed at a single glance, thereby also serving as an important aid for memorization.[85]

Unlike Richardson and Ames, his fellow Cambridge Ramists, Perkins did not develop his own Ramist encyclopedia.[86] However, he did claim that "arts must be learned and taught with an order. First the general arts should be taught, i.e., grammar, rhetoric, and dialectic. Afterward the particular ones that are derived from these, namely, arithmetic first and then geometry. Afterward come optics, then astronomy, next physics, and finally ethics and politics."[87] Here the medieval division of the liberal arts into the linguistic arts of the *trivium* and the mathematical arts of the *quadrivium* has become superimposed onto a Ramist methodical movement from the more general to the more particular. Notably absent in Perkins's encyclopedia is metaphysics, the mainstay of scholastic philosophy. Like Ramus, he likely thought this to be superfluous as a separate discipline, given logic's role as an analysis and anatomy of being.[88]

In his early dialectical works Ramus had inveighed against Aristotelian scholasticism as corrupting both philosophy and theology.[89] His own desire was to unify philosophy and eloquence, completing the humanist aspiration to employ rhetoric and logic in the analysis of Scripture and other seminal texts.[90] Perkins shared fully in this Ramist project of an eloquent philosophy, attacking Dickson for his "barbarism" of style and his "Dunsicality."[91] While he could certainly praise Aristotle,[92] he could still be highly critical of his logic.[93] As a Ramist, he himself had no doubt that method was the crown of logic.[94] He also

---

84. See Johann Thomas Freige, *P. Rami Professio Regia* (Basel, 1576).

85. *Libellus de memoria*, c. 4 (*Handbook on Memory*, 6:533–34).

86. See William Ames, *Technometria*, 52–62, in *Guilielmi Amesii Magni Theologi ac Philosophi Acutissimi Philosophemata* (Cambridge, 1646). A manuscript of Richardson's encyclopaedia is also located in Trinity College Dublin, MS 711.

87. *Libellus in quo dilucide explicatur*, 40 (*Antidicson*, 6:512).

88. For Ramus's view of logic as including metaphysics see Ramus, *Scholae in Liberales Artes*, 933–37, 942, 959.

89. Ramus, *Aristotelicae Animadversiones* (Paris, 1543; facsimile edition Stuttgart: Friedrich Frommann Verlag, 1964), 64v.

90. James Veazie Skalnik, *Ramus and Reform: University and Church at the End of the Renaissance* (University Park: Penn State University Press, 2021), 63–87.

91. *Libellus de memoria*, "Epistola" (*Handbook on Memory*, 6:526, 541).

92. *Handbook on Memory*, 6:546–47.

93. *Libellus de memoria*, c. 4 (*Handbook on Memory*, 6:533, 543).

94. *Libellus de memoria*, c. 4 (*Handbook on Memory*, 6:533).

attacked strongly the use of the demonstrative syllogism, which underpinned much scholastic argumentation.[95] Despite the fact that other sixteenth-century Reformed theologians such as Peter Martyr Vermigli were engaged in a comprehensive rehabilitation of Aristotelian ethics, Perkins remained highly suspicious of it.[96] He could also be biting in his attacks against medieval scholasticism for its undue mixing of philosophy and theology, holding that they do not "lay the foundation of their study upon the rock, but upon the waters— that is, not upon the Scripture, but upon Aquinas, or some such summist."[97] Of course, such views must be seen in context. Elsewhere, Perkins could draw deeply on Aquinas, Scotus, and a whole host of other scholastics. Yet even here he shows a marked preference for the Augustinian and voluntarist theology of the late medieval and early modern period over the Christian Aristotelianism of the thirteenth century with its harmonization of nature and grace.[98]

While Perkins never used the term "Christian philosophy," it nevertheless may still serve as an accurate designation of his thought. The term *philosophia Christiana* itself derives from Augustine and, since Etienne Gilson, has often been used to identify an Augustinian and Franciscan stream of theology standing at a critical distance from Aristotelian scholasticism.[99] Its employment by Ramus in his attempts to reform the University of Paris meant that it became a prominent aspect of the sixteenth-century Ramist program, with Polanus himself referring to the growing split between two different "families of philosophers"—one following Aristotle, the "Prince of Gentile Philosophers," and the other following Ramus, the "Christian philosopher and hieromartyr."[100] In Germany this division fueled a bitter controversy over the relation of philosophy

---

95. *Handbook on Memory*, 6:543.

96. For detailed discussion of this see Luca Baschera, *Tugend und Rechtfertigung: Peter Martyr Vermiglis Kommentar zur Nikomachischen Ethik im Spannungsfeld von Philosophie und Theologie* (Zürich, TVZ, 2008).

97. *Commentary on Galatians*, 2:4–5.

98. See *Problem of Forged Catholicism*, 7:242–43, 246–47, 254, 270, 283, 288, 298–302, 318, 321, 326, 333, 354, 376, 386–87, 398, 405–6 for positive citations of Alexander of Hales, Scotus, Richard of Middleton, Francis of Meyronnes, Thomas Bradwardine, Gregory of Rimini, Marsilius of Inghen, Pierre d'Ailly, Thomas Capreolus, and Nicholas of Cusa. Muller, *Grace and Freedom*, 16–18, notes Perkins's deep debt to Dominican and Augustinian sources on the doctrine of grace. Perkins's knowledge of the Scotist school is also impressive.

99. For the Augustinian and Franciscan tradition of Christian philosophy see Étienne Gilson, *The Philosophy of St. Bonaventure* (London, 1938) and Joseph Ratzinger, *The Theology of History in St. Bonaventure* (Chicago: Franciscan Herald Press, 1971), 119–34, 160–62.

100. Amandus Polanus von Polansdorf, *Syntagma Logicum Arisotelico-Ramaeum ad Usum Imprimis Theologicum Accommodatum* (Basel, 1605), "Epistola Dedicatoria."

and theology, with Ramists often defending an explicit Christian and scriptural approach to philosophy.[101]

While this controversy was less intense in England, its presence certainly registers in the work of William Ames who followed in the footsteps of Bonaventure in arguing for an exemplaristic and illuminist *reductio* of all human arts and sciences to Scripture.[102] Notably, a similar kind of impulse can be detected in Perkins. In his *Commentary on Hebrews 11* Perkins contrasted sharply the knowledge of God accessible to philosophy and to faith saying:

> Now then, whereas general faith brings understanding of many things which reason cannot reach unto, here, such as be students in human learning and which labor to attain to the deepness and perfection of it are taught with their travel in human studies to have care to join faith and knowledge of religion. For there are many things which our understanding by reason cannot conceive and many truths which philosophy cannot reach unto—nay, many also which it denies. But faith is able to persuade and demonstrate them all, and it enlightens the mind and rectifies the judgment, when as philosophy has left the mind in darkness and the judgment in error.[103]

Perkins is clear that there are truths which "reason cannot see and therefore philosophy will not admit"—not only the Christian mysteries of the Trinity and incarnation but also others such as the creation of the world or immortality of the soul. It is only through combining faith and reason to yield a "sound" philosophy, that these will become accessible. Indeed, Perkins is adamant that "religion hinders not human learning, as some fondly think, but is a furtherance and help or rather the perfection of human learning, persuading and proving and convincing that which human learning cannot."[104]

Later in the work, Perkins makes fully explicit his adherence to scriptural philosophy. Praising the eloquence of Scripture, the staple of the Puritan plain style, he has the following to say:

> For if we yield that rhetoric is good and lawful and practiced in the Scripture, then it must needs follow that it is there practiced in the best manner. For shall the divinity there taught be the soundest? The history there

---

101. For a detailed discussion of this dispute see Zornitsa Radeva, "At the Origins of a Tenacious Narrative: Jacob Thomasius and the History of Double Truth," *Intellectual History Review* 29, no. 3 (2019): 417–38.

102. William Ames, *The Philosophical and Theological Treatises of William Ames* [*PTT*], ed. Lee Gibbs (Lewiston, N.Y.: Edwin Mellen Press, 2013), 346–52; and idem, *Technometria*, 3.

103. *Commentary on Hebrews 11*, 3:21.

104. *Commentary on Hebrews 11*, 3:21–22.

reported the truest? The conclusions of philosophy, astronomy, geometry, arithmetic, cosmography, and physic there delivered, the surest? The music there practiced, the exactest? The logic there practiced, the sharpest? The laws there enacted, the justest? And shall not the rhetoric there practiced be the purest?... Let them study God's books, and there they shall find not only divinity but knowledge and learning of all sorts.[105]

Perkins's understanding here clearly draws on Augustine's *De doctrina Christiana*, a work he used in the composition of his *Art of Prophesying*, and resonates with the scriptural encyclopedism of Hugh of St. Victor and Bonaventure.[106] Like Ramus, he drew on these figures to offer his own evangelical version of the *prisca philosphia* developed by Ficino and the Florentine Platonists, tracing logic and other sciences back though Cicero and Plato to Solomon, Noah, Abraham, and even Adam.[107]

In his *Golden Chain* Perkins offered his own condensed Ramist and encyclopedic analysis of the Bible, prefacing the work with a chart showing the way in which the "body of Holy Scripture is distinguished into sacred sciences" including theology, ethics, economics, politics, ecclesiastical discipline, the Jewish commonwealth, prophecy, and academics. Significantly, he divides these further according to an overarching Ramist dichotomy in which theology is taken as principal and all the other sacred sciences as "attendants" or "handmaids." He also defines the purpose of these in a characteristically Ramist manner in terms of their practical utility, holding that the "body of Scripture is a doctrine sufficient to live well," that theology is a "science of living well and blessedly forever," ethics a "science of living honestly and civilly," prophecy "the doctrine of preaching well," and so on.[108] While Perkins' identification of other sciences as "handmaids" resonates with the famous opening of Aquinas' *Summa*, his desire to derive philosophical sciences from Scripture fits much closer into an Augustinian and Franciscan paradigm of Christian philosophy, harmonizing well with his Ramist and Scotistic vision of theology as a practical science.[109]

---

105. *Commentary on Hebrews 11*, 3:188.

106. Augustine, *De Doctrina Christiana*, 2:31:58–37:55

107. *Libellus in quo dilucide explicatur*, 36 (*Antidicson*, 6:508); cf. Petrus Ramus, *Scholae in Liberales Artes*, col. 312. For Ramus's own *prisca philosophia* see extensively Nelly Bruyère, *Méthode et Dialectique dans l'Oeuvre de la Ramée: Renaissance et Age Classique* (Paris: J. Vrin, 1984). For the wider context of this in French and Italian Neoplatonism see D. P. Walker, *The Ancient Theology: Studies in Christian Platonism from the Fifteenth to the Eighteenth Century* (London: Duckworth, 1972).

108. *Golden Chain*, 6:9, 11.

109. It should be noted that Perkins never says this classification of "sacred sciences" is exhaustive and his *Commentary on Hebrews* would suggest the inclusion of other sciences. For the Ramist and Scotistic dimension of practical theology see Richard Muller, *PRRD*, 1:324–54.

Reforging the Golden Chain

As a Puritan Ramist, Perkins sought a logic attuned not only to the structure of reality but also to Scripture and the mind of God. For him, as for other English Ramists, it was axiomatic that the Holy Spirit had made use of logic in inspiring and composing the Bible.[110] In his *Exposition upon the First Three Chapters of Revelation* he thus stoutly defended the legitimacy and utility of logic for theology:

> Hence observe the lawfulness of the art of logic, for divisions are lawful (else the Holy Ghost would not here have used them), and so by proportion are other arguments of reasoning. And therefore that art which gives rules of direction for the right use of these arguments is lawful and good. Those men then are far deceived, who account the arts of logic and rhetoric to be frivolous and unlawful, and in so saying they condemn the practice of the Holy Ghost in this place.[111]

For Perkins, following contemporary Ramist exegetes, every book of the Bible therefore had an intricate logical and systematic structure.[112] Indeed, like Piscator, he could even hold that the "sum of the Scripture" could be expressed in a single syllogism. Taking its major proposition from the Old Testament and its minor proposition from the New Testament this affirmed the identity of Jesus as the promised Messiah come to save humanity from their sins.[113] Analyzing, revealing and imprinting this logical pattern of Scripture on the soul thus became not only the job of the theologian, preacher, or exegete but also of the ordinary Christian.[114]

For Perkins, logic was thus not an extrinsic tool, however indispensable for the theological task, but something intrinsic to the Bible itself. Such an understanding is quite in conformity with his Christian philosophy with its commitment to a scriptural logic. For while all scholastics were deeply concerned with the logical analysis of Scripture, within the Augustinian and Franciscan tradition there was an influential movement toward formulating a scriptural logic transcending the Aristotelian logic of the schools.[115] The

---

110. See, for example, Richard Bernard, *The Faithfull Shepheard* (London, 1607), 25.

111. *Exposition of Revelation 1–3*, 4:410; cf. Thomas Aquinas, *Summa Theologiae*, 1a q. 1 art. 5 and Bonaventure of Bagnoregio, *On the Reduction of the Arts to Theology*, trans. Zachary Hayes (St. Bonaventure, N.Y.: Franciscan Institute, 1996), n. 1–14.

112. *Exposition of Revelation 1–3*, 4:409–10; *Art of Prophesying*, 10:301. See, for example, Johannes Piscator, *Commentarii in Omnes Libros Novi Testamenti* (Herborn, 1638), 2.

113. *Art of Prophesying*, 10:292; cf. Piscator, *Commentarii*, 3.

114. *Art of Prophesying*, 10:301.

115. For the wider Augustinian and scholastic tradition see Gillian Evans, *The Language and Logic of the Bible: The Road to Reformation* (Cambridge: Cambridge University Press,

anti-Aristotelian bent within Ramism clearly lent itself to this tendency, as can be seen in Ramus himself.[116] In the seventeenth century a number of English Ramists became explicit in their adherence to a scriptural and supernatural "logic of faith."[117] While Perkins did not go as far as this, he presses toward an understanding of Ramism as a kind of revealed, scriptural logic. At the very least, one can say that the natural, rather than unnatural or artificial character of Aristotelian logic, makes it ideally suited to understanding the logic to be found in Scripture.

Since Scripture is understood as having its own logical pattern, it follows that theological system should seek to replicate this as closely as possible. Such indeed had been the aspiration of Melanchthon whose *Loci Communes*—often hailed as the first Protestant systematic theology—had advocated a new kind of theological method in which Scripture itself, and specifically the book of Romans, governed the selection, order, and presentation of material.[118] Perkins too recommended immersing oneself in the logical structure of Romans, as well as the gospel of John, as a preliminary to all theological education,[119] but as a Ramist he took this a step further. For since Ramist logic itself conformed to the logic of Scripture, it followed that a Ramist methodological treatment of theology would naturally conform itself to this underlying biblical and divine order. It was for this reason that he recommended preachers and theological students to organize their commonplace books methodically according to "heads of every point of divinity."[120] For by doing so it would allow students to "diligently imprint" on their "mind and memory the substance of divinity described with definitions, divisions, and explications of the properties" giving them a much better insight into Scripture's own logical structure.[121]

While Perkins's *Exposition of the Creed* is often seen as his most complete systematic work of theology, it is undoubtedly his *Golden Chain* which represents his most innovative and influential work. For although not a full "body of

---

1985). For the late medieval logic of faith, see Michael Shank, *Unless You Believe, You Shall Not Understand: Logic, University and Society in Late-Medieval Vienna* (Princeton, N.J.: Princeton University Press, 1998, and Hester Goodenough Gelber, "Logic and the Trinity: A Clash of Values in Scholastic Thought, 1300–1335" (PhD diss., University of Wisconsin, 1974), 265–72.

116. See Petrus Ramus, *Commentariorum de Religione Christiana Libri Quattuor* (Frankfurt, 1576), 15, 329.

117. Simon J. G. Burton, *The Hallowing of Logic: The Trinitarian Method of Richard Baxter's Methodus Theolgoiae* (Leiden: Brill, 2012), 243–51.

118. See Philip Melanchthon, *The Loci Communes of Philip Melanchthon*, trans. Charles Leander Hill (Eugene, Ore: Wipf & Stock, 2007), 62–72.

119. *Art of Prophesying*, 10:301.

120. *Art of Prophesying*, 10:302.

121. *Art of Prophesying*, 10:301.

divinity" by any means, this work was pioneering in its application of Ramist logic to theology. The whole work offers an in-depth Ramist analysis of the scriptural "order of causes of salvation and damnation" according to an intricate pattern of branching dichotomies.[122] In fact, even the title *Golden Chain* can be seen not only as a reference to the chain of salvation in Romans 8:28–30, but also as an allusion to a celebrated motif in Ramus's dialectic. For, like other Christian Platonists, Ramus was deeply attracted to the Homeric and Platonic image of the golden chain attached to the throne of God and binding all things together in heaven and earth, regarding this as the exemplaristic basis of his own logic and mathematics.[123] Perkins too understood method as "golden," holding that "by grasping it, an infinite series of items can be so bound together that one item easily follows upon another."[124] Yet it seems clear that he reconfigured this popular Neoplatonic and Ramist motif in a markedly voluntaristic fashion.[125]

Right from the beginning of *A Golden Chain* Perkins makes clear that all theology must be grounded on Scripture. In comprehending within itself all the "sacred sciences," the Bible also includes theology as the "science of living blessedly forever." Such a blessed knowledge "arises from the knowledge of God" but also "likewise from the knowledge of ourselves because we know God by looking into ourselves."[126] For Perkins, both Scripture and the human soul become a glass or mirror in which we may see God. For Perkins, the "written Word" is thus "the first and perfect pattern of the mind and will of God."[127] Likewise, the elect human soul becomes a mirror of the divine nature. For predestination, as Zanchius states, impresses on it "a lively form and image of God, foreknowing us, loving us," so that by "beholding of these forms and impressions in ourselves, we shall easily be brought to the knowledge of those patterns (as it were), which are in the Lord Himself."[128] The pattern of the divine will and divine decrees thus becomes woven through both the Bible and the human soul and the purpose of *A Golden Chain* becomes to present a detailed and methodical analysis of these so that this pattern can in turn be even more deeply imprinted on the believer's soul.

---

122. For discussion of Perkins's systematic theology see Muller, *Grace and Freedom*, 25–30.

123. Petrus Ramus, *Petri Rami Mathematicae Praefationes: Prima*, in *Petri Rami Professoris Regii, et Audomari Talaei Collectaneae* (Paris, 1577), 167, and *Aristotelicae Animadversiones*, 2r–3v. Yates, *Art of Memory*, 240, notes the Neoplatonic valence of this image and its importance in Ramus's wider system.

124. *Libellus de memoria*, c. 4 (*Handbook on Memory*, 6:533).

125. For Perkins's voluntarist shift, see Muller, *Grace and Freedom*, 8–9, 19.

126. *Golden Chain*, 6:11.

127. *Commentary on Galatians*, 2:18.

128. *Case of Conscience*, 8:620–21.

For Perkins, all of theology follows a basic Ramist division into God and His works. Following Aquinas, Scotus, and the scholastic "metaphysics of Exodus," he describes the nature of God as determined by His name *Yahweh* as "I am who I am." Yet significantly he immediately couples this with His name Elohim as indicating the divine persons.[129] From the start then, as Muller has argued, Perkins's discussion of God is explicitly Trinitarian, something which conditions all his subsequent discussion. Yet at the same time the Trinitarian character of God becomes neatly enfolded in a Ramist couplet of the divine nature and persons. For Perkins the nature of God is His "lively and most perfect essence" as expressed in His divine simplicity and infinity.[130] In his *De Religione Christiana* Ramus had claimed that only God could define Himself since the "logic of God" is beyond all rational and logical description.[131] Notably, Perkins is in full agreement with this, claiming that God's divine simplicity means that He is "void of all logical relation in arguments," so that Ramist categories such as subject, adjunct, whole part, genus, species cannot be properly applied to Him.[132] Nevertheless, following an Augustinian and scholastic pattern of accommodation his own analysis of God clearly treats him according to different, logically distinct attributes, neatly organized into Ramist doublets.[133]

For Perkins, the "Trinity of the persons in the unity of the Godhead" is the "mystery of all mysteries."[134] In *A Golden Chain* he argues for a distinction of the persons according to their "incommunicable properties" and their communion by which "each person is in the rest." In his *Exposition of the Creed* he makes clear that the distinction between the divine essence and persons is "in mind" and designates the difference between an absolute and relative account of the Godhead.[135] In arguing this he seems to fuse both a Dominican relational and Franciscan emanational account of the Trinity.[136] In the same way,

---

129. *Golden Chain*, 6:12. For the metaphysics of Exodus see Étienne Gilson, *Thomist Realism and the Critique of Knowledge* (San Francisco: Ignatius Press, 2012). See also Thomas Aquinas, *Summa Theologiae*, 1a q. 2 art. 3 and John Duns Scotus, *A Treatise on God as First Principle*, 1:2.

130. *Golden Chain*, 6:12.

131. Ramus, *Commentariorum*, 15.

132. *Golden Chain*, 6:12–13.

133. *Golden Chain*, 6:12–18.

134. *Exposition of the Creed*, 5:27.

135. *Exposition of the Creed*, 5:24–27.

136. See Russell L. Friedman, *Medieval Trinitarian Thought from Aquinas to Ockham* (Cambridge: Cambridge University Press, 2010), 5–49. John T. Slotemaker, *Trinitarian Theology in Medieval and Reformation Thought* (Cham: Springer, 2020), 49–77, has recently argued that we should be careful of driving a wedge between them. Perkins does not use the language of emanation but he does emphasize that the persons are constituted by begetting and proceeding, and the relational language in his *Golden Chain* comes across as distinctly muted (*Works*, 6:20–22). Perkins's emphasis on the "incommunicability" of the divine persons has an important Victorine

Perkins's discussion of the divine life as that by which "the divine nature is in perpetual action, living and moving in itself" resonates with Aquinas, while his understanding that the self-moving divine nature is in "perpetual operation" through the three attributes of "wisdom, will, and omnipotence" also reflects the characteristic dynamism of Bonaventure or Scotus.[137]

Perkins argues that before creation the Trinity took eternal delight in each other and in the divine decrees.[138] Offering a Ramist analysis of the divine works he defines these as those which God does "out of Himself" and for the sake of His glory and divides them dichotomously into the divine decrees and the execution of the divine decrees. Imprinting a definite Trinitarian pattern on them, he holds that they are common to the whole Trinity, although with a "peculiar manner of working" always referred to each divine person.[139] As has therefore rightly been said, "It is impossible to understand predestination without realizing that God's decrees flow from the inner life of the triune God."[140] Elsewhere, Perkins also makes clear that predestination—God's decrees concerning humanity[141]—must be understood as centered on Christ. Indeed, he espoused a "Christological supralapsarianism" in which the decree of predestination logically precedes the decree of both creation and the fall.[142] In this, like his contemporary the Scottish Ramist Robert Rollock, he clearly follows Scotus, albeit restraining the speculative tendencies of the Franciscan's approach.[143]

While Perkins's doctrine of predestination is clearly biblical, Trinitarian, and Christocentric in character, it is important not to miss its logical character. If it is right to understand divine predestination itself "as a golden chain that runs from eternity past to eternity future,"[144] then the Ramist, methodical

---

and Franciscan heritage. See further Lydia Schumacher, *Early Franciscan Theology: Between Authority and Innovation* (Cambridge: Cambridge University Press, 2019), 158, 175, 196.

137. See Aquinas, *Summa Theologiae*, 1a q. 18. For Franciscan dynamism see Michael Sylwanowicz, *Contingent Causality and the Foundation of Duns Scotus' Metaphysics* (Leiden: Brill, 1996), 103–20.

138. *Exposition of the Creed*, 5:50.

139. *Golden Chain*, 6:23.

140. "Preface to Volume 6," in *Works*, 6:xix.

141. *Golden Chain*, 6:26.

142. "Preface to Volume 6," in *Works*, 6:xviii–xix.

143. For Rollock's Christological supralapsarianism see Brannon Ellis, "The Eternal Decree in the Incarnate Son: Robert Rollock on the Relationship between Christ and Election," in *Reformed Orthodoxy in Scotland: Essays on Scottish Theology 1560–1775* (London: Bloomsbury, 2015), 45–66. For the Scotist influence on Rollock through Ambrogio Catharinus see Aaron C. Denlinger, *Omnes in Adam ex pacto Dei: Ambrogio Catarino's Doctrine of Covenantal Solidarity and Its Influence on Post-Reformation Reformed Theologians* (Göttingen: Vandenhoeck & Ruprecht, 2011), 74–77, 240–70.

144. "Preface to Volume 6," in *Works*, 6:xvi.

valence of this must not be downplayed. In *A Golden Chain* we significantly find an implicit logical ordering of the divine decrees according to the three principal attributes of intellect, will, and power. Thus, he argues that "God's foreknowledge is conjoined with His decree and indeed is in nature before it." However, Perkins is quick to add "yet not in regard of God, but us." Indeed, he is clear in arguing that "things do not therefore come to pass because that God did foreknow them; but because He decreed and willed them, therefore they come to pass." This decree of God is "in order and time before all other causes," and "with God's will is conjoined an effectual power by which the Lord can bring to pass whatever He has freely decreed".[145]

Perkins's language of natural priority here is reflective of Scotus. It is therefore highly significant to find him citing approvingly the fourteenth-century Scotist Francis of Meyronnes in his *Manner and Order of Predestination* as distinguishing election and reprobation according to four logical "signs" or "instants of nature."[146] As was widely recognized in the seventeenth century, Scotus had been a pioneer in applying Aristotle's principle that "what is first in order of intention is last in order of execution" to the logical ordering of the divine decrees.[147] Perkins clearly followed him in this, although like Ames, seems to hesitate over whether this logical order is properly intrinsic to God, perhaps coming closer to Davenant's opinion, drawing on Gabriel Biel, that such a logical ordering is an accommodation to human understanding.[148] Perkins, we will recall, desired to trace the "patterns" of predestination in the human soul back to their origin in the mind of God,[149] and in this light it is scarcely surprising to find in him a definite convergence of a Scotist and Ramist logical ordering of the divine decrees.

Like Calvin, all of Perkins's theology is therefore driven by a definite Scotist "finalism."[150] According to this, creation, fall, and covenant can all be seen

---

145. *Golden Chain*, 6:23–24.

146. *Manner and Order of Predestination*, 6:320. Muller, *Grace and Freedom*, 57, 147 also notes his connection to the instants of nature framework but not the specific Scotist character of this. For Scotus's instants of nature framework see Antonie Vos, *The Philosophy of John Duns Scotus* (Edinburgh: Edinburgh University Press, 2006), 245–49.

147. See, for example, Richard Baxter, *Richard Baxter's Catholick Theologie* (London, 1675), 2:44.

148. William Ames, *Bellarminus Enervatus* (London, 1632), 3:279–80; and John Davenant, *De Praedestinatione et Reprobatione* in *Dissertationes Duae* (Cambridge, 1650), 108, 209.

149. *Case of Conscience*, 8:620.

150. This was the important claim of Heiko Oberman, *Initia Calvini: The Matrix of Calvin's Reformation* (Amsterdam: Koninklijke Nederlandse Akademie van Wetenschappen, 1991), 10–19. See also Richard Muller, "Scholasticism in Calvin: A Question of Relation and Disjunction," in Wilhelm Neuser and Brian Armstrong, eds., *Calvinus Sincerioris Religionis Vindex: Calvin*

in terms of both a biblical and logical unfolding of the eternal divine decrees. Indeed, conforming to a Scotist ordering of intention and execution, Perkins is clear in arguing that creation and fall must both be seen as means to achieve God's end of glorying Himself.[151] Notably, they can also be seen as a Trinitarian and Christological unfolding of the divine purpose. We may see this clearly from his *Exposition of the Creed* where Perkins offered an important correlation between the inward and outward actions of the Trinity. Inward actions he understands as those which constitute the divine persons, namely the communication of the divine essence from the Father to the Son and from Father and Son to the Holy Spirit. Outward actions are the works of creation, preservation, and redemption and while they are common to the whole Trinity, these must be carefully distinguished according to the order of the divine persons. Following Basil, he can therefore hold that "the Father is the cause that begins the work, the Son puts it in execution; the Holy Ghost is the finisher of it."[152] Put another way, Perkins held that the Father creates by the Son and Holy Spirit, the Son by the Holy Spirit and from the Father, and the Holy Spirit from the Father and the Son.[153] Creation naturally bears a Trinitarian imprint and elsewhere Perkins followed a distinctive Franciscan emphasis in identifying this, at least implicitly, with the stamp of the "admirable and unspeakable wisdom, goodness, and power of God" which causes us to "make haste from the creature and go forward to the Creator to praise and glorify Him."[154]

To trace this Trinitarian and Ramist pattern through all of Perkins's theology would take us too far afield. However, it is important to note its imprint on his covenantal theology. The relation between Ramism and covenant theology has long been a matter of controversy. While Moltmann seems right to suggest that the two were often closely entwined, his polarizing of scholastic and federal theology has rightly been discredited.[155] For our purposes it is enough to note the twin roots of the logical ordering of the divine decrees and the metaphysical understanding of the divine covenant or self-binding in late medieval, Scotistic

---

as Protector of the Purer Religion (Kirksville, Mo.: Sixteenth Century Journal Publishers, 1997), 247–65.

151. *Golden Chain*, 6:26–27.

152. *Exposition of the Creed*, 5:43.

153. *Exposition of the Creed*, 5:43.

154. *Exposition of the Creed*, 5:52. For extensive discussion of this triad see Burton, *Hallowing of Logic*, 95–147.

155. Jürgen Moltmann, "Zur Bedeutung des Petrus Ramus für Philosophie und Theologie in Calvinismus," *Zeitschrift für Kirchengeschichte* 68 (1957): 295–318. For Richard Muller's critique of this see *PRRD*, 1:183–84.

theology, without for one moment denying other influences or the fundamental biblical imperative which drove the Reformed codification of this doctrine.[156]

For Perkins, anticipating the explicit formulation of the covenant of redemption in the seventeenth century, the roots of the covenant surely lie in the delight taken by the persons of the Trinity in each other and the divine decrees.[157] Notably, he positions covenant as the pivot between the "eternal foundation of election" and the "outward means of the same." Covenant itself he defines as God's "contract with man concerning the obtaining of life eternal upon a certain condition." It is expressed in terms of both "God's promise to man" by which He "binds Himself to man to be his God"—a clear application of the late medieval dialectic of divine absolute and ordained power—and "man's promise to God" to devote himself to God and perform the conditions of the covenant.[158]

Significantly, Perkins then goes on to divide this covenant into two, becoming one of the earliest Reformed theologians to codify the distinction between the covenant of works and the covenant of grace. The covenant of works referred to that made by God with humanity in paradise on "condition of perfect obedience" to the moral law as expressing "the eternal and unchangeable wisdom of God."[159] By contrast, the covenant of grace referred to that "whereby God freely promising Christ and His benefits exacts again of man that he would by faith receive Christ and repent of his sins."[160] Indeed, since all three divine persons are "appeased" through Christ's sacrifice on the cross, it follows that covenant must be understood as fundamentally Trinitarian and Christocentric in character.[161]

While covenant theology should not be reduced to a monolithic influence, it is notable that the early pioneers of this doctrinal division—Caspar Olevian,

---

156. For the covenantal emphasis of late medieval theology see William Courtenay, "Nominalism and Late Medieval Religion," in *Covenant and Causality in Medieval Thought: Studies in Philosophy, Theology and Economic Practice* (London: Variorum Reprints, 1984), 26–59. For a valuable discussion of precursors to the Reformed covenant of works see J. V. Fesko, *The Covenant of Works: The Origins, Development, and Reception of the Doctrine* (New York: Oxford University Press, 2020), 11–32. *Golden Chain*, 6:18 draws prominently on the distinction between the absolute and ordained (actual) power of God characteristic of this movement.

157. *Exposition of the Creed*, 5:50. For detailed discussion of the Trinitarian covenant of redemption, see J. V. Fesko, *The Covenant of Redemption: Origins, Development, and Reception* (Göttingen: Vandenhoeck & Ruprecht, 2016). For the Ramist Ames as an early pioneer of this doctrine, see Jan van Vliet, *The Rise of Reformed System: The Intellectual Heritage of William Ames* (Milton Keynes: Paternoster, 2013), chap. 3.

158. *Golden Chain*, 6:65.

159. *Golden Chain*, 6:65–66; *Exposition of the Creed*, 5:75.

160. *Exposition of the Creed*, 6:153.

161. *Exposition of the Creed*, 6:61.

Robert Rollock, Dudley Fenner, and Perkins himself—were all Ramists.[162] In fact, it is difficult to avoid the impression that the covenant of works should be seen as the means toward the covenant of grace, placing them both within that logical framework of intention and execution we have already seen to be highly conducive to Ramist analysis. Ultimately, Perkins's Ramist conviction that logic must be attuned to the natural and divine order of things, helped him to communicate a powerful Trinitarian, Christocentric, and covenantal vision of theology which proved highly attractive to many of his Reformed successors and still continues to draw many today to study the works of this noble Puritan.

---

162. See Moltmann, "Zur Bedeutung," 295–318.

Contributors

Wyatt Graham, PhD—Executive Director, The Gospel Coalition Canada

Raymond A. Blacketer, PhD—Independent Scholar, currently working on a new translation of John Calvin's *Institutes of the Christian Religion*

Matthew N. Payne, PhD cand.—Research Student, University of Sydney

J. V. Fesko, PhD—Harriett Barbour Professor of Systematic and Historical Theology, Reformed Theological Seminary

Joel R. Beeke, PhD—President and Professor of Systematic Theology and Homiletics, Puritan Reformed Theological Seminary; Pastor of Heritage Reformed Congregation, Grand Rapids, Michigan

Matthew Hartline, PhD cand.—Research Student, The Southern Baptist Theological Seminary; Associate Pastor, First Baptist Church, Cobden, Illinois

David M. Barbee, PhD—Assistant Professor of Christian Thought, Winebrenner Theological Seminary

Andrew S. Ballitch, PhD—Associate Pastor, Westwood Alliance Church, Mansfield, Ohio

Roger L. Revell, PhD—Anglican Minister; Research Fellow; Faculty of Theology and Religion, Oxford University

Dee Grimes, PhD—Instructor in Biblical Spirituality, SIM missionary

J. Stephen Yuille, PhD—Professor of Pastoral Theology and Spiritual Formation, The Southwestern Baptist Theological Seminary

Simon Burton, PhD—John Laing Senior Lecturer in Reformation History, School of Divinity, University of Edinburgh